Beulah Davis Dooley
1998

MERCENARIES, MISSIONARIES AND MISFITS

Adventures of an Under-age Journalist

MERCENARIES, MISSIONARIES AND MISFITS

Adventures of
an Under-age Journalist

Tarquin Hall

[signature: Tarquin Hall]

THE MUNCASTER PRESS

Published in 1996 by
THE MUNCASTER PRESS
P.O. Box 16PB
London W2 7TH
United Kingdom

ISBN 0-9527412-0-2

Printed and Bound in Great Britain at
Redwood Books, Trowbridge, Wiltshire.

Contents

Dedication

To my dear departed Nims, who went to the Happy Mousing Grounds after eighteen memorable years. He was a faithful companion, an intrepid traveller, the scourge of rodents from the Thames to the Golden Horn, a most distinguished pussy cat.

Prologue

By the age of eighteen, my desire for further formal education was at an all-time low. It seemed as though I had spent my entire life studying in a classroom or cramming at a desk for this or that exam. I could not stand to read another text book or stare at another blackboard.

Studying the world from afar left me feeling that I might miss out on the best years of my life. What I needed was some adventure – and journalism seemed to be the key.

And yet immense pressure was being placed upon me to go to university. Parents, teachers, relatives and friends all stressed the tremendous opportunities which might lie ahead should I take the place offered to me at one of Britain's more renowned 'centres of learning'. 'Qualifications are vital things these days,' cautioned some. 'You can't do without them,' pointed out others.

True or not, I had made up my mind to travel and work abroad. Through first-hand experience and practice, I would acquire the necessary skills in writing and, perhaps, photography with a view to becoming a fully fledged journalist. If my plan were to fail and at the end of the four years I were to find myself unemployable in my chosen field, then I had promised my parents that I would go to university.

Being young, naive and impatient, my scheme lacked specifics – it was more a question of throwing caution to the wind. I decided my first port of call would be the United States, since my American mother had relatives on the East and West Coasts. I hoped they might help me find a job on a local newspaper. Beyond that, I wanted to travel to the Developing World, perhaps India or Africa. But when and how were questions I could not yet answer.

In the event, I spent those four years working, living and travelling in parts of America, Asia and Africa.

This book is about some of that time. It is not an 'A to B' travel narrative, nor does it recount every step of my journey in strict chronological order. It is not an autobiography.

Essentially, this is a collection of adventures, anecdotes, travels, encounters and episodes. It is about some of the places I visited, but mainly about the people I met – including a few mercenaries, missionaries and misfits. For it was they who, even in the strangest places and under the most difficult circumstances, gave me the odd piece of advice and the occasional floor to sleep on which helped me on my way.

Tarquin Hall
London 1995

Part One

America

ONE

The Best Hotel in New York

*... was almost caught up in a shoot-out ... walking
along minding my own business when three shots
rang out and a teenager dropped to the pavement
... Dozens of police cars arrived, sirens wailing ...
and a helicopter buzzed overhead ... Doesn't seem
like anyone's going to give me a job on a newspaper, not even emptying waste baskets. I'll have
to take that job in the hotel while I figure out how
to get into journalism ...*

Diary, 11 July 1988

'This is *the* hotel in the Big Apple, my man, the *only* hotel,'
said Sam, the black Mississippi-born page who was
showing me the ropes on my first day on the job. 'Liz
Taylor stayed here and spent five thousand dollars in one
night. Remember, style don't come cheap.'

Sam, who was studying to be a physical exercise
teacher in his spare time, fast-paced along the main
corridor in the basement of the Hotel X towards the laundry room where he had promised to find me a uniform. I
followed behind, trying to keep up, still clutching a knapsack that contained the pair of black shoes and white
shirt I had been asked to bring to work.

'We get everyone in here,' continued Sam as he
passed a room service waiter who carried a delicately
balanced breakfast tray. 'Stars, Mafia bosses, corporate
executives, astronauts. Last week, we had the head of
Boeing in the penthouse. Tipped me a Lincoln. He's a
good man.'

We passed one of the main kitchens and I caught a glimpse of chefs in their tall white hats, almost lost in a sea of steam and smoke, slaving over huge pots and sizzling pans. The next door on the left was an office.

'That's human resources,' said Sam. 'Any bullshit, go to them.'

At last, we reached the laundry room. Baskets brimmed with sheets and pillow cases, and a pile of shirts lay in front of two gyrating washing machines. An elderly Portuguese woman in a black wig pushed a heavy, hissing iron back and forth over a pair of trousers.

Sam opened a locker and pulled out a uniform: a pair of trousers with a red stripe running down both outside legs, a white jacket with silver buttons, red shoulder straps and lily-white gloves. Once changed, I looked like a cinema usher.

'You're now a page, my man,' he said, inspecting me with a discerning eye. 'Your duties include delivering messages, faxes and telexes, fetching anything the guests want from outside the hotel, giving out the occasional key ... oh, and last but not least, making sure the ash trays in the foyer are empty and sparklin'.'

Adjusting my collar, Sam explained that it was the bellboys' job to carry the guests' bags. 'We all belong to a union, here. So don't be interferin' with other people's work or you'll land yourself in a world of shit. Understand?'

'Understood.'

I followed Sam as he did his errands. We spent much of the first day travelling around the city, picking up unusual items for the guests. People in the streets spying our uniforms would salute us or shout: 'Hey, did you guys just jump ship?'

On our way back to the hotel, we stopped off to buy some foreign newspapers, *Le Figaro*, *The Times* and *Der Spiegel*, from the closest and friendliest newsagent, owned by a Sri Lankan who specialised in pornographic magazines. Once Sam had collected up all the papers, he added a couple of packs of cigarettes to the bill.

'Anything you want?' he asked. After a moment's hesitation, I reached for a cold drink.

'Always make sure you get somethin' on the bill,' insisted Sam. 'The guests are so damn rich, they never notice a few extra bucks. Getting the papers always pays for maa smokes.'

We returned to the hotel and entered through the main entrance. The foyer was full of immaculately dressed people, all correct and presentable, oozing charm and pampering one another. Perfect white teeth gleamed and sparkled.

A flow of guests moved through the lobby: Gucci bags, servants carrying lap dogs, skiing equipment, Fifth Avenue shopping bags and the occasional work of art. As Sam and I stood by the concierge's desk observing the scene, a guest who was checking out ordered his bags to be taken to his waiting limousine; a cleaner scurried towards the restaurant like a rodent caught in a truck's high beams; heels clip clopped across the floor.

For a moment there was silence and then a loud guffaw resounded across the room as three people responded to a joke told by an ageing executive carrying a cane. A concierge lit a cigarette for a woman wearing a wide-brimmed hat that dipped down, covering the top half of her face. The right-hand lift hummed open and I recognised the comedian, Richard Pryor, with his entourage following dutifully behind.

The grand foyer was dimly lit with chandeliers and sunken ceiling lights that bathed it in a mellow orange glow, creating a sophisticated, relaxed ambience. The scent from three giant bouquets of exquisitely arranged flowers filled the air. The walls were decorated in an exclusive hand-painted wallpaper depicting a French landscaped garden, complete with spouting fountains, creeping vines and rose beds. What an incredible contrast it was to the dingy, claustrophobic and disorganised staff rooms which lay behind the scenes of the Hotel X.

Sam stood to attention near the main doors. 'It gets pretty tough puttin' on this act all the time,' he whispered, pretending to give me some instructions.

'How do you mean?' I asked.

'Being good and polite to all these folk,' he said in his southern Mississippi lilt. 'Sometimes I just wanna bust their heads open.'

Guests continued to glide across the black and white marble floors, oblivious to Sam's real feelings. 'The men and women staying in this hotel have money beyond your wildest dreams,' said Sam. 'Some of them got it the old-fashioned way – they inherited it. Others made it the hard way – they earned it. And a good few married it, stole it, or even killed for it.'

'Wow. Do you really think so?' I asked.

'Are you kidding, man? Where the hell have you been?'

'England,' I replied.

Sam was called over to the main desk by the senior concierge, an Italian who had arrived in New York in the thirties on one of the immigrant boats. I was left standing on the edge of the foyer watching the scene. Never before had I seen such an array of chic and expensive outfits. The guests in the hotel, particularly the women – some of whom I recognised from glossy magazines – dressed like models straight off a cat walk. It was not uncommon to be asked to collect packages from the most expensive shops in New York. Only that morning, Sam had been sent to a smart chemist where he paid out over five hundred dollars for just three items of make-up and perfume.

'To these people,' my new friend continued when he returned, 'cash is little more than an inconvenience. These are some of the richest people in the world. What you have to do is encourage them to share a little of their wealth with you. We're talkin' about amounts they won't even notice, but will make all the difference to you when you wanna take a lady friend out at the end of the week. So, how you goin' to accomplish this?'

I shrugged my shoulders.

'Why do you think these people come here? I'll tell you. Because this is a small hotel, only two hundred rooms, and it's very private. These men and women wanna be taken care of. They crave personal attention, so get a little note book and write down the names of all the regulars. When you're in the elevator or out on an errand, memorise their names. They like you to remember. They pay you to remember.'

Sam started to point out some of the guests. 'See the tall guy over there with the blue tie? That's Louis Lecomte, a regular. He just sold his partnership for two billion dollars, cash. The guy don't fool around. Remember his name. Here comes another one: Mr Nash and his fifth wife. She's French; you can tell by that look. He helped finance Reagan's campaign for the governorship of California and later his march to the White House.'

Sam bent his head closer to mine, his arms behind his back. 'The story goes,' he whispered, 'that a while back he was havin' dinner in Washington when the President was talkin' about some missile sites they planned on constructin'. He suggested that Mr Nash build 'em. Nash bought up the largest concrete companies in the state. Now he's one of the richest men in the world.'

Sam continued his run-down on some of the better tippers, not forgetting to mention the man who had left five thousand dollars for the staff last time he checked out. 'One last pointer,' advised Sam, 'don't be shy about waitin' for a tip. Remember, thank yous don't pay the bills.'

He introduced me to all the bellboys: Pridip, Paul, Wang and Geoff. They were a friendly and welcoming group like most Americans. The States is, after all, a country of immigrants where everyone has come from somewhere else, so tolerance and a willingness to accept a newcomer is the general rule.

Geoff offered to show me one of the penthouse suites. That morning, it had been vacated by a member of Britain's Royal Family who had jetted in to New York on a three-day Fifth Avenue shopping spree. The design of the suite was breathtaking. Arched windows led out onto a spectacular glass conservatory where we found a half-finished bottle of Bollinger '69 standing in a chiller full of watery ice. It was selling on the hotel's wine list for hundreds of dollars.

The bellboy rinsed out a couple of coffee cups, filled them with Champagne and took some potato crisps from a walnut-veneered cocktail cabinet. We relaxed on a comfortable couch in front of the windows from which we could see the whole city.

'This is the life!' said Geoff as we clinked coffee mugs and toasted the health of the Big Apple.

* * *

The cheapest place to eat near the hotel was a diner called Marty's. Bright and cheerful with glitzy mirrors on the walls and ceilings, and shiny red plastic seats, it became my regular haunt.

The waitress was called Barbara, pronounced 'Barbrar', or 'Barb' for short. She had pretty, soft eyes, but was hard and tough: 'tough as any Wall Street hot shot', as she put it. Barb and I seemed to build up an understanding and, knowing that I was new in town, she enjoyed filling me in on life in the Big Apple.

'How ya doin' today, Tarkin?' she asked as I walked in one Sunday shortly after starting work at the hotel. 'Get you somethin'?'

'What are the specials today?' I asked.

Barb rattled off a list as rhythmically as a paddle steamer chugging down the Mississippi: 'Dixie fried chicken, Caesar salad, Belgian waffles, hot beef sandwich ...'

I ordered some bacon and eggs 'sunny side up'. Barb walked over to the open kitchen and shouted out the orders to the Canadian cook: 'One Swiss on rye; one eggs over easy, hash brown on the side and decaf; one eggs sunny side up and bacon – crispy; one Pepsi – free ...'

Some of the other regulars filtered in. First came Rob, a sports fanatic who worked as a 'stats', or statistics, man for CBS Sports. The job required him to feed a constant flow of information and statistics about players and games into the earpiece of an on-screen commentator. Rob lived, breathed and dreamed sport. His brain was bulging with baseball averages, football goals, basketball history and any other fascinating or facile fact you might ever wish to know about the American sporting scene. All you had to do was give him the name of a player or a team and, like Mr Memory in *The Thirty-nine Steps*, he would automatically rattle off a long list of information.

I had only a passing interest in American sports' coverage and for Rob, this was unforgivable. To him, I was an ignoramus, a non-believer, and there were moments when, realising how little I knew, he would clasp his hands over his sweaty face and with that contorted, desperate expression that is the hallmark of the fanatic everywhere, shout, 'What kind of person are you? You don't even know who Babe Ruth was!'

Next through the diner door were Sidney and Tommy. Their names went together like oil and vinegar or Laurel and Hardy. They were an inseparable duo – both balding and divorced, they seemed to have been buddies since always. Both men claimed to have been the victims of the US Government's atomic bomb experiments, thus explaining their lack of hair. The fact that everyone was quite sure that no atomic bombs had ever been detonated in the vicinity of the Bronx failed to deter them from acting out their parts.

Sidney and Tommy always found something to complain about: if it wasn't the weather it was the Government, and if it wasn't the Government, it was the cost of 'cwarfee'. When they weren't complaining, they were doling out advice, most of it lousy, a little of it quite sound.

Sidney and Tommy sat down next to me. 'How ya doin', kid?' asked Tommy, who was wearing a T-shirt that read, 'Just Visiting this Planet'.

'Fine, thanks.'

'You been doin' much readin' lately?'

'A bit.'

'Well, I'll tell you somethin'.' Tommy moved to the edge of his seat to pass on his advice. 'If you wanna be a great writer, ya gotta be a great reader. And you know who told me that?' He paused, waiting for everyone to bend an ear in his direction. But the diner regulars had heard it all before and, with the exception of myself, no one listened. 'Henry Miller when I met him in Paris,' said Tommy. 'Now what da ya think of that?'

'Sure, Tommy – and I'm Jackie Onassis,' intoned Barb.

One of Tommy's friends was a journalist who worked for Press International. His name was Frank Renard. He wore tan cotton summer suits and stripy blue shirts which always had ink blotches around the breast pockets. Frank joined us that Sunday morning, carrying copies of the *New Yorker* and *The Economist* under his arm.

'Sorry I'm late,' he said, shaking my hand and asking Barb to bring him a cream cheese bagel, 'I had to call my father in Maine. He's eighty-two and he still can't keep out of trouble ...'

Frank grew up in Maine, in Kennebunkport, the site of George Bush's summer residence. His father managed the local supermarket and, through hard work and guile, Frank won a scholarship to Brown University where he studied English. During the Vietnam War, he had been drafted into the army and worked as a journalist on the *Stars and Stripes*, the American forces' newspaper.

'Vietnam was a crazy time. It was a real mess,' he

said, sitting across from me in the booth, his back straight, 'but I wouldn't have missed it for the world. After it was all over and we pulled out, I thought about becoming a foreign correspondent and going on to Thailand or something. I wanted a family, though. Always wonder what would have happened if I had stayed. Guess my life would have turned out pretty different ...'

Tommy and Sidney were playing poker in the next booth. Frank asked me how my plans were coming along. There seemed something odd about discussing my future with an almost total stranger, but Americans always seem prepared to chip in with some friendly advice when needed.

'Why don't you want to go to college?' asked Frank.

'The kid doesn't wanna go,' interrupted Tommy, who was listening in on our conversation. 'He's right. He should get out and see the world.'

'Have you tried for a job on a newspaper?' Frank asked.

'The kid tried,' interrupted Tommy again. 'No one's going to give him nothin' with no track record and no lousy degree. He doesn't have a lousy degree.'

I asked Frank how he thought I might go about getting some writing experience. The journalist considered for a moment. He straightened his tie clip. 'Why not spend a year or so working your way around the States? Just do anything to bring in some cash. Meantime, write on the side. It'll be easy here. You speak the language and it's a culture you're at ease with. Then, go and base yourself in some "hot spot", like Beirut. Use the money you earn in the States as a back-up fund and freelance.'

It didn't sound like a bad plan – quite exciting, in fact. But it didn't really answer my question about how I might go about gaining some writing experience.

'Do you know the story about the kid who wanted to go to Carnegie Hall?' asked Frank, who had picked up a New York accent during his nine years in the city.

'No.'

'Well,' he continued, warming to the idea of spinning a yarn, 'there's this kid and he's trying to find Carnegie Hall. But he's only young and he gets lost.

'So he goes up to a guy on the street and says, "Hey, mister, how do I get to Carnegie Hall?"

'"Well," says the guy on the street, "there's only one way of getting to Carnegie Hall that I know of. You gott'a practise, son. Practise."'

'Practise ...' I said. 'But practise what?'

'Write about anything,' replied Frank. 'Start off with something simple. Doing articles is like telling a tale, you need a striking beginning, gripping middle, and a great ending. Go to places where you can live cheaply, and if you've got imagination and can develop a nose for news, you'll always find quirky angles and stories. Then, the trick is to persuade an editor to publish.'

Frank said he would be happy to look over my first efforts and give constructive criticism; he seemed delighted at the prospect of taking me under his wing. Did he have any further advice?

'Have you read Waugh's *Scoop*?'

'No,' I said.

'Well, get hold of a copy. I think you'll enjoy it.'

* * *

The enthusiasm for my project shown by the regulars in Marty's left me with a feeling that anything was possible. I read *Scoop* and decided to take Frank's advice. I would work in the Hotel X and save as much money as I could, while writing in my spare time. I would then travel across America in search of suitable subjects for articles of interest to editors in England.

After that, there were a number of other countries I wanted to visit. Topping the list was India where a school friend, Tariq Khan, was working as a journalist and doing exactly what I wanted to do.

Frank Renard had advised me against attempting current affairs stories and pointed me in the direction of light features. My first attempt was about New York skyscrapers; the second on New York street food. Looking back, I took far too much time on unnecessary research, and the articles seemed to take me days to write. Finally, however, I made print-outs on Frank's computer, showed them to him for comment, and eventually sent copies 'on spec' to several British newspapers. Then I waited impatiently to hear from the editors.

Back at the Hotel X, I was beginning to learn how things worked behind the scenes.

I got on well with the bellboys and managers, but the concierges were a different matter altogether. The youngest, Philip, pronounced 'Phileep', treated me as his personal slave. Yet when it came to ingratiating himself with the guests, he would bend over backwards. 'Good evening Mrs Lancon. You're looking radiant tonight,' he gushed on one occasion. 'I have your theatre tickets here,' he continued. 'They're the best in the house. Oh, you don't know how much trouble it was getting hold of them. The show is so, so popular. No matter, we do our very best ...' Mrs Lancon blushed. The female guests generally savoured this kind of pampering.

'I've also booked a table for two at Le Cygne,' continued the concierge greasily. 'The maître d' is a personal friend of mine. Your limousine is waiting outside, so have a wonderful evening. I'm so, so envious.'

Mrs Lancon handed him a fifty dollar bill which he pretended not to notice and, with a haughty expression on his arrogant face, brushed it under a theatre programme. Only minutes later, I heard 'Phileep' and another concierge gossiping: 'I gave Mrs Lancon her tickets,' he whispered. 'They cost her a fortune. What a waste. She wouldn't know a good play if she found one in her panties ...'

'Phileep' was the most disagreeable of all the

concierges. A cocaine addict, he was overly sensitive and insecure, and on one occasion I saw him burst into tears after addressing an English Lord as 'Sir' and being ticked off for doing so. 'Phileep', who seemed to find my Englishness threatening, took a special dislike to me.

But after one specific incident, he never troubled me again. It was all thanks to Don Ameche, the late actor.

The veteran Italian-American arrived at the Hotel X one evening in late November. There was nothing extraordinary about a Hollywood star checking in. I had escorted Clint Eastwood up to his room, and run errands for Billy Crystal and Dan Aykroyd.

The night before Ameche's arrival, I happened by coincidence to have seen the star in his latest role as an impoverished Chicago shoe shiner in the film, *Things Change*. Through a series of bizarre incidents and coincidences, the shoe shiner finds himself in the most luxurious hotel in Lake Tahoe, California, where the hotel staff mistake him for a wealthy Mafia boss. As the film progresses, the head concierge ingratiates himself more and more and personally escorts him up to the penthouse suite, trying his best to make an impression.

Standing in the foyer of the Hotel X, I now saw the exact same scene being played out again in front of me. As Ameche entered, 'Phileep' rushed over towards him. The bellboys were all busy, so he snapped his fingers at me to take the actor's bags.

'Mr Ameche,' he said, 'it's such an honour to have you here. We are so, so glad you chose the Hotel X. Please let me help you. If there is anything you require ...'

But Ameche wasn't listening. I sensed that he found this situation as irritatingly ironic as I did. He caught my eye and, with a smile, he gave me a knowing wink.

The concierge stopped in his tracks and I followed the actor into the lift. Upstairs, Ameche began unpacking and, taking off his shoes, he asked me to give them a shine as he had an important engagement the next day.

'I would do them myself,' he said, smiling kindly, 'but I left my shoe shine kit in Chicago.'

* * *

One afternoon, not long before I left the Hotel X and began my travels around the US, I was particularly busy. The Marharani of Jaipur, while dining in the restaurant, had burst a blood vessel in her nose and had been rushed up to her room. In the hotel café, the black pianist was doing his best Ray Charles impression, his fingers tinkling over the ebony and ivory keyboard. And the mysterious toy boy who spent every afternoon with the gentleman occupying suite 506 was making his way to the door with his leather bag of goodies tucked under his arm.

An impeccably dressed middle-aged woman who smelt like a herbaceous border approached the reception desk where I stood. She reminded me of a Siamese cat as her hair was sleek and shiny, and she walked on her toes. The clothes she stood up in were alone worth more than I lived on for a year, and her diamonds could have set me up for life. She made an enquiry about her dinner reservation and in the process, overheard me talking to another guest.

'Excuse me, sugar. Are you from England?' she purred in her soft southern accent.

'Yes, madam.'

'Oh, I've just been over there,' she said faintly. 'I love the Royal Family and your little old English gardens and the guys in those furry hats at Bucking-ham Palace ... I visited Didcot. Do you know it?' I told her I did, even though I had never heard of the place, and she waxed poetic about Big Ben, Harrods and cream teas. 'Well, gotta go,' she said, finally, 'take it easy, now.'

That evening, Gus, the podgy, Polish doorman who had cheeks as puffy as burger baps, went home suffering from a toothache. I was ordered onto the door.

23

It was getting colder and the days were growing shorter and sharper as the New York winter approached. However, as I paced back and forth in front of the main entrance, trying to think of ways to sell articles to newspapers, I took comfort from the fact that I had on Gus's thick, cashmere coat.

Towards midnight, a silver limousine with tinted windows pulled up. I opened the back door and a woman's elegant leg appeared. I offered my hand, the lady clutched it and I drew her up towards me, recognising her as the southern lady with a love for all things English.

'Oh ... good evening, sugar,' she said.

Her breath smelt strongly of alcohol and she was swaying slightly. 'Why, it's my friend from D..D..Di.. Did ...'

'... from Didcot, madam,' I added, inaccurately, but promptly.

'Oh, y'all know what I mean,' she said giggling, waving her hand past her face. 'How are you tonight, then, sugar? I was hoping I was ga..ga..going to see you again.'

Her tall, handsome, broad-chested and very rich husband was getting out of the car and tipping the chauffeur. I escorted the lady to the door.

'Well, guess I should be getting to bed,' she said.

As she wished me good night, she slid her hand between my legs and squeezed gently. Closing her eyes, she heaved a great sigh, whispering, 'Sweet dreams, sugar.' She staggered forward into the hotel foyer.

Her husband, who had his back turned, now walked towards me.

'Good evening,' he said. 'It's a clear one tonight, isn't it?' He pressed a note into my hand.

'Th..th..th..thank you ... sir,' I spluttered, clearing my throat and trying to look composed.

The gentleman disappeared into the Hotel X.

Two

Cordon Bleu Rattlesnake

Sweetwater is a world away from the Big Apple.
What a country of extremes this place is. Hardly
anyone here has even been to Dallas ... Called Pete
who started at Bristol (university). He couldn't
believe I was in Texas. Said I was missing some
great parties ... Got yet another rejection letter for
one of my articles! 'Doesn't quite fit our editorial
needs.' That seems be the line they all use ... Am
going to try and write something for the local
paper here.

Diary, 26 January 1989

I saved enough money working at the Hotel X and
started travelling around the States in search of stories. I
explored Chicago and the Lake Michigan area, then
travelled up to see Toronto, took the train back to the
East Coast, and made my way down to Philadelphia,
Baltimore and Washington DC. I spent ten days driving
through Virginia, Tennessee, Mississippi and Texas.
Finally, after a quick stop-off in Dallas, I arrived at 702
James Street, Sweetwater, Texas, the home of Sally
Twigger, one of my family's oldest friends.

Sweetwater had just two attractions: the museum
and the red-haired cashier at K-Mart, a superstore chain.
The museum had an extensive collection of American
Indian, or 'native American', arrow heads. The tall,
slender cashier had beautiful, friendly, large brown eyes.
She gulped when she heard me speak and asked me to
say her name out loud because, I suppose, she found my

pronunciation intriguing. I was happy to oblige.

'Amanda,' I read from the name tag on her becoming uniform. Her breathing grew shallow, her cheeks blushed, her eyes flashed. 'Oh ma Gawdd,' she said.

That was the first and only time I have made such an immediate impact on a woman. Many times since, I have asked women if they would like me to say their names for them out loud. Yet when they agree – and this is rare – it never seems to have quite the same effect as it did in K-Mart that day.

Sweetwater, which was once voted 'All-American City' of its class, had a population of thirteen thousand. The original planners and architects must have thought the oil boom would last forever and Sweetwater would grow to suit the monstrous size of its amenities. The mall contained hypermarkets which make the average Tesco look like a street corner newsagent; and a car park, the size of an airstrip, where I only ever saw two or three cars parked.

The town was comprised of cloned Legoland houses neatly positioned on either side of straight streets; a remarkable number of churches, complete with hell-fire evangelical preachers whose congregations were permanently stoked up to boiling point; and a liquor store on every corner with so many sophisticated security systems and flashing lights that as you entered you wondered if you would ever get out again.

For Sweetwater's teenagers, life revolved around the High School football team, the Prom and the High School Yucca Gloriosa beauty pageant and, of course, the Drag, the main road leading from Sonic, the drive-in burger joint, to the drive-in bank. Everything was drive-in in Sweetwater. It was just another middle American town: same shops, same architecture, same video stores, same bars, same diners ...

And yet Sweetwater had something to rival all the others, an event which attracted people from across the

States during an annual week of festivities, namely the world's single largest rattlesnake round-up.

Never having heard of a rattlesnake round-up, I was naturally curious to learn more. I asked Sally if she could fill me in.

'It's the most exciting event in this one-horse town,' smiled Sally, who was sitting in her bedroom where she still kept her late husband's collection of hunting rifles and pistols in a case by her bed. 'Rattlesnakes are vicious reptiles, a dangerous nuisance to ranchers and townsfolk alike,' she continued. 'Several times I've found them in the backyard. They're terrifyin'.'

Sally explained that as few people feel sympathy towards snakes, hunting has become a popular sport in the area. Disappointingly, I had missed the round-up itself in which snakes are paraded through the town on floats. However, Sally said that I might be able to go hunting, and a couple of phone calls put me in touch with a group of seasoned rattlesnake hunters. Would they be going out soon?

'Matter-a-fact, we leave tomorrow at first light,' an old timer replied.

This sounded like a suitable subject for a feature with photographs, the first that I had attempted.

I spent an hour locked in my room at Sally's, ensuring that not a speck of dust remained on my camera or lens, sharpened a brand new box of black and yellow striped pencils until they would have served well as skewers, and went to K-Mart to buy a fresh note pad. I was so enthused that I could only spare a few glances and moments for the gorgeous Amanda.

The very next morning, I found myself squeezed into the cabin of a rusty Ford pick-up lurching across the rocky plains towards rattlesnake country. I was seated between two elderly men straight out of a Steinbeck novel: on my right, an oil-rig worker who talked interminably about his many ex-wives. On my left, the driver, a man called Joe, a home-grown Texan who was retired from the cattle business and living in a pre-fabricated house in the middle of a desolate ranch.

Joe's pure white hair flapped in the gusty wind. His face looked like a charred piece of toast, and as he chewed on Red Man tobacco, his square jaw moved up and down rhythmically. A worn hand offered me the packet. I accepted, taking a small pinch of what looked like finely chopped, damp seaweed. I dropped it into my mouth. A bitter-sweet taste pricked sharply on my tongue and, to Joe's delight, I quickly spat it out, coughing and spluttering.

Joe began talking in his slow Texan drawl, a soothing accent that might have hailed from the west of England.

'Son ... before we starts huntin', we'd best warn you that there's three rules which need to be adhered to, if you catch my meanin',' he said, sucking on a false tooth and adjusting his worn baseball cap. 'No smokin', no drinkin' and no shootin'.'

His wise face broadened into a friendly grin. I asked what he meant.

'Cos, smokin' is bad for you and can cause fire. Drinkin', the women don't like and it makes us clumsy – and shootin' is downright dangerous for everyone, on account of the ricochet.'

He chewed a little more and then continued elaborating on the ins and outs of rattlesnakes.

'Snakes, see, they don't retain heat like us humans, so durin' the winter they hides in holes and go to sleep. A lot like my friend Billy,' Joe joked, referring to another hunter who was sprawled out in the back. Billy didn't seem to register the comment.

'We gotta kill those vermin,' he continued, 'lest they kills the cattle. We're doin' everyone a real favour.'

Joe also explained that snakes have no insulating layer, fur or sweat glands. During the winter months they hibernate, venturing out only very occasionally for brief periods in search of bright sunshine. If the temperature drops to near freezing, they risk death. During the summer months, they use the sun to regulate their metabolic rate by basking for hours out on the open plains.

We continued along parched, pitted roads. Joe and his friends seemed to take life in their stride: a relaxed, detached approach allied to their own brand of common sense. If a mushroom cloud had suddenly formed on the horizon, Joe might have said, 'Hey fellas, look over thar. That look like a hydrogen bomb to you?'

'Yep, guess so,' and he would have just kept on driving down the road, in the knowledge that life should never be taken too seriously – and besides, there were snakes to hunt.

The land, which looked as if it had been ironed flat, stretched out in all directions. Lonely nodding-donkey oil pumps and outcrops of mutated rocks were etched upon the horizon. It was as if this silent territory had been abandoned, doomed only to be inhabited by slithering and crawly things with hundreds of legs, the sort of creatures we used to show girls at school to make them scream.

Scrubland gave way to dried river bed, and dried river bed back to scrubland. It was the backdrop to a thousand Westerns and I found myself idly imagining cowboys and Indians doing battle all around us, the thundering of hooves, the crack of pistol fire, the cries of the wounded, the whoops of victory ...

'What a lonely place to die,' I said out loud, although I was not quite sure why. Joe nodded and spat a mouthful of tobacco juice out of the window.

'Yep.'

The sun was on the meridian as we drew to a halt at the bottom of a hillock. An enthusiastic young Texan who had been in the back of the truck jumped out with such a spring in his step that he seemed almost airborne, pointed and shouted, 'Last summer we caught those suckers just lyin' out thar in the sun. All we had to do was pick 'em up.'

We unloaded our equipment and climbed the hill warily, avoiding sharp cactus underfoot.

'Snakes live in holes in rock faces,' said the oil-rig worker, who had just finished showing me a knife wound which he swore he had earned in Vietnam. 'They usually face away from the wind.'

Cautiously, we approached a rock face and then stood still and silent. I asked if snakes could hear. 'Hell no!' Joe bawled, heedlessly, 'but they senses heat.'

I was allocated my hunting equipment: one five-foot stick with a sharp hook attached to the end, one set of long thongs, one small tank of petrol complete with pump and hose, one dustbin and one pair of thick plastic leg guards. Our group of six were split into three pairs.

I teamed up with Joe who crept around on the rock face humming to himself while looking for snake holes. Soon, he located a nest and pumped petrol deep into it. Joe told me, as he kept the petrol pumping, that the fumes are supposed to force the snakes to slither out, but once in a while the gas overwhelms them and they die inside. We crouched down with our equipment at the ready – anticipating the slightest movement. Without warning, the swollen head of a Diamondback surfaced at the entrance of the hole. I dropped my stick and thongs and jumped back.

'It's a four-footer!' shouted Joe – he could tell by the size of its head. Seeing us, the snake tried to re-enter its den, but with a lightning movement, my partner caught the hook on its lower jaw and, clamping the thongs firm-ly below its head, he gave a tug as if he were reeling in a fish. Slowly, more and more of the snake appeared, until finally the entire creature had emerged from the hole.

'Bet you ain't seen nothin' like that in England!'

'Thank God, no,' I breathed.

The unforgettable, loathsome hiss and rattle is a noise which will never leave me. I felt a chill shoot straight down my spine and right through my body to the ends of my toes. The captured reptile lashed out with its tail, wriggling and writhing for life.

'How's that, son?' asked Joe, holding up the struggling prey and encouraging me to take a closer look. 'Course if I should loosen my grip, he'd go for us, no mistake.'

The snake measured close to four and a half feet; a substantial length these days as fewer snakes reach their full growth due to regular culling. A fierce Diamondback can grow up to seven feet long. The other men gathered round, admiring the first catch of the day, and in an authoritative manner, Joe announced that each of the notches on the rattle represented one year of the snake's life.

'That's bull!' interrupted the oil-rig worker. 'The rattle is the hard part of the tail that remains when the snake moults – about four times a year!'

'No, three times!' interrupted another.

When the jostling had subsided, my partner plunged our quarry unceremoniously into a dustbin and slammed down the lid. The petrol fumes inside finished it off quickly. I quizzed the hunters about the rattlesnake's bite. Was it as deadly as I had heard? 'It depends,' was the general opinion; none of the hunters had ever been bitten.

'My wife came huntin' once,' said Joe, who was proud of having been the first to catch a snake that day. 'The only time in her life and she got bit. She was OK though.'

The oil-rig worker interrupted: 'Few people die; it depends upon an individual's tolerance to the venom. Some animals can resist its ee-ffects better than others. A rat can tolerate six times as much venom as a guinea pig.'

* * *

By the end of the day, we had captured a total of sixteen snakes of varying sizes; ten lucky ones were put into another bin where they slithered around at the bottom, like the trimmings from one of Medusa's hair cuts. Later, these snakes would be sold to a snake farm.

'I think it's time we went and slugged back a few cold ones,' announced the oil-rig worker, who had caught too much sun and was thirsty like the rest of us.

'Cold ones?' I asked.

'Beer,' he replied.

'Yep,' said everyone in unison, a signal to pack up our gear and set off for Sweetwater.

Had the American Indians taken any particular interest in snakes, I asked the hunters, once we reached the local bar. Joe had heard that the Hopi Indians worshipped snakes as gods and after a delirious dance lasting nine days, washed them religiously and housed them in a sacred place. Then, as a display of courage and nerve, the Indians would carry the snakes about in their mouths and finally let them loose in the wild.

The purpose of all this?

'To bring rain, 'course,' said Joe, 'everyone's always prayin' for rain in these parts.'

More practically, snakes have other uses. Rattlesnake sells for nine dollars a pound. Boots, belts, bags, wallets and hat trimmings are all manufactured from the skins.

'And that ain't all,' said Joe, 'we even eat 'em.'

'You eat snakes?' I said, surprised and vaguely disgusted. Could I really bring myself to eat one of those reptiles?

'Sure, they ain't bad with a bit of sweet potata.'

And before dropping me at Sally's, Joe wrote out a recipe for mouth-watering Diamondback on the back of an old cattle-feed form:

> Skin snake and cut into three pieces.
> Dip in milk and egg.
> Roll in mixture of flour and corn meal.
> Salt and pepper.
> Deep fry in oil.
> Serve hot.

THREE

I Become a Cowboy

My feature on snake hunting turned out well.
Pictures look good. Am sending it to The Times. *I'm*
sure they will be interested ... Am getting a bit
worried about cash. Have spent far too much and
have now got to decide what to do. Can't stay here
forever, but as things stand there's no way I'm
going to make it back to New York, let alone India.

Diary, 4 February 1989

'How'd ya lyke to work on a genuyyne cowboy ranch?'
asked Sally as we were looking at some of my rattlesnake
photographs.

'A real one? With real cowboys?' I asked.

'Sure. It's owned by a friend of a friend of my couzin.
He's an oyle man.'

Sally knew that almost all my savings were gone.
Having not sold any of my articles, I had little choice but
to take another casual job.

Sally arranged an interview with the oil man, Rowdy,
who cut an awkward figure: he had a bulky lower half,
but his arms were thin and gangly. His thick black hair
was permanently slicked back with gallons of gel and oils,
and he wore purple-framed glasses and flared trousers as
wide as the span of an eagle's wings. He spoke glibly, but
bore little resemblance to some of the smooth business-
men I had spotted in Dallas. He was a collector of kitsch
and lacked all sense of taste, did everything as big as possible – except when it came to writing pay cheques – and
loved nothing better than to hear the sound of his own

voice.

As well as drilling for oil, Rowdy was hiring workers for his new venture, raising and training horses on a nearby ranch.

'This 'ill kill two burds with one stone,' he laughed, sensing a good deal. 'You can come work for me and y'all can teach my daughters all about England. I promised them a vacation thar and now they won't have to go!' He laughed the laugh that only rich men can laugh.

'What about wages?' I asked.

'Fifteen dollars a day, seven days a week, plus room and board. It ain't much, but y'all enjoy the fresh air.'

The pay was extremely low; I had been earning ten times as much at the Hotel X and I wasn't sure if any amount of fresh air would make up for it. Still, my taste for adventure had been heightened: the prospect of working with horses and cowboys was appealing thanks to all those Western re-runs I had watched as a child on British TV on Saturday mornings. Besides, I had never worked on a farm, except the odd day spent turkey plucking and egg collecting and, no doubt, it would provide me with colourful material. I asked Rowdy if I needed anything special for the job.

'A pair of sturdy blue jeans – Wranglers, they're the best. Some tough workin' gloves and some strong ridin' boots. As I said, ranchin's a tough life,' replied Rowdy, who was long-winded.

Feeling poor, I hesitated to ask the price of boots. He immediately drew up his legs from underneath his polished mahogany desk and plonked his feet on the top of it. Fragments of dirt fell off and scattered among his business papers like fleas jumping from a drowning dog.

'See these here boots,' he pointed, 'made out of alligator skin – o-n-e..h-u-n-d-r-e-d..p-u-r-r..c-e-n-t. Cost me two thousand dollars – but y'all don't want to pay that, now do you?'

'Not particularly,' I replied, 'can I get some a bit

cheaper?'

"Corse you can. I'll take you to the best place in town.'

En route to the shop in Rowdy's Cadillac, which came complete with a sound system obviously designed for Wembley Stadium, he told me something of the history of cowboy boots. The oil man was a mine of information about all things Texan. He had an impressive memory; a mind like an open encyclopedia.

'The present-day boot – it ain't changed much since them old days,' he began. 'Our boots are still made of top grade leather. See mine – they got a high arch and a slightly rounded toe. That's the business. The heel varies from a flat one-inch rise to the more popular one and a half to two-inch form.

'The soles – these are thin to give the rider a feel of the stirrup. That thar heel can prevent the foot from slippin' through. Plain or fancy, my boys prefer hand-made boots to factory-manufactured ones,' continued Rowdy, 'and they're willin' to spend considerable sums to get the pair they want.'

Armed with these useful tips, I bought a black pair of 'ropers' for thirty dollars and Sally lent me one of her late husband's old Stetson hats.

* * *

It was two days before Sally drove me out to Rowdy's Abeliene Ranch again. Along the road, signposts read, 'Drive Friendly in Texas'. It was true that each time we passed a car – even in a queue – drivers waved at us. Naturally, we waved back.

As we drove along, Sally discreetly contributed some advice, pausing thoughtfully: 'While you're out here, remember that they're goin'a think you speak funny. Remember it's "peekan" not "pikaan" and "ranch" not "raunch". Don't swear and whatever yuu do, don't blaspheeme by sayin' Jeesus or Christ: they take religion seerious in these parts. You should always call the men "Sir" and the women "Ma'am" and ...,' she paused again, 'well – the Texan girls, they're real pretty and they can git carreed away and flash their eyelids and smile a lot and ...'

'What do you mean?'

Shyly, she continued. 'Uh. Well. Just reemember. No harsh swearin', specially in front of the wimen, be respectful, and spend more tyme with ther sons than ther daughters. Texan men are armed!'

'Oh, right.' I nodded in comprehension. Enough said.

We headed on towards the three thousand acre ranch located in Apricot Canyon. As gigantic as it seemed, by comparison to some of the other Texan ranches, this was a small patch. We turned off the main road, rattled over a cattle grill and passed in the shadow of steep escarpments which led up to a higher plateau. Eventually, the car, now coated in fine dust, pulled up in front of a group of old stone frontier-like buildings. This was the centre of the ranch which Rowdy dramatically referred to as 'HQ'.

As it turned out I was very lucky because the Abeliene Ranch was one of the few remaining authentic ranches left in the Wild West. It came complete with genuine cowboys, most of them descendants of some of the first men and women who had worked this land, handing down their skills from generation to generation for nearly two hundred years. Practically all the work and chores on the ranch were still done without the use of modern, electrical equipment.

As we stopped, a figure was pulling on a long rope ringing a bell, its monotonous clang resounding over the whirling of a windmill on the tower above us. Rowdy appeared from a doorway and with a wave of his hat and a 'how do' smile, he invited Sally and me to join him in the cook shack where chow was about to be served.

The cook shack was more than just a shack. It was a fine, sturdy structure made of solid granite with a broad chimney and thick pine doors; the sort of friendly, welcoming place of which many cowboys must hold fond memories. Inside, Rowdy carefully hung his hat on a polished brass hook and invited us to wash in a fine old porcelain basin.

A wide open fireplace crowded with crackling logs dominated the dining room. In front of it sat three cowboys, the light of the flames flickering across their stony faces. The room fell silent and, slowly, they all looked up towards us. I must have been as much of a strange sight to them as they were to me. My baggy British cotton trousers, blue striped Marks and Spencer's shirt and running shoes, branded me a 'seetee boy'.

Rowdy introduced the cowboys: Chuck, Elly, Sonny, Duke, Bubba and George, the manager. Sonny, a Mexican, had pitch-black eyes and brown skin; Elly was a mix of Scots and English, although he claimed to have some Cherokee in him; and Duke's family, the Macdonalds, had originally come from Aberdeen – as far back as anyone could remember, they had been in the cattle business.

The cowboys all had short, finely cropped hair and moustaches. They looked like practical-minded men who, because of the nature of their lives, their environment and the rigours of the cruel climate, had maintained a high level of common sense and quick wittedness. Although rugged individuals, each knew that being a member of the team meant survival for all.

We shook hands, the cowboys listening discreetly to my accent. All of them were dressed in uniform, tight worn jeans and scuffed boots decked with spurs which jingled quietly when they moved. They all nodded their heads sternly in welcome, their gaze never leaving my face. Rowdy was the only one smiling. They must have wondered what on Earth I was doing there.

As we sat down, there was a general stir and conversations were rekindled. Maria, the jolly, plump Mexican chef who wore flamboyant skirts, served us each a plate of spicy beans and *fajitas*. She was a talented cook and a tough lady, seemingly having more children and grand-children than the Old Woman Who Lived in a Shoe. Occasionally, she prepared our meals in the open, using black cast-iron pots hitched up over red-hot fires which gave the food a wonderful smoky flavour. Among her specialities were succulent young quail trapped on the ranch; crispy chicken-fried steak in breadcrumbs; fresh fish brought up from the Gulf of Mexico; gritty home-made corn bread; beef *fajitas*; red beans cooked in pig fat and okra; and sweet peach cobbler.

Rowdy, who ate with a napkin tucked into the top of his shirt, launched into one of his Texan lectures, appro-priately enough about cooks.

'In them old trail days,' he said, leaning over his plate, 'the cook was the most important person. He travelled on a chuck wagon or travellin' kitchen and had to be more than a chef. Upon him fell any domestic duty. He was a doctor, barber, seamstress, blacksmith, and keeper of the peace. It was his job to look after all the provisions need-ed on the drive, from needles to bedrolls. He was damn busy on the trail. He had to pack and unpack the chuck wagon twice a day and cook three meals ... Some things don't change. Right Maria?' joked Rowdy, but no one ever laughed at Rowdy's jokes.

Once we had finished eating, Maria, who always had a smile for other women and a curt 'Yes, Sir' for the men, brought Rowdy and Charmayne, a cowgirl who had joined us, mugs of steaming coffee and tea for Sally and me. Rowdy stirred several sweeteners into his, complaining of high blood pressure. He then gulped it down before excusing himself for a few minutes while he went 'to take care of some pressin' business. Y'all understand.'

Meanwhile, I couldn't help overhearing a conversation between two cowboys sitting two tables away. One, sport-ing a bright red and green checked shirt, exclaimed aggressively, 'I got me a couple of coons last night.' He drew hard on a cigarette. 'They were goin' through my trash and I pumped 'em full'a lead.'

I turned suddenly, wondering what they were talking about. Then the second man moaned, 'Yer, dirty scum, ain't they. My wife, though, she don't like me killin' 'em. Says she feels sorry for 'em, if you can believe that. God knows why. They have no respect for nothin'.'

I had seen some racial prejudice in New York, but this was monstrous. Were these two men discussing what I thought they were discussing? I must have looked quite pale, imagining that I had fallen amongst racists who went about mercilessly killing black people and discussed it in public over a meal.

Sally asked me if I was OK. I whispered to her that the men two tables away were discussing a murder one of them had committed.

'I think we should leave,' I said under my breath.

'I think you've misunderstood,' she said, giggling. 'One of 'em is describing how he killed two raccoons.'

'Raccoons?' I said.

'Sure. Coon is short for raccoon.'

'What's a raccoon?'

It was then that Sally described the nocturnal vermin with their striped faces. In the early hours of the morning, they rummage mischievously through rubbish bins and make a general nuisance of themselves, climbing and ranging over the rooftops.

'Oh,' I said, feeling just a little foolish.

* * *

Assuring me that I was in safe hands, Sally returned to Sweetwater. Charmayne, who was chubby and rosy-cheeked and married to one of the cowboys, took me to my lodgings, a cosy bunk house with wood-panelled walls and a fireplace. The four-poster bed was covered with a hand-made American quilt with geometric patterns similar to those I was to see in the Islamic world.

Charmayne helped me unpack. 'What are we goin' ta call you, then?' she asked.

'Well, my name's Tarquin.'

'We'll never get that,' she said. 'We'll just have to be calling you Tark.'

I asked the cowgirl about how things worked on the ranch and found her as knowledgeable as Rowdy.

'This is a permanent ranch,' she told me. 'Way back, before barbed wire came along, life centred around the round-up and the long, long drive to market. That took months and crossed thousands of miles. There were two round-ups a year. The first was as soon as the grass turned green, and the second in the fall.'

Charmayne left me to change into my jeans and boots, and later took me for a guided tour of the HQ. As we approached the stables, I could hear gentle neighing and whinnying. Hairy heads peaked out from their stalls. At one end, the smith was working on the hooves of a frisky colt, and Dolly, an energetic black labrador, was romping about flipping stones in the air.

I was handed a shovel and a rake. Charmayne instructed me to clean and re-bed all thirty horse stalls. She opened the door to one of them and, to my horror, it was brimming several feet deep with ripening, steaming, stinking horse shit.

'You can't be serious,' I said. 'Rowdy never mentioned anything about mucking out stalls.'

'Aha, that sounds like Rowdy,' replied Charmayne over her shoulder as she left me to my task.

Duke, one of the younger cowboys – a gifted rider with whom I was to become good friends – was saddling his horse round the back of the stables. I asked him why the stables had not been cleaned for so long. Grinning sheepishly, he replied, 'Cause the Mexican who used to shovel it out got a kneecap kicked clean off by a geldin' called

Wild Thaing. Since then we ain't been able to find no one to do the job.'

He left me speculating as to what terrible fate might befall me. This wasn't exactly the sort of work I had imagined doing on a cowboy ranch. I had been led to believe that I would be riding horses and branding steers.

For ten days I wallowed in, shovelled and stank of horse manure. It was so rotten that the methane gases and fumes made me feel nauseous and dizzy. I was Hercules, working through his labours in the Aegean stables: it was several worlds away from the marble foyer of the Hotel X. Meanwhile, my fellow ranchers were cautious and distant; to them, I was a pale, lily-white, feeble city boy – a 'greenhorn' – who wasn't used to hard work and hadn't yet proved himself. They didn't make allowances for me just because I was from England: New York was as foreign to them as London and none of them had even visited the Big Apple. As far as they were concerned it was infested by 'yankees', and that was as good a reason as any for not going there.

At first, I found their isolated lives and lack of interest and knowledge of current affairs irritating. A few days after I arrived, as I was eating in the cook shack, one wizened old timer who had never left Texas asked me, 'So, how d'y'all get here from England? Did you fly or did you drive?'

I silently laughed to myself at the time, amazed that he didn't register the Atlantic Ocean due to his ignorance of geography outside his 'patch'. However, my feelings of superiority were short-lived. After only a few days on the ranch, I was a wreck: my hands were blistered, my back ached and my muscles felt like jelly.

All this meant that I quickly developed a healthy respect for the ranch workers' skills and prowess. Duke, for example, could take a car engine apart, repair a water heater and fix just about any electrical or mechanical appliance. His motto was: 'If I'm goin' to use it, I want to know how it works'. I, on the other hand, for all my familiarity with geography and current affairs, lacked manual dexterity and, at the time, could hardly mend a plug.

* * *

It took me nearly two weeks to clean and re-bed all thirty horse stalls, and gradually I began to win the cowboys' confidence. A particular incident greatly contributed to my growing acceptance.

One freezing February morning, I was just finishing breaking the ice in the stalls' water troughs. A voice called out to me. It was George, one of the most accomplished horsemen in Texas, a born cowboy who ran his life according to proven axioms. He asked me to help him and some of the other hands 'doctor cattle'. Obediently, I followed him to a penned-off area a few hundred yards north of the HQ.

When I arrived on the scene, Duke, Bubba and Chuck were chasing a brown cow with a bloated stomach into the cattle chute, which resembled a medieval torture chamber with metal gates and clamps which came crashing down with resonant clangs as soon as the animal charged inside. George ordered me to take the animal's temperature with a thermometer. My first instinct was to walk up to the cow's head where I attempted to insert the rod into her mouth, but the salivating tongue kept pushing it out.

'Tark. Um ... wrong end,' said George sarcastically, then pointed to the cow's rear.

Hesitating, I put on my gloves and, reaching through the bars, lifted up the turd-encrusted tail. Grimacing, I inserted the rod into the cow's arse.

'You enjoyin' that, Tark?' asked George, chuckling to himself. Just then, more green crap oozed out onto my gloves.

'Every minute of it,' I said.

George concluded that the cow had a pocket of air trapped in her stomach. He attempted to release it by pushing a long length of plastic tubing down the animal's throat and then sucked on the end as hard as he could, but to no avail.

'This cow's goin'a die 'less we get this air out,' said George, now worried. 'This lady's worth five hundred dollars so we best work hard to save her.'

Without further ado, he took a knife from his belt and stabbed it into the animal's side. A mix of methane, blood, air, bile and nauseating gases spurted out. The wounded beast made a sound like a cross between a lion's roar and the blast of a fog horn. Then, with George urging us to help out, we all stood around the chute and squeezed the cow's stomach from either side to ensure that all the air was out, a putrid task which ended with Duke and me being splattered with the remaining stinking contents.

The stab wound was left to heal naturally. Berating us for being 'a couple of faggots', George released the animal. The heavy metal gates flew open and the cow shot into the yard like a fanatical bargain hunter during the New Year sales. She tossed her head in the air, hind legs kicking out, mighty hooves sending clumps of mud and pebbles flying in all directions. Then, as if the animal realised she was making an undignified exhibition of herself, she suddenly stopped, not ten yards from where I stood out in the open pen.

I was shocked by this, as cows in England don't generally behave in such a manner; they are placid creatures who stand around in fields, chewing cud, discarding cow pats and mooing occasionally. But this was a Texan cow and, evidently, Texan cows were different, more bullish.

She exhaled heavily through her wide, moist, soft nostrils, looked me straight in the eye and drew a hoof back and forth over a rock like a butcher sharpening his knives. This was one angry bovine. Duke, who was now standing well out of harm's way on the edge of the yard, gestured to me: 'Chase her up through that open gate, Gringo!'

I gulped. I inched forward, my head down, half-heartedly swinging my arms above my head. 'Go on. Move,' I said feebly.

'That ain't the way,' shouted George.

The cow stood there looking mean, steam rising from her back. 'Get out of here,' I repeated.

'Tark, you better get out,' bellowed Chuck.

But it was too late. The animal lowered her head, lining me up in her sights. I turned and ran like a cowardly matador, but her hooves thundered towards me and she caught me below the ribs. The air was punched out of my lungs and stomach, my hat flew off, and I was thrust backwards three or four feet across the yard.

Luckily, the cow zoned in on my hat which it duly stamped, crushed and ground into the dust. Then, she prepared to charge again. Having caught my breath just in time, I managed to grab hold of the railings and pulled myself up out of reach of her butting head. She smashed blindly at the bar below. I jumped down on the other side of the railing and dusted myself off. A cluster of hats soared into the sky as the cowboys hollered and laughed like a pack of coyotes.

'That's enough foolin' around thar!' shouted George, who had enjoyed the whole spectacle as much as everyone else. 'We got cattle to take to grazin', there's gates need fixin' and I want those bronks broke. So come on!'

The cowboys reluctantly stubbed out their cigarettes and made off in all directions, leaving the cow still fuming, still bucking, still tearing my poor hat to shreds.

* * *

During the following weeks, I learned that although cowboying is fun, the air is fresh and it's a free life, it's also incredibly hard work and, not surprisingly, nowhere near

as glamorous as Hollywood portrays. I can now understand why a limit of only seven years was traditionally the
average time spent on the range before seeking a more
settled existence in the towns of the West. By tradition,
the American cowboy has been underpaid, overworked,
deprived of sleep, and prone to boredom – and drink – and
has been poorly fed (although this aspect has greatly
improved).

The motives which led men to become cowboys were
seldom romantic. In the years following the Civil War, the
peak years of the range cattle industry, many young men
from the vanquished Confederacy found themselves without family, property or jobs.

The West was, if not the Promised Land, at least
a land that offered a new beginning. A smaller number
of Union veterans, especially those from New England,
were likewise drawn to the range. The origin of many a
cowboy in those early years was readily discernible in the
ragged remnants of a grey or blue uniform, serving as
work clothes.

Filling out the ranks of the cowboys were native
Americans, Mexicans, Blacks, Englishmen and Scotsmen.
The black cowboys were, for the most part, ex-slaves from
Texas ranches. The rest had moved west to escape the
constraints placed on them by local Southern politicians
in reaction to the North's reconstruction policies.
Mexicans, like blacks, formed one-seventh of the cowboy
population.

Day by day, I gradually became a familiar part of
the team and started to form friendships with Duke,
Bubba, Rowdy and some of the others. Then to my relief,
an illegal Mexican immigrant named Jesus arrived. A 'wet
back' – so called because many of his countrymen swim
the Rio Grande river to reach the US – he was hired to
take over my job of mucking out the stables.

I was offered full cowboy status and was accepted
enthusiastically as one of them. George appointed Duke

as my tutor and guide saying, 'You two hang around together like a couple of girls at a barn dance anyways.' Not only would I now have to learn how to ride, but Duke was also determined to have me thinking, acting and behaving like a true cowboy. He kitted me out with a proper tan Stetson hat to replace the one trampled by the cow, or 'your lady friend' as she was jokingly referred to.

'If you're goin' to be a real cowboy, you've got to know what this clothin' is all for and why we use it,' said Duke. 'Years ago,' he told me, 'hats came in a lot of styles. A little over a hundred years ago, Sam Stetson brought this one to the West. Since then, they've been number one around here.

'To us cowboys, a hat is a tool of the trade. It protects us from the Sun, y'all can drink out of it – that is if yar dandruff ain't bad – and y'all can use it to fan the old campfire. A Stetson is always the first thing to put on in the mornin' and the last thing to take off at night.'

Duke handed me a pair of spurs and showed me how to put them on. Spurs, also known as *espuelas* or grappling irons, are a necessary accoutrement. Each spur includes a rowel, shank, heel plate and spur button plus a leather strap to hold the contraption in place.

'These thaings,' Duke explained, 'they're used to control, but never, never, never to punish the horse. A man who uses his spurs to cut a horse don't last long around these parts. The first thaing y'all gotta do is to blunt the points. That's what we all do.'

I still had my work shirt, gloves and Wranglers. Jeans, I had been told, were first introduced by Levi Strauss who, in 1850, landed in San Francisco with a load of merchandise he hoped to sell in the Californian mining camps. Unable to move a supply of canvas and finding a demand for work clothes, Strauss made trousers and became an overnight success. He soon switched from canvas to denim, added copper rivets at the stress points and made an impressive fortune.

Duke handed me a red and white 'kerchief, or bandanna, to provide protection for my neck from the Sun; it could be used to cover my mouth and nose from dust when riding out on the plains. Now I really looked and felt like I was getting the hang of it. However, I still had a long way to go before I could claim to be a real 'hand'.

One of the mannerisms of the cowboy that I was determined to master was the walk. In the movies, I had seen countless shoot-outs between rough, unshaven, often drunk men standing at opposite ends of a street. Whether good guys or bad guys, they always walked in the strangest manner: with their hands hovering over their gun holsters, their bowed legs stiff and splayed, looking like thinner versions of sumo wrestlers. I had imagined this to be some affected gait that allowed them to draw faster. This was yet another romantic Hollywood Wild West image that was way off trajectory.

Duke gave me some leggings and after wearing them for only a few hours, I made the alarming discovery that cowboys walk in this ridiculous manner because they are in excruciating pain. While the leggings are designed to protect the inner thigh from constant rubbing against the saddle and the horse's side, they ripped out all the hairs on my legs and made my arse so sore that I could hardly sit down for days. Just moving in them guaranteed the splayed effect. The leggings were so tight that if I tried to bring my legs together, my eyes watered.

Once Duke had provided me with the whole kit, he gave me an appraising look. He stroked his blonde moustache, and led me towards the stables where he presented me with a frisky 'stud' called Chicken Joseph George.

From the start, Chicken Joseph George and I didn't hit it off. The lower half of my body felt as if it was being lashed with stinging nettles, so I wanted to take things slowly; George had other ideas and wanted to chase every mare in sight. At the beginning, I had little control, and every few minutes I was bucked off unceremoniously onto the hard ground.

'You ever ridden before?' shouted Rowdy, who stood with most of the cowboys watching me trying to learn to ride. At that particular moment, I was attempting to untangle my spurs from the stirrups. Splitting their sides with laughter and with tears running down their faces, all of them swore they had never seen anything as funny before.

'Pony trekking in Wales, if that counts,' I replied.

'You rode on a whale?' asked one man, incredulously.

'Tark. Stop screwin' around and get back on that stud and keep your ass in the back of the saddle,' shouted George.

There was nothing like the wrath of George as an incentive for getting something done. Once more, I mounted Chicken Joseph George, silently promising him a lifetime's supply of sugar cubes if he promised not to throw me off again. And lo and behold, he didn't.

The 'western' or 'stock' saddle is deep, unlike the English 'dressage' which requires the rider to stand in the stirrups and is used for recreational activities such as steeplechasing and polo. The stock saddle was used by working riders with no time for horsing around.

'Our saddle was introduced via Spanish Central America,' Rowdy once told me in one of his mini-lectures. 'Them conquistadors borrowed it from them Moors, the Spanish guys, who brought it from the Middle East, Arabia and so on. It sure is a practical seat when riding out in the open.'

Indeed, while it was the American East and Europe that, to a large degree, provided the cowboy manpower, it was Spanish Mexico that contributed the techniques and much of the jargon of the trade. The earliest Texan cowboys learned from Mexican *vaqueros*. These men were the heirs of Spaniards who herded a type of long-horn cattle on the plains of Andalusia long before their conquest of the New World. The round-up, branding, the western saddle, roping and cowboy clothing all originated with them.

The very idea of mounted herdsmen was almost entirely Spanish. In other European countries they usually moved about on foot. Words like *cincha* (cinch), *catallerange* (wrangler), *chaperejos* (chaps) and *reata* (lariat) entered the colourful vocabulary of the cowboy, revealing the origins of his trade.

The strong relationship between cowboy and horse is another of the most highly romanticised elements of the cowboy myth. Indeed, when the cowboy needed a good cow horse to do his job, he would change mounts with as little hesitation as any worker who needed to change his tools. Most cowboys did not even own their horses; they were provided by the employers since cowboys rarely had enough money to buy their own. Yet somehow, the legends that grew up around these horses inspired the creation of Hollywood's 'wonder' horses.

Chicken Joseph George, like the other steeds on Rowdy's ranch, were being bred and trained as 'cutting horses'; so called because they are literally used to 'cut away' or isolate cows from the herd. This is a technique used if a cow is lame, pregnant, diseased or ready for slaughter.

Many years ago, it was noticed that certain horses had a natural herding instinct, like a sheep dog. Ever since then, they have been bred selectively and trained for this purpose. On the surface, cutting a cow away from a herd may sound like an easy task. As I had learned from experience, however, cattle, although lacking stamina, are remarkably cunning, agile and stubborn animals.

One of my new jobs was to assist George in training sessions. On horseback, Duke and I would bring a herd of cattle, usually around a dozen or so, into one of the sandy enclosures and ensure that they remained at one end. When ready, George would approach the herd at a leisurely walk and, as he drew close, the cows would thin out along the edges of the enclosure.

Next, he would cut or isolate a cow from the herd and chase it to the opposite end of the pen. It was then that our job of preventing the rest of the herd from following was crucial. Once a cow was isolated, it would instinctively try to return to the herd, charging back at George and his horse, attempting to outmanoeuvre them. This was when the real excitement would begin. A well-trained cutting horse would automatically work to prevent the cow from returning to the herd without any prompting from the rider.

A typical round would see the cow trying to outmanoeuvre the horse, lurching left and then right. A swift, nimble cutting horse, with its head down, would literally jump from side to side, anticipating the cow's every move, the animals' two heads almost touching, eyeball to eyeball. The cow would charge over to the other side of the pen where the horse would block it off, bending down close to the ground, dashing sand in all directions. Then suddenly, they would both turn and charge off in another direction. Then another turn. And so on ...

My average day now comprised rising at 5.30 a.m. to feed the animals. After a breakfast of scrambled eggs, beans and bacon, grilled toast and jam, Rowdy and I would saddle up the horses and 'lope' or ride them for hours. In the afternoon, there were always hundreds of cattle to be herded across the vast, expansive plains of the ranch.

At the end of a satisfying hard day's work, I was usually ready for a cold beer in Sweetwater, like Duke's forefathers who enjoyed painting the town red at the end of a hard trail. A cowboy would always spend the hundred or so dollars he made on a drive in the cattle towns. After only a few days, the money would probably be gone on clothes, liquor and prostitutes.

'Hell-raising' by cowboys on a spree invariably met with the resistance of the townspeople and earned the cowboy a largely unfair reputation for violence. Despite all this, Charles Goodnight, whose long career in the West embraced every aspect of cowboy life, claimed never to have heard of any real cowboy, as distinct from any professional 'badman', being tried for a crime in the Texas Panhandle. He recalls only two fist fights in fifty years. Even today, however, the townspeople continue to look down on the cowboys while the ranchers resent the pseudo Marlboro cigarette, urban cowboy image promoted in the media.

* * *

Towards the end of my stay, the cowboys took me to a four-day round-up on another ranch a five-hour drive away. We left at three in the morning and drove in Rowdy's mammoth copper-coloured pick-up, which was almost as large as a bus and had a dozen side mirrors. Even George, who I only ever saw smile once – on the day his first child was born – was excited and keyed up. This was a chance for him to show off their best horses, which ranked among the most highly trained and well bred in the country.

At sunrise, we found the cowboys, dozens of them, warming themselves over a blazing wood fire where they had been camping out for several days. George parked amongst the other pick-ups and trailers. Hands were unloading bales of hay, saddles were being polished, horses were being watered, hay and feed were being distributed. Most of the cowboys had just woken up. One, wearing only a pair of jeans, was rinsing off shampoo suds in a bucket of cold water. Another brushed his teeth, swilling out his mouth from a tin mug. A cowgirl walked past and wolf whistled. 'Hey, Duke, you cute thaing,' she called out as we dismounted from the pick-up.

Duke blushed ever so slightly. 'Fiery one that,' he told me under his breath.

Once unloaded, we fed our horses and made camp, not far from the fire.

'It's goin' to be a real old-fashioned brandin',' Duke shouted, as we were saddling up the horses. 'None of that electronic shit or nothin'. They don't even use a cattle chute.'

Since I was now competent enough in the saddle, I was allowed to join in the herding. I galloped off over the miles of open range with Duke and George, and we found a few dozen cattle. This was where the cutting horse came into its own. On the way back to the pens, one cow suddenly charged off in the wrong direction.

'That one's yars,' shouted Duke.

I spurred my horse and gave chase, soon returning with the cow in front of me. 'You're beginin' to look like a real hand,' said Duke, slapping me on the back. ''Course your accent's still strange. When we goin' to get you t'say "ranch" right, with a hard "a" 'stead of that fag pronunciation of yars?'

Once all the cattle, which amounted to a few hundred, were assembled in penned-in areas, George was assigned the task of cutting away those cows which were pregnant or sick, and newly born calves which needed branding. He would isolate one and then lasso the animal's back legs, quickly tying his end of the rope to the cattle horn on his saddle. Then he would turn his horse around and drag the animal behind him. Another cowboy built like a heavyweight boxer would flip the cow onto its side and immediately another hand, like myself, would pin its neck to the ground while yet another would grip the animal's kicking legs and release the rope. Before the calf could break free, it would be branded with a hot iron with the mark of the ranch's owner.

Like so many ranch chores, it was dangerous and tough physical work: a steer suddenly pulling a rope taut could easily topple both horse and rider. Fingers could be peeled down to the bone and, of course, there was always the danger that George would lasso you instead of a cow and drag you through horse shit.

Duke pointed out the owner of the ranch, Buster Welch, standing amongst a group of cowboys. Wearing mirror sunglasses, a slight paunch hanging over his belt, he looked like a prison security guard. I already knew Buster Welch by reputation. Rowdy and the others had often talked about him; he was, after all, a legend, the most famous cutting horse rider in the West, five-time world champion. A rich, humorous, charismatic man, he had more than a little trouble with my name: 'What the hell is this boy's name?' he asked George, who was well respected by Welch.

'That thar's Tark'in,' he replied, 'but we have to call him Tark 'cause we can't pronounce the rest.'

'Tark'in!' the horseman replied. 'What the hell kind of name is that?'

'He's from England,' they chorused.

'Well,' said Buster, 'guess England's been there so long they've plain run out of names and have to make 'em up!'

* * *

In the fortnight after the round-up, I helped out at two cutting horse competitions and two more weeks rolled by until finally the time to continue my travels had arrived. I decided to go to San Francisco where my mother's sister, Jane, said she would be able to get me a job in a catering company. This, I hoped, would provide me with enough money to move on from America to India and start working as a proper reporter.

There was no room for sentimentality in the lives of the cowboys and the 'goodbyes' on the ranch were short and unemotional. Nevertheless, Duke, in spite of himself, seemed genuinely sad to see me go. As I was getting into Sally's car to return to Sweetwater, he handed me a pair of spurs.

'Thar you go, Tark,' he said. 'You may need these in San Francisco. You know what those Californian women are like!'

After that, Sally insisted on taking me on a six-day tour of Texas, stopping off in the cities of Austin and Saint Antonio, where I was shown tremendous hospitality by her family and friends.

There was, however, one piece of bad news. Sally broke it to me gently as we ate a last meal at a Dairy Queen fast food restaurant.

'I hate to spoil yaar evenin',' she said, looking down at her plate. 'But it's ... it's Amanda, the redhead at K-Mart you were so keen on.'

'Oh God. What's happened?'

'Well nothin' baad,' replied Sally, 'well nothin' baad ... baad. She wasn't in no accident or nothin'.'

'Well, what then?'

Sally looked up from her plate: 'She got herself hitched – married, I mean – in Hawaii. To a fifty-year-old mult-i-millionaire.'

'How did they meet?' I asked, astonished.

'In K-Mart. He came in one day to buy some jeans and whisked her off her feet.'

FOUR

'Keep Talking, I Love Your Accent'

... whereas before I only ever wanted to meet or spend time with people I liked, now I find myself anxious to meet anyone, from whatever background, however dreadful or strange or nice they may be. The same with places and situations. I find myself hunting for colour, the quirky, the ridiculous, the fascinating. The world has become my hunting ground. The game: 'good material'.

Diary, 13 March 1989

On the flight from Dallas to San Francisco, the passenger sitting next to me smelt like a rotting tea towel; clearly he had not bathed for several days. He appeared agitated. Next to him, sat a woman who looked as if she had been pieced together on a production line: her face had that plastic look and her silicone implants were disproportionate to the rest of her body. Her skin was so tanned it looked as if she was wearing a body stocking. She tried to make general conversation, but I was too tired to follow what she was saying.

As the huge airliner taxied to the end of the runway, I rested comfortably in my seat. A stewardess started to explain what to do in the event of an emergency.

None of my fellow passengers, with the exception of three young bucks who were busy eye-balling her trim physique, appeared to be paying the slightest bit of attention. The frequent flyers, some of them know-it-alls, and those who wished to personify images of hardened, seasoned travellers, displayed their arrogance and conceit by staring out of the windows. They glanced up occasionally, scrunching up their noses and nodding their heads superciliously, as if to say, 'I've flown a thousand times before'.

Abruptly, my neighbour shoved that morning's edition of the *Dallas Morning Post* into my lap.

'Look! Have you seen this?' he snivelled, in a voice that quavered as if someone was drumming on his back. He fixed me with a frightened look, every muscle in his face twitching.

'Look! Look! Look at the headline! My Ma warned me not to fly today,' he whined again nervously.

209 DIE IN AIR CRASH.

I quickly scanned the first few paragraphs only to discover that another American plane had crashed the day before. Admittedly, this was not comforting news, although I felt it unlikely that we were in danger. At any rate, I tried to calm my neighbour by joking and reminding him that statistically we were safer in the air than on the ground.

'No way, man,' he cried, 'this is a bad omen!'

Slightly annoyed, I said, 'Look, when your time has come, it's come. There's not much you can do about it.'

He went back to staring at the front page. The wheels left the ground and we soared into the air. The puffy clouds whisked by the window and Dallas quickly shrank to doll's house size.

As the 'Fasten your Seatbelts' light flicked off, I tried to relax once more but my neighbour, who sank his nails into the plastic arm rest, startled me again.

'The air-conditioning! The air-conditioning! It hasn't come on!' he shouted. His tongue darted snake-like in and out of his mouth; he grabbed my left arm and gripped it tight.

'It will come on soon. Get control of yourself,' I murmured

soothingly to him, managing to reclaim my numb limb.

Releasing his hold on me, he nodded and slotted his fingertips back into the now pitted arm rests. 'Everything's fine,' I assured the others sitting near us and reclined nervously back into my seat, forcing my eyes shut tight. Unexpectedly, one of the stewardesses scrambled down the aisle and burst into the pilot's cabin. Within seconds, the plane made a furious U-turn, swiftly losing altitude in the process.

'My God,' I thought. 'Perhaps my neighbour was not mad after all. Had he had a premonition?'

'Ladies and gentlemen,' announced the pilot in a cool, over-restrained voice. 'We have a slight technical difficulty and are returning to Dallas. Please pay attention to your air stewardess ...' Static crackled from the speakers.

'Oh God, man! Oh my God! Oh Jesus!' gasped my neighbour. 'This is it, man! We're all going to die! We're history. I knew it! My mother was right!'

His outburst was now accompanied by other hysterical passengers, some crying, some sobbing uncontrollably. The woman with the plastic face uttered a prolonged wailing noise and others embraced and consoled each other. There were so many Hail Marys that, for a moment, I thought we were flying into the Vatican. Even the most hardened of the snooty air travellers looked panic-stricken. Were we part of some corny American disaster movie, I asked myself?

Our stewardess, who was shaking like someone standing naked in a snow blizzard, took her place in the aisle.

'L..L..Ladies a..a..and,' she stuttered, wiping her perspiring brow, '... gentlemen ...'

She paused again, trying to control herself, trying to get into the routine she knew so well instead of sounding like a foreign language student.

'Please ... fasten your ... seat belts ... and ... and ...' She stopped again. We could feel the plane plunging earthward at what felt like ninety degrees. Her aplomb having totally abandoned her, she screamed, 'Get your heads down and grab the seat in front of you!'

My heart was pumping waves of adrenalin while my neighbour lowed pathetically, narrating the Lord's prayer, never quite getting past the 'thy kingdom come' bit. The seat in front of me was resting backwards, so I couldn't assume the crash position. Leaning over it, I asked the occupant, a woman who had 'cool' written all over her forehead, if she would kindly lift the lever and put her seat in the forward position. She brushed her hand through the air with a 'tut'. 'Wait a minute,' she said.

Dallas and its suburbia now loomed only a few hundred feet below. The engines were yowling like an untuned radio. It was as much as I could do to defy the pressing G-force.

'Look, you bloody woman, put your seat forward!' I shouted.

'Take a chill pill,' she said.

I forced her seat forward. She looked back at me over the head rest. 'Bad karma,' she muttered.

So was this it? I reflected, squashing my face up against the current issue of *Newsweek* and a complementary copy of the in-flight magazine. Was the great computer in the sky about to punch my delete button? Was I about to be blown into a pulp with dozens of hysterics and one bona fide fatalist? So much for my career in journalism ...

The captain's voice came over the speaker warning us to hold tight: we were about to go in. I crossed my fingers, tensing my arm muscles. Only a few seconds now ...

I sensed a sudden bump. The wheels screeched. The plane trembled as if it were just a mere toy about to be ripped into pieces by some sadistic child. The overhead lockers shook like soup blenders. Doors snapped open, bottles, cases, cameras, coats spilled everywhere; objects flew across the cabin. The Hail Marys crescendoed. The wheels continued to thump, crunch and screech until, finally, we came to a full stop. Passengers were already hurrying for the exits. Through my window, I could see fire trucks and a cavalcade of ambulances racing towards us, their flashing lights sending yellow, white and red whirling patterns skipping across the tarmac like a glorified disco.

Leaving our belongings on board, we slipped down inflated ramps into the arms of our rescuers. By the time I had my feet on the ground and managed to say, 'I've always wanted to do that,' the tail, which had caught on fire, was already covered in gallons of thick, creamy foam.

* * *

Once inside the terminal, everyone raved deliriously, whooping and hollering. Strangers told one another their stories, blurting out how they felt, and cried on each other's shoulders. Only the female Californian fatalist, who was already demanding another plane, and two inscrutable Chinese gentlemen, who had continued reading their newspapers during the entire emergency, remained calm.

I saw my former neighbour being carried away on a stretcher – fused into the crash position.

Two hours later, another plane and crew were ready for take-off. Only about twenty of us boarded. Of the others, many were too frightened to fly again that day and wanted their money back; and some vowed never to go up in the air again, heading towards the railway station and Hertz rent-a-car.

Upon our arrival at San Francisco airport, a camera crew were waiting. Like a pack of jackals, they headed straight for a young mother and her child.

'How d'ya feel?' the female reporter asked her, the cameraman moving in close, focusing his imposing lens. I tried to make good my escape, but they were in hot pursuit and, in spite of my evasive actions, finally cornered me. I unleashed a broadside: 'Bugger off. We've been through enough.'

The reporter looked at me for a moment with a quizzical smile and, ordering the camera man to 'roll tape', retorted, 'Keep talking, I love your accent!'

* * *

When I finally reached a hotel in the city centre, physically and mentally exhausted, I longed to collapse, clothes and all, onto the cosy, soft bed. As soon as my head touched the pillow, I began to drift off ... then some incredible force rocked the room and threw me out of the bed onto the carpet. A book shelf came crashing down within inches of my head.

I got up and stood under the door frame, dazed and stunned. There could be little doubt that this was one of California's famous earthquakes which, I later discovered, registered close to six on the Richter Scale.

The next morning, I called a friend in LA whose house had been destroyed recently by mud slides.

'What's going on?' I asked him, 'emergency landings, earthquakes – your mud slides. What's next?'

'I don't know, man,' he said, 'but my sister in Florida just got hit by a hurricane. Wiped out her place. If this keeps up, I might have to get religious or somethin'.'

FIVE

A Miasma of Cosmic Garbage

San Fran is beautiful, but much smaller than I imagined ... Watched the fog roll in from the Pacific this morning, engulfing the Golden Gate bridge within minutes. The fog horns started blaring and I could see Alcatraz in the middle of the bay ... Am going to meet the catering company people tomorrow. Aunt Jane says I'll be able to make a lot of money. Easily enough to make it to India, at any rate ...

Diary, 15 March 1989

The society wedding was to be held in one of San Francisco's Victorian gingerbread houses. The front door was situated high above the street with steep, winding steps leading to it, a nightmare for removal men. The window sills and frames were painted pastel blues and yellows. Inside, the rooms had mahogany-panelled walls and the air was thick and sweet with the smell of fresh polish. The staircase was solid and swept into the hallway like a lady's ball gown, and in several small side alcoves, light shimmered through stained-glass windows.

A woman with a beehive hairdo greeted my Aunt Jane and me at the door. It was my first day in San Francisco and I was exhausted from the events of the day before, but I tried to put a brave face on it. We were ushered into an oval room, decorated with balloons and streamers, which was packed with smiling people. There, we were greeted like old friends by a member of the family and took our seats in one of the rows of gilded chairs.

The show music, played by a small band in the corner, wafted gently around the room. An old oriental gentleman inched his way to the front where he addressed the guests. Apparently the Master of Ceremonies, he introduced the priest, who was a relation of the bride, before moving off dolefully to his seat.

The minister was dressed in a black leather jacket and Western cowboy boots. He slouched as he greeted us. 'Hi, how are you today?' he asked in a melodious voice, 'it's real cool to see everyone here. It should be one wild kind of a party and I know you all want to get down. First, though, we have the honour of marrying this couple.'

For a split second, I thought that Jane had brought me to the wedding rehearsal by mistake. I was about to suggest that we return later, when a little inner voice counselled: 'Tolerance, Tarquin. New ideas.'

'Marriage,' continued the Reverend, 'is a beautiful, wonderful thing and it's good to see a couple who are so downright suited ... keep out of the divorce courts, kids!' he joked. Everyone laughed. 'Jerry, can you explain why you want to marry this lovely girl?'

Jerry was a tall, fair-skinned, pinched-faced fellow and not especially eloquent: 'Well, she's a babe as you can see and we're great together. What more can I say?'

The minister put the same question to the bride.

'I love him – and he's rich,' she sniggered.

I nudged my aunt: 'Are these good friends of yours?'

'No,' she whispered, 'I met her in the manicurist this afternoon.' I looked around the room. How many more of the guests went to the same manicurist?

The priest was delivering something like a sermon, but instead of the usual references to the Almighty, religion and that sort of thing, he was quoting from the film, *Field of Dreams*.

'I now pronounce you man and wife.'

This was the only familiar part of the service that I recognised, apart from the kiss. The newlyweds moved into another room where four saxophonists in white jackets and pink bow ties started playing Scott Joplin tunes. Their band was called, The Nuclear Whales Saxophone Orchestra. I fetched my aunt a drink from the bar and, during a break, asked one of the band members, 'Why the name?'

'Hey dude,' he replied, 'it's a name.'

I had to agree and moved into the other room where a line of guests were wishing the couple good luck. My aunt and I shook hands with each member of the extended family, trying to think of something to say to all of them. They seemed genuinely pleased to meet us, but I'm sure in years to come, when they look through the wedding photographs, they will ask themselves, pointing at pictures of Jane and me, 'Who the hell were they?'

After I had wished the bride and groom all the happiness in the world, an object was placed in my hand. I looked down, expecting to find a plate of cake. Instead, I discovered ... a baseball cap. It was printed with the names of the bride and groom, and the day's date. An anorexic-looking woman told me to put it on.

'Is this a normal custom at American weddings?' I asked my aunt.

She nudged me and said gruffly, 'Whatever ... you ... do ... don't ... laugh!'

'OK, OK.'

I put on the cap. When we moved into the main room, I found that everyone was wearing baseball caps; many of them were fans of the sport. I thought back to my New York diner and how much Rob, the CBS stats man, would have appreciated this. Mingling amongst the guests, I met a variety of art dealers, television and media people and the mayor of San Francisco's doctor. The only person at the reception that my aunt knew at all well was an executive working in Silicon Valley who spoke about the arms race coming to an end. I asked him if he was worried.

'No,' he said, quite calmly, 'we'll just start doing

something else.'

'But what?'

'We'll find something,' he said confidently.

The executive soon left and Jane introduced me to a bubbly young woman who was something called a 'philosophy major' at Berkeley. Blonde and skinny, with a ring through her nose, her eyebrows had been plucked out. She was a 'health freak' and droned on about the cholesterol levels of the food on the buffet and how you should only drink 'one glass of wine because one a day is good for you and more is not.' She insisted on telling me that the yoghurt on the dessert table would have been put to better use as a face pack and how the dark bags under my eyes were due to a vitamin deficiency and not because I was suffering from sleep deprivation over the past few days, thanks to a near air disaster and various earthquakes. When I offered her some sugar for her coffee she said, 'I don't believe in sugar.'

'Hang on,' I stammered. 'Don't believe in sugar! Ghosts, the Loch Ness monster, UFOs, God, maybe – but sugar! How can you not believe in sugar! It's there in the bowl. You can touch it.'

She backed away from me, telling Jane that I was 'real tense'. If I happened to bump into her again during the rest of the evening, she called out, 'Smile!'

Later, The Nuclear Whales Saxophone Orchestra suddenly trumpeted the theme tune to *2001: A Space Odyssey*, at which point, two muscular models draped in American flags and wearing top hats carried in the wedding cake. It was a three-tiered structure with pink icing and some sort of phallic symbol on top. Doing a double-take, I moved over to gain a closer look. The bride, who was preparing to cut it, apparently noticed my amazed expression: 'It's a papier-mâché, baloney, Swiss cheese, salad and mayo sandwich,' she said.

'Um ... well ... of course it ... is ...,' I replied, not wanting to make her feel awkward. 'Tell me, though, why is

Acrobats in Greenwich Village, New York.

A stab at Ansel Adams: tyres on the side of the road, Oklahoma.

The splendour of Washington DC.

Venice Beach, California.

Rattlesnake hunter with catch, near Sweetwater, Texas.

Captured rattlesnake, near Sweetwater, Texas.

*The author and Chicken Joseph George take on an agile calf,
the Abeliene Ranch, near Sweetwater, Texas.*

*A traditional branding at a ranch owned by Buster Welch,
the cutting horse champion, Texas.*

Cowboys mind their herd, the Abeliene Ranch, near Sweetwater, Texas.

A cowboy poses in front of a traditional chuck wagon, together with the cook's pots, the Abeliene Ranch, Texas.

*The author's cousin, Alexandra Lecomte,
beside the Golden Gate, San Francisco.*

*Survivors of the Summer of Love:
hippies on Haight Ashbury, San Francisco.*

Live opera at an Italian café in San Francisco.

Instant everything: Las Vegas.

A man enjoys a Sunday afternoon hair cut, Memphis, Tennessee.

*The author aged 18 standing on the Prime Meridian, Greenwich,
just days before leaving for New York.*

there a papier-mâché, baloney, Swiss cheese, salad and mayo sandwich on top of the cake?'

She smiled across the room at her new husband. 'Well, I met Jerry at a ball game,' she explained, before handing out the cake to her guests, 'and the first thing he ever did was buy me a sandwich.'

I had no trouble guessing which kind.

My aunt, who had now crept up behind me, took me by the arm and led me away.

* * *

The wedding's excellent food had been provided by the catering company owned by Jane's friend, a wild-eyed Irish New Yorker called Jack. He had been a chef since the day he applied to a restaurant claiming to be a gourmet, despite having never even boiled an egg. He played the violin like a virtuoso, did most of his drinking before noon, and told the dirtiest jokes I had ever heard.

Jack was always on the lookout for waiters and general helpers, so he took me on board while I began making my plans for going to India. Working for Peaches Catering was great fun. The clients lived in many different districts of San Francisco and the Bay area. We catered for every kind of function imaginable, meeting people from all backgrounds and professions. A typical week found us at a barmitzvah held in a fringe art gallery; a wedding reception staged on a lighthouse for a Russian bride and a Japanese groom; an office party for the Gay and Lesbian League of America; and a stream of parties held in the Napa and Sonoma Valley wineries.

The company was successful in spite of the fact that Jack's catering events were often prone to mishap. En route to one wedding, the back of his company van blew open and the four-tiered cake flew out onto the freeway, disappearing under the wheels of the car behind. Looking back, all we could see was a squashed mess on the motorway. Not long after, Jack hired two black men who ended up brawling with some of the guests at a posh South African dinner party. And then there was the engagement party where Claudia, one of the waitresses, was found in a broom cupboard with the groom-to-be.

Jack's staff were a spirited but motley crew: several were unemployed actors and actresses – one having come close to stardom as a ghost in *Raiders of the Lost Ark*; another was a has-been film editor who spent three days a week recording voices for the *ET* ride at Hollywood's Universal Studios, and the rest were a mixture of high school dropouts and surfers.

Many of Jack's employees were involved in cults; two were 'scrambalologists' and constantly tried to persuade me to join. Despite my curiosity, I have always made a point of steering clear of such sects, if only because I have never been much of a joiner of groups. After thinking it over, however, I decided that a day spent at a scrambalology centre might make a good first-person story for a British publication.

I duly set off for the school in downtown San Francisco. On the pavement outside, a spry young man with a spurious smile was handing out leaflets and chatting up passers by, trying to persuade them to come in.

I knew a little about scrambalology because before I left England, I had spent one summer working for a businessman who had been a devotee for over a decade. Ian ran a building business which had an impeccable reputation for efficiency and first-class work. The man had more energy than a nuclear reactor. Like a puppet on a string, he walked in a correct manner, his back ever straight, his heels bouncing up and down like rubber balls. His life followed the cult's philosophies strictly: he rose early, never ate meat, steered clear of alcohol and was always overly positive. However, for someone who tried so hard, his effect on people was curiously negative.

His commitment to scrambalology could be measured

by the fact that every few months he travelled to Florida to have his negative ions 'sucked' out of him; what this involved was never exactly explained to me. In return, he donated thousands of pounds to the cult's cause.

The young Californian on the street walked and even talked in the same way as Ian. Thrusting a leaflet into my hand, he ushered me inside. 'You would be well advised to take our test, the results of which would reveal hidden realities about yourself!' he said.

I walked in. At a group of desks at the back of a well-lit room, a dozen young people who, like myself, were about to take the test. Most seemed to be approaching it seriously, their body language thoughtful and concentrated. The walls were plastered with colourful posters advertising the many books by the cult's founder. The scrambalology bible, which I had read while working for Ian, seemed to contain little substance. I didn't need a book to tell me that people with an enthusiastic, positive outlook tend to go further in life; to my mind, it was rather like saying, 'You must brush your teeth twice a day to keep them clean.'

The room was air-conditioned yet very warm, which created a dozy environment where everyone was continually yawning. I was presented with the test and instructed to answer every question 'without exception'. It was entitled 'The International Aptitude Test', or something with an equally meaningless but worthy ring to it. Yet the questions seemed to have little relevance to aptitude. How do your friends see you in a relationship? Are you negative much of the time? Are you ambitious? Do you enjoy sex? Do you feel insecure ...?

Haphazardly, I worked my way through, ticking any old square, then presented my completed form to a fat young girl suffering from severe acne. Having heard stories about how the cult enticed children and teenagers away from their parents and brainwashed them, I wondered if she was just such a case. The unfortunate girl assessed my answers and then plotted a graph that depicted my psychological make-up.

Just as she finished, three aggressive men in black jackets strode into the room like the evil knights out of a fairy tale. One of them stood in front of us and called a name, holding my tests in his hand. No one responded, so he announced it again – louder this time. Suddenly, I realised that he was calling the pseudonym I had given them. I quickly raised my hand. He pointed a bony finger towards a door on the far side of the room. 'Wait in there,' he said sternly.

I entered a small cell, the only furniture being a table and two chairs. I sat down in one of them; it was low to the floor and designed for resting but not relaxing; my head barely reached the top of the table. A tall man with a sombre expression walked in, remaining silent for two or three minutes. Then, for the following half an hour, he tried to disorientate and intimidate me: it was more like an interrogation than an interview.

Snatching the graph from the table, he studied it – and then stared at me. It was a stare which I shall never forget, as cold and dark as an icy sea. Although I tried to meet it, I felt compelled to look down. His pupils were large, his manner controlled, brooding, imposing. He looked down again at my chart and shook his head in an annoying fashion.

'Very bad, my friend. I really pity you. You are extremely selfish. You make no time for others. You lack ambition. In short, you are worthless!'

I wanted to ask him for his credentials. What gave him the right to analyse me? But I was curious to see where this would lead, so I said nothing.

'Your life will go steadily downhill if you do not do something soon. Yes, you might experience a few fleeting moments of happiness but you will always be depressed. I can offer you hope. I can offer you a way!' So saying, he offered me his hand. I refused it.

'You're worthless!' he roared, smashing his clenched fist on the table. 'You have no future. Do you want our help?'

'Yes, of course.'

'Good! Sign this paper.' He pushed a form towards me.

Having read it, I signed at the bottom, only just remembering to use my pseudonym.

'Now give me two hundred dollars.'

I asked him what the money was for. He told me that I was to start on a course that very evening. I tried to make some excuses, fudging my words; in truth I was rattled, such was this man's effect upon me. He shouted again: 'This is a decision that is going to affect your entire future. Give me the money!'

Explaining I had no cash, I managed to make good my escape, promising to return. Once outside, I wondered what had happened to the other young people taking the test. Had they been milked of two hundred dollars? I suspected many had. Some would probably become zealous followers of scrambalology.

* * *

California is the Cult State. People were always asking me what I was into and I'd reply, 'Well catering – at the moment.'

In the Berkeley bookshops, you could buy the works of Jung, Gurdjieff, Zoroaster, Freud, Maharishi, Osho, Reverend Moon, Billy Graham, the list was endless. Those looking for some sort of religion, -ism or sect could take their pick from Zen, black and white magic, psycho-analysis and goddess worship. Failing that, you could ponder the mysteries of the world. Are there UFOs? Does the yeti exist? Was Elvis a Martian? Or alternatively become a fitness fanatic and get into yoga, meditation or aerobics. The choice was mind-boggling.

On Haight Ashbury, which had become a trendy street full of middle-class boutiques, I met Rikki Prado, a former zoologist and sandal maker with a florescent orange beard who settled in Haight Ashbury at the height of the anti-Vietnam movement. I asked him why he had come to California.

'I came because the rent was cheap. Also, I was mentally diminished at the time and was on a quest for a new way of life. Jesus, man – in those days we did OK', he continued, 'now it's real hard to be here and be yourself.'

Kelly, a younger hippy who sat in the sunshine carving wooden pipes, gave me this reason: 'California will always manifest some unconventional activity like this,' she said, 'because California eats its young and spits them out as a miasma of cosmic garbage ... America is on a tilt and all the loose marbles roll into California.'

Perhaps D.H. Lawrence's words sum it up better than any other. 'California,' wrote the author in 1923, 'is a queer place – in a way, it has turned its back on the world, and looks into the void Pacific. It is absolutely selfish, very empty, but not false, and at least, not full of false effort ... it's a sort of crazy-sensible.'

Now that's a 'rad' way of putting it – man.

* * *

From San Francisco, I flew back to New York where I met up again with Frank Renard, my journalist friend. We talked over my plans for the future and I told him I intended to go to India. The fact that I still hadn't sold any stories did not seem to bother him. He reminded me that I had only been writing for a year without any formal training.

'What you need now is to get into some real reporting. I like your idea. That's just the sort of place for you. You're ready to take the next step.'

I prepared to leave America. I called Tariq Khan, my friend in Bombay, to tell him I was coming.

'Great,' he said, 'but hurry – or you'll miss the elephant god celebrations.'

Part Two

Asia

SIX

Part Man, Part Elephant

*It's been exactly a year since I arrived in New York.
Seems like a long time ago. I often felt
helpless and lonely then. Now, at least, I've learnt
to get around on my own and got used to my
own company. I've had to do so much for myself
that I was never allowed or encouraged to do at
school. I love it ... God knows what lies ahead. It
feels very much as if I'm graduating onto another
stage ...*

Diary, 2 July 1989

'Your reservation's confirmed, sir,' said the assistant in
the New York Air India office. A dot-matrix printer on her
desk spat out an itinerary. She read from it in a monotonous voice: 'Departing Newark, Sunday at 19.15, arriving Bombay at 23.00, the next day, local time.'

I was spending the day with Barb, the waitress at the
diner around the corner from the Hotel X, who was helping me arrange last minute travel details. The assistant
handed me my ticket. 'Enjoy your flight, sir.'

Everything now seemed set. As we left the office, I
ticked off the items from my list: film, ticket, money,
cameras ... I casually asked Barb what else I had left to
do. She shrugged her shoulders.

'You got a visa – right?' she enquired.

A feeling of sudden nausea swept over me. I had forgotten all about the visa. Glancing at my watch, I saw that
it was three o'clock. And it was Friday afternoon. Without
a visa, there was no way I would be able to leave on

Sunday. I grabbed Barb's arm and hailed a cab. Within the hour, we were inside the Indian High Commission.

A long queue snaked in front of the visa counter behind which stood an Indian bureaucrat with an oiled moustache and an expression about as warm as a cobra's smile. 'Visas must be being applied for in morning time and being issued in the afternoon!' the bureaucrat told an American who was booked on that evening's flight to Delhi.

The disappointed executive withdrew, stammering and muttering under his breath. The Indian puffed up his chest. There seemed little hope. When it came to my turn, I spun a white lie about how 'my company' had just faxed me demanding my presence in Bombay by Monday. The Indian eyed Barb and I suspiciously before giving me the same treatment as the American: no visas were to be issued in the afternoon. Gleefully, he pointed to a sign that spelled it out in black and white.

'Please,' I pleaded. 'This isn't my fault. I have just been notified ...'

'How do I know you are going to be leaving on Sunday?'

'Why would I claim to be going to Bombay on Sunday if I'm not?'

'We must be having proof,' he said.

I showed him my airline ticket and he also demanded to see my yellow fever certificate; I didn't have one of those either. He flicked his hand at me as if he were brushing away flies. Then, as I was about to back down, a conversation came to mind: I remembered a friend telling me stories about how the Indian bureaucratic mind operates and its response to a deep-rooted respect for the British. There was a good chance he had assumed that I was an American – after all, we were in New York. I tried a new tack.

'Now you listen here!' I bellowed like a grumpy old man giving a teenager a lecture. I brought my fist down hard on the counter: 'I'm not just some Yank, you know. I'm not just some filthy European. And I'm not just some Dago. I'm British, damn it! ... British!' I whipped out my passport, now thoroughly under the skin of the part: 'My great-grandfather fought for the likes of you on the North-west Frontier. He played polo with the Maharajah of Jaipur and lived in Bangalore for years. My father was brought up in Bombay ...' I paused for a moment and then threw in: 'He's a pillar of the MCC! Now I have to go to India on Sunday and you're jolly well going to give me my visa, aren't you, my good man?'

The bureaucrat looked dismayed. Waiting to see what his reaction would be, I stood there, angry, adjusting my collar. Everyone waited as the world seemed to stand still ... And then he started wobbling his head from side to side, as if his neck had turned to jelly.

'... Certainly sir. No being problem. You just filling in this form and ve'll be issuing you a visa. Thank you, sir. Thank you most, most kindly.'

He scuttled away mumbling to himself, 'North-west Frontier, Maharajah, Jaipur ...'

Victorious, Barb and I walked out of the building twenty minutes later. Now grasping my officially stamped passport, I felt rather full of myself.

'What did you think of my performance?' I asked in a supercilious way. My ranting, as usual, hadn't rubbed off on Barb; she was her usual down-to-earth self.

'What sort of jerk forgets to get a visa, anyway?' she said.

* * *

Madness: that was the only word to describe the scene at Bombay International airport. It was like Judgement Day at the end of time when, it has been prophesied, humankind will be weighed on giant scales outside Damascus. The conveyor belts were broken and several flight-loads of passengers were waiting impatiently for their luggage to arrive. A trio of mechanics, splattered in oil, were doing their best to repair the archaic machines; spanners and wrenches, bolts and grease were strewn across the floor.

An Ethiopian Airlines flight, which had just landed, off-loaded a couple of hundred African refugees all seeking asylum from the latest despot. Terrified members of a touring Swiss orchestra clung grimly to their instruments while a group of German tourists made a clamour that a full stadium of British football hooligans would have been hard-put to equal.

Many of the passengers grabbed any person who looked vaguely like an official. In one corner, two Arabs were shouting at an innocent janitor dressed in a grey boiler suit; and an over-excited American was taking out his impatience on a security guard. With a drawn-out groan and crunch of cogs, nuts and bolts, the conveyor belt suddenly lurched into action. The exhausted crowd surged towards it, sending the mechanics diving for cover.

Slowly, one by one, our belongings appeared. It was amazing to see what Asians bring back on international flights: fans wrapped in brown paper, fridges packed in polystyrene, electric heaters and microwaves still in their boxes, cumbersome air-conditioners and televisions which needed to be carried away by gangs of porters. I felt like a contestant on a game show watching a display of prizes as the conveyor belt slowly wound round.

Tariq Khan had come to pick me up at the airport. Somehow, he had taken advantage of the confusion, dodged the security, sneaked past customs and found me struggling amongst the frenzied crowd.

In appearance, my friend had changed very little from how I remembered him: short, with wiry black hair, piercing eyes, a prominent forehead and a puckish grin. People likened him to Omar Sharif without the moustache. At school, Tariq was best known for his daring escapades. Once, he stripped all the lead off the gymnasium roof, which he smuggled into the forest and melted down into ingots, later selling them to a scrap metal dealer for a tidy packet. What I most admired about Tariq was that he rarely – if ever – got caught.

Since those days, he had travelled extensively, visiting every continent with the exception of Antarctica. He had written a captivating travelogue about his adventures in India, Africa and South America, as well as numerous monographs. And to top it all, he had found the time to learn to fly light aircraft. He never stopped working and was now writing a new book as well as articles for the British and American press. Tariq, who was three years older than me, was an operator and the first foreign journalist I had met in 'the field'.

My friend helped me with one of my bags and led me through the crowd. Customs officials decked out in spotless white uniforms, a striking contrast to their grubby surroundings, rummaged through hand-held suitcases, rucksacks and dufflebags.

'Put your passport in this,' he instructed, handing me a red leather cover with the British coat of arms stamped on the front. 'When you pass through customs wave it in their faces and shout "diplomat!". They won't stop you.'

I asked him where he had managed to get one of those.

'Oh, that. Available in any British post office.'

His ploy worked. I was ceremoniously ushered through the mêlée, like royalty. In a few minutes we were ensconced in a dilapidated yellow taxi, crunching towards downtown Bombay.

'I didn't think the British gave their diplomats special passports,' I said, amazed.

'They don't,' replied Tariq, smiling the smile of someone who lives outside the system.

Pelting rain beat against the window as our taxi driver carefully inched his way through the rutted roads and deep puddles.

'This is the greatest show on Earth,' said Tariq, enthusiastically. 'Bombay is the craziest, zaniest, most amazing place you'll ever be. Things happen here. Things are going on all the time. And if most of it were happening anywhere else, people would pause and stare and shout "incredible!" Here, no one bats an eyelid.

'This is a haphazard place where nothing dares stop moving or else it will collapse and die and be eaten. The cockroaches are the prey of rats, which are the prey of cats, on which dogs thrive. When the dogs die they are scooped up and made into glue. This is sniffed by street children who buy it for four pence a pot. When they asphyxiate themselves, they're taken off and cremated and their ashes are used to fertilise rice, on the crumbs of which cockroaches thrive ... then it all begins again and hasn't stopped for the last four thousand years.'

The taxi stopped at a set of traffic lights. Beggars, who looked more alien than human, like the survivors of a nuclear holocaust, raised themselves up from crouched positions on the pavement and slowly weaved their way in between the cars. Some were armless; others legless. A few moved their tortured torsos on makeshift skateboards. A blind man, whose mutated face was melted like a candle, held a child up to the open window. The infant's arms were twisted, its hands deformed; it seemed to be pleading for someone to put it out of its misery. The man stretched out an open leprose hand.

'*Ek rupia, ek rupia* (one ruppee, one ruppee).'

To my astonishment, Tariq shooed him away. He noticed my surprise.

'Lesson number one,' replied Tariq, who was now an expert on India, 'in Bombay you have to be cruel to be kind. There are millions of people suffering here like you have never seen people suffer before. They have nothing. They'll do anything to survive. That child's arms and hands were probably broken deliberately by its parents so they could use it for begging.

'I know a lot of people who haven't been able to hack it here because they want to help every unfortunate on every street corner. People don't think, they react, which doesn't help the situation. You have to keep calm and remain detached ... You can't become over-identified with Bombay or it will literally turn you mad.'

The taxi passed the Gothic Victoria Terminus, lit up by powerful lights, and a late-night market outside a Zoroastrian temple with pillars in the shape of winged lions. Tariq, in his inimitable fashion, had somehow finagled membership of the Royal Bombay Yacht Club which, I discovered later, was almost impossible to join. He was now living there. I didn't enquire as to how this had been accomplished.

As far as his budget would allow, my friend liked to do things in style. He saw no point in being uncomfortable. Tariq always wore brogues, meticulously ironed shirts and kept a blazer handy. He travelled with an electric toothbrush, plenty of hair gel and aftershave. His eldest sister once told me that when he was in Jordan during the Gulf War, his mother rang in a panic, concerned that her son might be thinking of travelling into Iraq.

'Don't worry. There's no chance of that,' she replied, 'There aren't any five-star hotels left in Baghdad!'

We stopped briefly so that Tariq could show me his favourite stall in Bombay, owned by a blind man who sold greeting cards and knew each one by touch. Within the hour, we pulled up under the grand stone porch of the Royal Bombay Yacht Club.

We were greeted by the Indian director who called himself the Admiral. His title was only a nickname since he had never served in the forces; still, he ran the club and staff as if he were commanding a ship.

The Admiral wore a three-piece suit, carried a silver pocket watch on a chain, and had whiskers like an elderly walrus. He spoke fondly of London where he had worked as a secretary before the War. Indeed, the Admiral was more English than the average Englishman and he told me he had dedicated his life to becoming a 'true gentleman'.

Our host led us inside to sign the Club's register and 'have a spot of tea'. The door to his office had been salvaged from a cabin on HMS *Delhi*. It was a sturdy piece of oak with a thick glass window and brass fittings – the Admiral's most cherished possession. The office itself was set out as I would have imagined Rudyard Kipling's newspaper bureau to have been. Nowhere was there any sign of modern office equipment – no calculators, computers, printers or plastic files – only manual typewriters, piles and piles of yellowing forms and crusty ink wells.

Here, as in tens of thousands of offices across India, the sub-continent's zealous love for paperwork thrived. Three scribes beavered away at documents of every description and another was responsible for preparing the day's restaurant menu, which he printed out meticulously in longhand on pristine pieces of white card. An old British safe with a chunky lock stood against one wall and piled high on shelves running up to the ceiling were the club's records and accounts going back at least fifty years.

As Tariq waited, I signed the book and quickly gulped down a cup of the Admiral's excellent mellow tea.

'Call on me any time,' he said. 'I'm a wizard at bridge and a dab hand at chess, too.'

* * *

A toilet cleaner who doubled as a bellboy helped me up to Tariq's room with my bags. He was a Christian whom the Admiral had delegated as our 'man-servant'. A quiet man, he lived on a diet of lentils and leftover butter supplied to him by a friend working in the club's kitchen.

Stepping into our room, which the Admiral called our 'chambers', was like entering an unopened time vault from British colonial days. Three wicker fans, whirling frantically, hung from the high ceiling in a vain effort to alleviate the stifling humidity. In a far corner, there was an antique weighing chair. A fridge stood by the door, stocked with soda water and freshly cut limes, and, next to it, a glass cabinet crammed with faded newspapers.

The period furniture, chairs and solid tables all crafted from dark mahogany, would have complemented a musty old library; while a cupboard, with fixed wooden hangers, seemed designed for navy uniforms. Although it was scratched, worn and touched up, it had the bearing of former imperial days. There were two beds, made up with freshly laundered sheets, wide enough to accommodate portly old sea-dogs. Lamps stood on each side, the stands made out of camel bladders.

Best of all was the view. In the distance, the lights on navy frigates and fishing boats bobbed around in the Arabian Sea, and down below, beyond a square garden, stood the elegant Gateway to India, built in 1911; to its right, the Taj Mahal Hotel, where rich Indian families go each Sunday to try to marry off their eligible sons and daughters. Tall Sikhs in blue turbans and suave uniforms stood to attention in front of the doors like officers on parade.

'So what's your game plan?' asked Tariq, as we sat down in two coarse armchairs frayed with age.

'I'm trying to become a journalist, so I thought I'd try to get a job on a local English language newspaper here.'

'Why don't you go to Afghanistan,' replied Tariq, quick as a flash. 'I just came back. That's the place for you ...'

Afghanistan. I wasn't sure I wanted to go to a war zone. It sounded incredibly dangerous.

'It is,' said Tariq, 'but I can give you some contacts who'll look after you. Go to Peshawar on the North-west Frontier,' he continued. 'It's the centre of the Muhjahidin *jihad*, or holy war.'

'Right,' I said, reeling, the word 'Afghanistan' going round in my head.

Tariq opened a soda water. The top fell onto the floor and spun around on the polished boards. He bent down to pick it up.

'Well that's settled then. Afghanistan it is,' said Tariq, who was extremely enthusiastic about my plans for the future. 'In the meantime, stay here for a couple of weeks. You have to see the festival of the elephant god, Ganesh. His birthday celebrations start tomorrow. You're just in time to see the whole bonanza.'

* * *

I showered and changed and Tariq took me on a guided tour of the club. In the heyday of the British Empire, the rooms and corridors, chambers and verandas must have sparkled; now, however, its former glory had faded. The lift was unreliable; the kitchens were run down; the felt on the billiard table was worn and dull; the ground floor was infested with sewer rats ...

And yet, it still retained much of its majesty and charm, a decaying relic of a bygone age, cherished and preserved by the well-to-do Indians, albeit with limited funds. Sweeping staircases decked out in hanging plants led onto long corridors with stone floors. There were lounges with reading lamps, a dark library, a rather for-lorn ballroom, a small shop stocked with chocolate, fruit and soap powder, none of which could be purchased with-out the vouchers available at the front desk. There was even a barber's shop, fully equipped with a grand leather swivel chair, where you could get a shave for ten pence.

The dining room had a nostalgic air. Photographs of World War Two destroyers and paintings of yachts hung from the walls. Corroded yachting cups, plaques and ships' colours were displayed in alcoves and, above the bar, portraits of British admirals in full regalia.

The restaurant was run by a comic collection of elderly waiters who, in spite of their rheumatism and arthritis, remained staunchly at their posts. They reminded me of a group of old Soviet leaders at a reunion. Many of them had dedicated their entire lives to the club. All were grey-haired; some deaf; others toothless; one had a predominant, hunched shoulder thanks to a lifetime of carrying heavy trays of food above his head. He and his colleagues treasured their jobs with an admirable sentimentality and were consistently polite. Their reply to any request was, 'Yes, of course, sir. Right away, sir. It is my duty, sir.'

Every evening, the dining room was frequented by ex-Indian naval officers who reminisced fondly about the British Raj and the Burma Campaign. You were guaranteed hours of entertainment by old sailors, spinning tales of the high seas. That first night, Tariq and I sat at a table underneath a glass cabinet which contained a handsome model sailing boat with three masts and a web of rigging. My host gazed over the menu.

'Fish again,' he said, disappointed. 'They have fish here for every meal. It's always cooked exactly the same way, but it's never given the same name twice.'

One of the waiters, Vikrain, brought us our drinks in bottles on a tray and, with shaking hands, he poured them out, almost missing my glass.

'The chef has an atlas of Europe and every day he names the fish after a new capital or country,' continued Tariq. 'Last night it was "Fish Bel-gee-um". The night before that it was "Fish Parisian". On another occasion it was plain old "Scunthorpe Sole". Still, it's a small price to pay for staying here.'

He raised his glass of sweet Thums-up cola, the local brand. 'Welcome to Bombay.'

* * *

The annual birthday celebrations in honour of Ganesh, the Hindu elephant god who traditionally rides on a mouse, is the most eagerly anticipated event in

Maharashtra in western India. Held during eleven days of late August and early September, millions upon millions of Hindus visit specially erected shrines dotted throughout Bombay. Hundreds of spectacular hand-painted idols, some over thirty feet high, are venerated by the people. On the last day, the idols are paraded through the streets, carnival-style, by the thronging masses who bring the city to a standstill. As a finale, the idols are taken down to the Arabian Sea and immersed in the water.

I had arrived just in time for the beginning of the festival. One of Tariq's contacts, a journalist called Krishna, agreed to take us to a shrine where we hoped to see the unveiling ceremony of the largest idol made that year.

We arranged to meet him in the foyer of the Taj Mahal Hotel. As we sat waiting on one of the comfortable sofas, Tariq continued my Indian education, reiterating that while in Bombay I should expect the unexpected. In the process of gathering research material for his latest book about the city, he had interviewed the most peculiar collection of Indian characters. One was a man who worked part-time as a bank clerk and part-time as a god; another who believed he was a ghost and not a man at all. And Tariq had even tracked down the owner of some of the rarest gemstones in the world who lived like a pauper and could only afford a pair of bedroom slippers ...

'This is a writer's paradise,' said Tariq. 'Material just comes at you the whole time.'

No sooner had he uttered these words, than two respectable-looking men dressed in suits approached our sofa. Without asking either Tariq or myself, they squeezed unceremoniously into the space next to us. For more than five minutes, they said nothing and looked intensely into each other's eyes. Then the older man started to speak.

'It has been so, so long since I have seen you and for vely, vely long, I have waited for this day ...' He blew his nose on a silk handkerchief and stuffed it back in his top pocket. 'It is my honour to have asked you here to inform you of something of the greatest, Greatest, GREAT-EST importance!' he proclaimed.

Tariq and I glanced at one another, expecting them to start discussing the marriage of their children or something equally consequential. The second man seemed delighted by the first man's words and grinned like the Cheshire cat, wobbling his head, 'Thank you. Thank you.'

'I have asked you here to tell you ...,' continued the first man, pausing and lifting his hand in the air while twisting it as Indians often do as they talk. 'I have asked you here to tell you that you ... that you ... that you ... THAT ... YOU ... ARE – MY FRIEND!'

'Achha, achha. Thank you. Thank you – thank you kindly,' acknowledged the second man, wobbling his head and smiling at his peer.

The first man was leading up to something: 'But YOU!' he continued, moisture in his eyes, 'you are not only my friend. But you are ... you are ... you are – my BEST FRIEND!'

'Achha, achha. Thank you kindly.' He grabbed the first man by the arm. Tears started to well up in the second man's eyes. 'MY BEST, BEST FRIEND,' he reiterated, shaking his head from side to side like a child who misses its parents.

'Oh, thank you, thank you.'

They sat in silence for a few long seconds, both still staring at one another. What would come next?

The older man continued again, slowly. 'But more than that my dear, dear fellow. Not only are you my best, best friend ... You are ... you are ... the ... THE ... BEST ... FRIEND ... ANY CHAP ... EVER HAD.'

The second man was now in a state of near hysteria. Grabbing the first man by the shoulders and hugging him, he bawled through his tears, 'Oh, my vely, vely best, best friend. You do me such honour. Thank you. Thank you. With friends like you, we human beings, frail things that we are being, would all be being FRIENDS!'

He pulled his head back from his friend's shoulder to look him straight in the face. 'Never did I think this auspicious day would come when I should ever be blessed by having such a vely, vely good friend such as yourself. Oh my dear, dear friend!'

Tariq and I sat, perplexed and amused but not laughing, which would have been rude. This went on and on and on for no less than fifteen minutes. By the time they finally got up and left, their shirts soaked with tears, they were completely out of control, kissing, hugging, embracing and shouting, 'FRIENDS! FRIENDS!'

No one in the foyer of the Taj Mahal Hotel even raised an eyebrow.

'See what I mean,' said Tariq, who was busy writing down notes on the conversation in his bulging note book. We sat in the foyer for a further twenty minutes. At length I wondered out loud whether Krishna was coming.

'He'll be here in three and a half minutes,' said Tariq casually looking at his watch.

'How do you know?'

'Krishna is always precisely forty-seven minutes late.'

Sure enough, as Tariq had predicted, Krishna appeared three and a half minutes later. He was wearing an open, untucked Hawaiian shirt, a gold chain around his neck, and fake crocodile boots. Krishna, who was in his early forties, fancied himself as the original machismo stud, and sure enough he had the hairy chest to match the image. Yet the rest of his incongruous physique didn't add up to much: he was stubby, had one eye socket much larger than the other, buck teeth coated in plaque, and was bent over like a hunchback.

I learned later the reason for his malformation when I visited him in the *Times of India* building. His office, where he had worked for twenty years, was located under some stairs, and because of the overhead slant, there was not even enough room for him to sit up straight at his desk. His left eye was permanently fixed into the left-hand corner of its socket and consequently, like a chameleon, Krishna had developed the ability to read or write while looking to his left.

Tariq introduced me to Krishna and we ventured forth in search of the largest Ganesh idol.

'Bombay is a teeming city, containing the largest slums in Asia, all built around the relics of an empire,' said Tariq like a walking guide book. 'The architecture is an astounding mixture of florid Gothic styles characteristic of the eighteenth and nineteenth centuries, mixed with contemporary designs.' We passed a number of older buildings which told of the city's boom years. 'When the American Civil War created a shortage of cotton in Europe and the British built the Suez Canal, new trading opportunities developed,' Tariq continued.

Krishna led us through a flower bazaar brimming with sweet-smelling buds and blooms. We were swallowed up by a mass of humanity. The market echoed to the sound of Hindi which coursed from the lips of Bombayites, enthusiastically buying special wreaths of orange and yellow pansies for the celebrations. Further on, bullock carts, black and yellow cabs, and carefree sacred cows took up their positions in what is a permanent traffic jam throughout this city of twelve million and rising. Krishna took us through back streets until we stopped in front of a white circus tent. Before we entered, a dwarf with pixie ears asked us to take off our shoes and leave them amongst the piles of other pairs.

The tent was dimly lit by hundreds of flickering candles and in the centre, a group of devotees with red dots painted on their foreheads burnt incense, creating clouds of thick, acrid smoke. A crowd of barefoot Indians of all ages filled the interior, alert and facing the far end in anticipation. Soon after we arrived, a white curtain was drawn back to reveal a towering Ganesh idol, garishly painted pink, orange and blue with a twisted trunk, sitting on a platform and wearing a golden crown.

Everyone gasped. Many piously intoned a prayer. A group of shaven-headed men wearing orange togas who looked like monks, arranged wreaths at their god's feet. Some lit candles, others were prostrate in worship, while still more stretched out motionless on the ground. Just as a woman fainted to the floor, her eyes wide open, a rapid drum beat began and a high-pitched, erratically-played wind instrument joined in. A train of young girls wearing flowing *saris* threw petals into the air and giggled uncontrollably all at once like children in a playground. I felt as if I had entered an opium smoker's dream.

Krishna led us into a small adjoining tent. Dozens of people were dancing frantically in a circle around an old man who was covered in bright paint and sat cross-legged on the floor, meditating. At a clap of hands, his revellers were ushered out. We sat down in front of him. The ancient Indian's eyes remained shut and, to our surprise, he spoke English in an affected Victorian British accent, pronouncing words like India with an 'r' at the end.

'Our friend Krishn-aar tells us that you have certain questions about our Lord Ganesh that beg to be asked,' he said, as a few remaining disciples lit incense sticks and wafted sweet-smelling smoke in our direction. This was true; Tariq and I wanted to know more about Ganesh.

The old man cleared his throat before saying, 'The Ganesh Ganapati – the *adi pati* of ganas – is the god of wisdom and success, and the remover of *vighna* or obstacles. He is also known as the Vighneshwara. Our Lord is worshipped before every important event, even by other gods. Brahma worshipped him before creation, Vishnu before vanquishing Bali, and Seshanaga before carrying the Earth on his head.'

It took me a few minutes to comprehend all that he had said. It sounded like something out of a Greek myth.

'Why has Ganesh the body of a man and the head of an elephant?' asked Tariq.

'According to tradition,' the sage continued, 'one of

the female goddesses, Parvati, was barren but wanted someone she could trust and call her own. She rubbed off some dirt from her body and mixed it with oil. From this, she fashioned a little boy and breathed life into him. Then, she instructed him to guard her home.

'Later, her husband, who had been away, returned and a fight broke out, and the husband cut off the boy's head. Parvati was inconsolable and demanded that the other gods revive her son. They agreed to bring the first head of an animal found sleeping while facing north.'

This, of course, turned out to be an elephant and they placed its head on Ganesh's shoulders.

Krishna was anxious to return to his office so we thanked the old guru and left. As we made our way to the *Times of India* building, I asked Krishna what he thought of such legends.

'It's being fairly mad, my friend,' he said. 'But India is having much of this kind of thing. Anything is thought possible in our country because the Hindu religion is allowing for everything and anything. It is being so very diverse, you see.

'You can be calling yourself a Hindu and being worshipping one god, or be seeing all the gods as aspects of the one god, or be having a favourite god like Ganesh. Most Indian people are believing these things because they are always being told that mad things are true.'

He continued by giving an example. 'If you stand up on that box in the middle of that crowd and shout, "Pigs can fly!" no one will be surprised or thinking you are mad. Many people will be believing, Tarquin sahib.'

* * *

Ganesh's birthday was a week away so I spent the time with Tariq, who was busy writing an article about the Indian film industry.

Bombay produces over three hundred major feature

films every year – even more than Hollywood. Their popularity lies in the fact that a large proportion of India's more than nine hundred million strong population are illiterate and live in abject poverty. To these unfortunate masses, the glitz and glamour of the silver screen is a welcome form of escapism. As Anupam Kher, one of India's most accomplished actors, explained to Tariq: 'We are dream merchants. What the normal man cannot achieve, he sees his hero achieving on screen. For those three hours, he can forget his misery, poverty, debts and hardships.'

Tariq was spending his afternoons at the studios, conducting interviews and making contacts. He took me along to Film City in northern Bombay where thousands of frenzied fans were crowded around the gates, waiting to catch a glimpse of India's leading actress who was due before the camera that day.

On the set, hundreds of wires and cables ran across the floor in all directions like multi-coloured pythons: thick ones; short ones; ones with old-fashioned, cumbersome wooden junctions. On the rickety scaffolding overhead, barefooted helpers in rags scurried about like mice on rafters, fixing lights, changing filters, checking connections, while people on the ground pointed up at them, shouting directions.

Apart from the director, everyone seemed confused and flustered, but all the same, the polished, stylish, finished product would appear in the local cinemas within a matter of months. A band of sitar players was practising behind a Sun god temple set, and a snake charmer sat training his prop. Dead centre, stood an old Bolex camera fixed to a metal clamp, which in turn was fixed to a block of wood, which sat on top of a sturdy stool. In Heath Robinson style, four men assisted with the complicated process of operating it: one was in charge of keeping it clean, two more, armed with a metal tape measure, calculated the focal distance required and adjusted the lens accordingly, and another operated the camera.

The crew were preparing to film a wedding scene. The actress was well endowed with the proportions which Indian males seem to find so appealing. She wore an elaborate purple costume decked with silver frills and matching satin veil like something out of a Middle Eastern pantomime. A dozen extras were instructed to take their places and vied for centre stage like mosquitoes attracted to light.

Dressed entirely in flowing black robes and wearing sunglasses, the lanky, suave director was smoking so much that he looked as if he was about to catch fire. He lounged back in his own monogrammed chair, while constantly being fanned by an obedient servant. Everyone moved into position on set when he firmly announced, 'Silence.' The little men who had been selling tea and samosas flitted away. A young boy with a clapper-board stood in front of the camera. 'Action!'

Watching from the sidelines, the producer stood with his arms crossed across his chest. He looked as jumpy as a football coach; Tariq had warned me that Indian producers are generally a bundle of nerves. Films are usually financed privately, unlike productions in the West which enjoy the patronage of production companies. To make matters more difficult, no insurance company will provide cover for an Indian film as the safety standards on the sets are so poor. Only two months earlier, one of the best producers had been bankrupted when a film set burnt to the ground, killing many of the crew and cast.

Producers also have to contend with the fact that Indian actors and actresses will never commit themselves to just one film and may be working on as many as ten projects at a time. They are almost always late – often they do not turn up at all – which causes lengthy delays and sends production costs sky rocketing.

In Hindi films, the spoken scenes are almost thrown together, the emphasis being on the glamorous dance sequences with less attention given to the plot. When actors and actresses sign up for a film, it is rare that they see a finished script; they are usually given only a bare outline of the story and, based on that, decide whether to commit themselves. Often the script is written as the film progresses and the stars are fed their lines just a few minutes before they go on camera.

The films are mainly epic, fairy-tale stories whose characters usually include princes and princesses, thieves and brigands and the perennial love-sick heroes and heroines, all spiced up with modern action scenes. Many are staged like plays with the actors and actresses often speaking straight into the camera. When there is the slightest hint of a romantic interlude, the cast start to dance, miming to the latest Indian hit tunes.

Tariq finished his interviews and we left the studio with Anupam Kher, the star, whose car was mobbed by the mêlée of fans who screamed, prayed, and tried to break the windows in an effort to touch him.

Indian films have become such a part of the fabric of the culture that the actors and actresses are literally worshipped as deities. Tariq recalled how he had lunched in a Bombay restaurant with a famous actor who once played the god, Vishnu. When the waiter recognised the star, he dropped everything and bowed low in obeisance. Tariq asked the waiter to explain himself. The man replied, somewhat surprised, 'That man is god! Haven't you seen him before?'

* * *

The Ganesh festival continued all over the city. Every night, politicians distributed sweets amongst the poor; firework displays and dances were held in the streets; and children crowded into fairgrounds. Devotion and divinity filled the air.

On the big day, Ganesh's birthday, the streets were packed with millions who made their way to the Chowpati beach. There, the clay idols were slowly immersed in the warm waters of the Arabian Sea. Waving multi-coloured flags and banners, the Hindus chanted sacred hymns and threw red dust into the air which, from a distance, resembled smoke signals. As we photographed the finale, I asked Krishna why some of the idols we had seen had snakes coming out of their stomachs.

'It is because of another one of these most colourful Hindu stories,' he explained. 'They say that Ganesh was one day eating very many *modaks* (sweet rice balls for which he is said to have a weakness) and went riding on his mouse. But Vasuki the snake was sliding in front of them, scaring the mouse, and Ganesh is falling off. His belly burst and the *modaks* fell out. So he is putting them back in and tying his stomach with the snake.

'The Moon and his wives laughed when they are seeing this spectacle and Ganesh is cursing them. That is why the Moon is having a scar. He also forbade man from looking at the Moon on his birthday.'

The frenzied, joyous celebrations went on throughout the night and into the early hours of the morning. At dawn, I returned to the beach to find groups of Indians armed with buckets and spades, digging up and taking away sand. This would be transported to the countryside around Bombay where it would be scattered ceremoniously in the fields in the hope that Ganesh would grant a bountiful harvest.

On the beach, confetti and garlands lay wet and shredded across the sand, together with half-dissolved bits of the elephant god. I contemplated picking up a piece as a memento but decided, out of respect for Ganesh, that I should leave him to the ravages of the Sun and sea.

I returned to the Yacht Club to have a last lunch with Tariq and pack up my belongings. The Ganesh festival had drawn to an end and so had my time in Bombay. I was eager to travel on to Peshawar and the North-west Frontier, the land of the wild Pushtuns.

SEVEN

Mercenaries, Missionaries
and Misfits

*... pollution, sewage, spices, smoke from
kebabaries. They blend together to form an
indescribable smell. If I were to capture some in a
jar and opened it ten years later, I am sure it would
transport me back, as if I had never left ... I'm
surprised I don't have culture shock ... There's so
much to write about, I'll need a lifetime's
supply of notebooks and pens ...*

Diary, 10 September 1989

Peshawar was seething with intrigue. The fortified city, a
former outpost of the British Empire lodged between the
Indus Valley and the Khyber Pass, sits on one of the most
unstable borders in the world, a stone's throw from the
ever-turbulent country of Afghanistan.

Capital of the infamous North-west Frontier Province,
Peshawar is now a reluctant part of Pakistan, a country
that only forty-five years ago was a patchwork of wild
tribal territories. The people are still struggling to come to
terms with their modern national identity. During the
1980s, Peshawar was the ultimate border town, volatile
and unpredictable, and liable to revert into open anarchy
at a moment's notice. It acted like a magnet to an extraordinary mélange of assassins and con men, political
spies and gun runners, murderers and all manner of
villains, crooks and thieves, who fed off the misery of the
three and a half million Afghan refugees and the confusion caused by the war in Afghanistan which started after

the 1979 Soviet invasion of the country.

An American war correspondent called Sean, whom I had befriended, was as fascinated by this collection of characters as myself. 'Who are all these people?' I asked him, as we walked in the Old City one day not long after my arrival in Peshawar. We had just passed a Westerner who was wearing a camouflage-patterned khaki outfit with a killing knife sticking out of his belt.

'Mercenaries, missionaries and misfits,' he said, 'that's what I call them. This is a haven for them.'

Indeed, you couldn't get away from such people in Peshawar. Scheming smugglers were making millions selling stolen US Stinger missiles to the Iranians. Countless aid workers and missionaries, many of whom didn't know the difference between a Sunni and a Shi'ah, were forever rushing to some emergency meeting. Within mammoth house-forts surrounded by bodyguards who made body builders look like wimps, multi-billionaire drug lords – some of the richest men in the world – lived in ultimate air-conditioned luxury.

Second-rate mercenaries pounded the pavements looking for employment. Journalists with overly vivid imaginations filled the telex office. Forlorn Russian mothers waited hopelessly for news of their sons who were missing in action. And representatives of every espionage agency in the world watched and waited, plotted and schemed.

No one knew or understood what was going on, but everyone was desperately trying to find out, while at the same time endeavouring to project a veneer of confidence. Nobody trusted anyone, and if they appeared to, it was only because they were after something.

These unorthodox individuals often turned out to be something other than they pretended to be. Even at Dean's Hotel, a complex of colonial-style white bungalows with green tin roofs and elegant verandas, the guests and staff were spying on one another. The long-haired Australian backpackers were being watched by the waiters; the waiters by the cleaners; the cleaners by the managers; the managers by the taxi drivers; the taxi drivers by the Australians, and so on ...

Anyone wanting to write a spoof on a John le Carré thriller would have found rich pickings in Peshawar. But there were so many twists in the plot that the reader would suffer nervous exhaustion trying to unravel the clues.

Daily bombings and explosions had become a way of life. After each incident, the informers and spies would filter in to the bazaars to sniff around – and to start rumours. You could be certain that by nightfall dozens of different theories and opinions would be circulating via the tea houses and caravanserais about who was responsible for planting that day's bomb.

Gossip abounded, theories formed. Cousins, friends, uncles and neighbours whispered that the culprit was none other than the notorious KHAD, the KGB-trained Afghan government's secret service. The truly paranoid would insist that it was the agents of India stirring up trouble. And a few might postulate that some obscure Middle Eastern group was accountable.

Then came the speculation about the true target of the bomb. Who had he really been? Was he, as the police affirmed, a mere spice trader? Or was it true that he was a money launderer for the CIA? Or perhaps a Saudi Government agent countering Iran's influence over western Afghanistan's Shi'ah population?

The following morning, the editorial in *The Frontier Post*, or 'The Heroin Post' as it was known, would, no doubt, take up the mystery, concluding, somewhat predictably, that the bomb could have been planted by any one of several dozen groups, or perhaps just some cousin equalling the score in an ancient tribal blood feud.

* * *

I walked through the old British Cantonment Area with its wide, well-swept streets, parks and gardens, trees and lawns. I peeked through the gate of the Peshawar Club before making my way to Saddar Bazaar. The main pot-holed street, its gutters filled with decaying, discarded vegetables, had come to a standstill as it was Friday, the holy day of Islam. Hundreds of barefoot men, wearing baggy light-coloured clothes and small white prayer caps, stood in rows facing towards Mecca. As the prayers began, they moved in unison, bowing and crouching on prayer mats.

I reached Dean's and sat down in a blue cast-iron chair on the shaded lawn. I ordered tea with lemon, but the waiter brought it with lime; I was slightly annoyed, but you don't argue in Peshawar. As I took the first refreshing sip, a skinny Sindi in scruffy clothes limped over towards my table. He was brown and greasy and dragged his left foot behind him like a giant cockroach whose lower body had been crushed. Splatters of dried lentil soup clung to his shirt.

'Which country?' he asked, attempting a smile but failing.

Although I felt some pity for this unfortunate man, I didn't like the look of him. 'Japan,' I replied curtly.

'Japan. Japan ...' he repeated the word several times as if it were in code. He eagerly eyed a packet of oral rehydration salts that I had just bought to help alleviate a severe case of Peshawaran diarrhoea.

'Papers!' he said suddenly, pulling out a grubby note book while trying to assume an air of authority.

'What do you mean "papers"? Who are you?' My friend Tariq Khan had warned me not to trust anyone in this part of the world.

'Officer of police. Give passport.'

'Do you have an identity card?'

'Plain clothes police. No identity,' he said.

'Well I'm sorry. If you don't have any ID then I'm not going to show you my pass. Move away now, I'm having tea ...'

'... Papers or trouble for you.'

'No!' I said firmly.

He walked away, his clubbed foot making a trail across the recently watered lawn. For the next five minutes, like a perverted voyeur, he glared and glowered at me from his position under a nearby mulberry tree. Months later, I was to encounter the same man again, this time loitering on a street corner wearing a Salvation Army hat and a bandage around his forehead, asking for money for Afghan refugees.

Sitting at another nearby table on the lawn at Dean's, reading a week-old copy of the *Philadelphia Enquirer*, was an American wearing a red tank-top pullover, dark glasses and an arrogant smirk. Evidently, he had overheard our conversation.

'Guy's an Ear,' he said, 'just hangs 'round and sells information to anyone who's buying ... May I join you?'

He sat down, calling for more tea, and asked what had brought me to Peshawar. For caution's sake, I told him that I was a tourist. What did he do? His eyebrows twitched as if infested by voracious fleas and he moved his chair a little closer to mine. 'I'm in with the Muhj-ahi-deen – the Afghan freedom fighters ... these guys are really kicking commy ass.'

He took a spent, brass rifle cartridge from a pocket and threw it into my lap.

'That's from Herat. A memento. I'm in with one of the high commanders. I'm personally helping him run a consignment of weapons – heavy stuff – over the border. If you want, I can arrange for you to go ... to Afghanistan. I bet you'd like that, huh?'

For a moment, I thought about playing him along, but I had already met a dozen characters just like him in the few days I had been in Peshawar. They were a dime a dozen. I declined his offer.

'Come on man! Where's your sense of adventure?

Opportunities like this only come along once in a lifetime.'

'Not interested, thanks.'

He finished his tea and moved on to another table where he tried to sell the idea to a group of backpackers who were desperately seeking some adventure. Was he really in the big time, I wondered. Or was he just another show-off? I doubted whether anyone cared very much, anyway.

As for myself, events had moved along quickly since my arrival in Peshawar. A British photographer, who was just leaving Pakistan as I arrived, tipped me off that the Associated Press were looking for a 'snapper' to be based in Peshawar to cover events in the North-west Frontier and Afghanistan. Naturally, I jumped at the chance and went to meet the Pakistan Bureau Chief in Islamabad. I took along a number of my American pictures which he flicked through.

'Who have you worked for before?' he asked.

I didn't know whether to tell the truth. I decided to lie. 'Just local papers,' I said. But it did the trick and soon I was taking the occasional picture for the Associated Press.

The pay for each picture, however, was not immediately forthcoming and for the first few weeks I had to stay in a hotel called the Quetta. It was tucked in behind a bakery and a travel agent that was never open, just across the road from Dean's. I was not exactly sure why I was staying in that particular hotel, only that a taxi driver at the train station, who happened to be the proprietor's nephew, had insisted that it was the best place in town.

It was one of Peshawar's cheap doss houses boasting a small parking area in front, full of stolen cars and goats with sizeable appetites who nibbled at the ankles of passers-by. The rooms were filthy, rank and dim; the walls, which were crawling with bugs, at times actually seemed to move, and the beds were made up with old tablecloths, the pillows just pieces of foam taken from car seats.

The courtyard, however, was sunny and echoed with the sounds of laughter and voices of travellers exchanging stories, describing adventures and exotic destinations. At dusk each evening, I sat amongst the other guests writing notes about Peshawar, listening to the Muslim call to prayer, the wild dogs barking and the shouts of joy from children playing cricket nearby. These sounds blended and mingled with the buzz of the swarms of Vespa rickshaws on the main road, creating a strangely magical atmosphere.

* * *

One night, shortly after I arrived, the Quetta's proprietor, Ali, a bluff, overweight man with one glass eye, who was forever bragging about his sexual exploits during his time in America, sat down next to me with a terrified expression on his face. We had already become friendly, having shared a meal or two together, and he had told me many stories about Peshawar.

Ali asked me for advice: 'What am I to do?' Limply, he held a letter in one hand; I could tell that it did not portend good news. He was shaking, as if in the grip of a malarial fever, his shirt soaked through with sweat, his one good eye twitching spasmodically.

The letter was from his first cousin, who was serving time for triple homicide; in it he vowed to kill Ali for having stolen his inheritance. Ali translated the note, the tears trickling down his face: 'Do not fear, oh cousin!' the letter stated in the Pushtun chivalrous style. 'It is my honoured and sworn duty to finish you. Your death will be painless. Do not fear, I will kill you quickly with a Kalashnikov. Prepare yourself to meet Allah, the Great Designer ...'

I was unable to offer Ali any real advice about his

tricky predicament, but he thanked me anyway and went to seek sympathy from the chapatti seller across the road.

Hearing Ali's outpourings, the two new arrivals of the day, who were sitting at a nearby table eating sticky, orange chicken tika, fell about on the floor like two clowns. One was a Welshman with cropped red hair and a vicious, scarred face. His friend, a Londoner, looked equally sinister. Stuffed into his back pocket was the latest edition of *Soldier of Fortune*, the magazine for mercenaries. Both men were decked out in the mercenary uniform of fatigues and Dr Martens.

Curious about my two fellow countrymen, I struck up a conversation. They had spent the afternoon at Darra Adam Khel, a smuggler's village near Peshawar where you could buy all manner of weapons. The Welshman showed me a pen-gun which he had bought. Boasting that it would make the perfect assassin's weapon, he aimed at a Coca Cola bottle and fired, narrowly missing a tourist. The bottle shattered, spilling its frothy contents on the ground, but the tourist, a Swede, remained calm and casually carried on with his conversation.

The Welsh mercenary pulled out a dog-eared pack of cards and invited me to join them. I could hardly refuse; as they cheated at poker, they regaled me with their life stories.

'We fuckin' started out in the fuckin' paratroopers, didn't we,' began the Londoner, who was from Ealing. 'We thought it would be right cushy; then those fuckin' bastards sent us to fuckin' Belfast.'

After attempting to murder his commanding officer, the Welshman was thrown out of the forces; the Londoner went to fight in the Falklands. Later, they met up again and joined the French Foreign Legion and, after further confrontation, entered the South African Security Forces.

It was in Africa that they found their true callings in life: murder, rape and theft. 'I 'ate Pakies, Wops, Krauts, Paddies, Frogs, Chinks, Dagos, Kiwis, Yanks, Commies,

Jews, but most of all, I – HATE – FUCKIN' – NIGGERS,' said the Welshman who said he was deported from South Africa after killing a murder suspect by throwing him out of a fifth-storey window. The Londoner was also expelled soon after, he claimed, for shooting a black burglar and then 'finishing him off with a couple of rounds to the 'ead.'

'Fuckin' right. We could fuckin' do anythin' in Bongoland,' they laughed, slapping their thighs as they reminisced over their evil escapades.

Hour after hour, I listened to an inexhaustible reserve of horror stories; each more terrible and grotesque than the one before. They had no respect for anyone or anything and their perverse attitudes left me with a feeling of total revulsion. The Welshman, who could be heard masturbating vigorously in his room at night, was in Peshawar to look for employment with the Muhjahidin. He didn't want to know about the enemy, he just wanted to kill people. I asked him why he didn't simply go into the middle of London and start shooting commuters.

'I fuckin' well would,' he replied before heading off with his mate to try and find some local prostitutes, 'but, like, I'd probably get fuckin' caught and fuckin' put away, wouldn't I?'

The two men headed off into the bazaar where I had no doubt that they would bring harm to somebody.

* * *

The next evening, in a corner of the courtyard, as I sat eating a succulent lamb pilau which I had bought take-away from a nearby Afghan restaurant, a stream of tracer bullets streaked across the sky like shooting stars, followed by the ack-ack sound of machine-gun fire.

At first, I imagined that there were gun battles going on, like the ones in Los Angeles or New York. But Ali, now his calm, hospitable self again, explained: 'This is a nightly custom. People in Peshawar step out of their homes, point their Kalashnikovs into the air. Then they start blasting. When their clips are spent, they turn around and calmly head indoors. Very, very mad.'

A Swiss tourist, who was travelling from Europe to Australia, chimed in with a comment in his impeccable English: 'What none of them seems to take into consideration is that when bullets are fired into the sky, they don't simply keep going into outer space. There is, after all, such a thing as gravity. Bullets come down and what's more, if there is not a strong cross wind, they tend to land in or around the same place from where they were discharged.'

On one occasion, a Moroccan doctor, who regularly played tennis at Peshawar's American Club, had just served an ace when a bullet whizzed by and clipped off the end of his nose. Other instances were even more tragic. At a wedding held just before I left Peshawar eighteen months later, clansmen firing a salute accidentally killed the bride, the groom and four guests.

Such weddings were held in the summer, during which time the level of evening gunfire increased ten-fold. At one wedding, the daughter of a chief of a local clan married the son of another powerful chief and the celebrations, which were held in a village adjacent to the airport, continued well into the night. During the revelries, a light Fokker aircraft was coincidently attempting to land. The pilot, who was flying into Peshawar for the first time, was startled to see what looked like a gun battle in progress near the runway. With tracers streaking across his approach, he radioed the tower. The police rushed to the scene, and after much argument, negotiation and threats, put a stop to the shooting.

The pilot, who had been circling for nearly an hour, began his approach again. By now, however, he was so tired and disorientated in the darkness, that he thought the street lights along the canal marked the runway and, tragically, flew straight into a pylon, killing himself and all the passengers.

As I continued to watch the tracers and listen to the machine guns, a filthy young man with troubled eyes and a nervous twitch took an ice-cold drink from the fridge. He wrenched off the metal cap with his teeth and sat down in front of me.

It was offensively obvious that he hated bathing and had no interest in personal hygiene. In order to pay off his bill, he had spent the morning cleaning out the hotel's archaic sewerage system. Bits of stinking excrement now festered under his finger nails. Using a splintered matchstick, he gouged out flakes, letting them drop into his lap.

If his intention was to draw attention to himself, he was succeeding. For many of the other guests, this spectacle proved gut-wrenching. They beat a retreat to their rooms, the revulsion apparent on every face.

At a glance, you would never have guessed that he was from Sussex. He had the sallow apricot complexion of a Central Asian, a Semitic nose, brown Romany eyes and wore the *shalwor kameez*, baggy pants and long shirt, found in one style or another throughout the Islamic world. I judged him to be a Middle Easterner, but only until I noticed the elaborate tattoo on his forehead that proclaimed the word 'FUN'.

'*Salam-alaik-um* (peace be upon you),' he stated.

I was even more confused by his rural Sussex accent, but said hello, catching a glimpse of his bare right arm which was almost completely covered in colourful tattoos. 'Tarquin Hall,' I said, acknowledging him.

'My name,' he replied proudly in English, at the same time extending a faeces-encrusted hand, 'is Abdul.'

Not wanting to get my hands dirty, I told him that I was about to eat supper. He got the message.

Abdul was not his real or original name; that was Simon, and he was from Petworth. His father was Spanish, which explained the bronze complexion; he had once been a punk rocker and then a skinhead, which explained the tattoos; and he had recently converted to Islam, which said something about his choice of native clothes.

Only a few months earlier, he had been lazing in Regent's Park in London when he stumbled into the middle of an anti-Salman Rushdie march. Having nothing else to do, he joined in the protest, burning effigies and numerous copies of *The Satanic Verses*.

'I didn't know nofink about Rushdie or any of the Muslims or nofink,' he said.

Yet they accepted him and for someone who had been an outcast much of his life, this friendship and fellowship proved overpowering.

'I soon convarlerted to Islam,' said Abdul. Exactly what he had 'converted' from was unclear, although he assured me that some sort of conversion had taken place. 'Then I journeyed to the battlefields of Afghanistan and joined my Muhjahidin brothers. We've been fighting the evil Communist invader.'

Having returned from Afghanistan, Abdul had spent the past three months in Pakistan training as a medic with a sympathetic French doctor.

'I want 'a return, like, to the battlefields. You knaw what I mean. I've got skills now. Medical ones. But my commander says I 'ave to 'ave this removed.' He pointed to the 'FUN' tattoo on his forehead. 'They fink it reads "ALLAH",' he said, 'and 'fink it's blasphemous or some-thin'.'

The more I learned about this misfit, the more I realised that they were doing everything conceivable to rid themselves of him.

The French doctor he had been working with had promised to arrange for plastic surgery on his forehead at a local hospital and his problems seemed solved. In the meantime, Abdul spent his days cleaning the hotel for his keep and trying to persuade the local chicken farmer to let him marry one of his daughters.

A week later, I happened to meet Abdul in the street. He was looking even more disturbed than ever. I asked him what was the matter.

'It's the tat-oo on me 'ed,' he bawled, massaging his brow. 'The doctor told me 'at they 'ave to take skin from my arse for the operation, like, because everywhere else is cover' in tat-oos.'

'So what's the problem?' I asked.

'I can't 'ave a piece of my arse on my for'ed, it's unclean,' he wept. 'What if my Muslim brovers find out ...? They won't wana know me. They won't wana hug me. I'll be shunned – cast out.'

I thought it remarkable that Abdul should be concerning himself with personal cleanliness. But why would they find out if he didn't tell them?

He lowered his head piously and spoke in his strong rustic accent. 'Allah moves in mysterious ways, knaw-what-I-mean?'

* * *

To the Pushtuns, who believe they are one of the Lost Tribes of Israel, the Ben-i-Israeli, Peshawar is simply *Shehr*, the city. Despite the presence of electricity, cars and some other modern amenities, the effect on the character of the Old City has been minimal. It remains untamed; a place so ancient that its origins are forgotten.

The labyrinth of narrow streets in the Old City make up what is effectively a gigantic rabbit warren. When walking in downtown Peshawar, it is a definite advantage to be agile and fit; good eyesight is also a benefit as hardly any sunlight permeates down to ground level.

During each exploration, I discovered new areas, new nooks, new crannies. Many places were impossible to find a second time: it was as if they had been movie sets dressed for *A Thousand and One Nights*, and then carted off to some other studio. I always half-expected to see a group of eunuchs march through the Chowk Yadgar square leading a train of veiled concubines to a magnificent harem; or look up and see a flying carpet sailing by; or perhaps even a giant genie materialising from the spout of a brass lamp, lying in a pile of antiques in an open bazaar stall. And for all I knew these things actually did happen – only when my back was turned.

Turbaned men, daggers hanging from their belts and bandoliers strapped around their chests, sat on *kilims* in smoke-filled tea houses, talking over the affairs of the city. Anonymous faces appeared at the windows, watching – always watching. Cloaked figures emerged from dark, cobbled alleyways down which only the truly brave ventured.

Women, who might have been young or old, beautiful or ugly, shuffled by under their pastel-coloured *burkas*, the all-covering cloaks which resembled shuttlecocks. Slanty-eyed Turkomen with furry hats and dreamy expressions sauntered past Palestinians with their characteristic black and white patterned head gear. Dark-skinned Hindu and Sikh money lenders counted out their precious rupees, while Baluchi nomads bartered for their winter provisions.

No one had a job in Peshawar; everyone seemed to own a shop. Pushtun culture still frowned upon those who worked for others – independent was the thing to be and having a shop was what counted, no matter what you sold. There were bazaars for everything: birds, hats, money, vegetables, captured Soviet military clothing, even some for buying false teeth and dentistry, noticeable thanks to the painted signs of giant dentures hanging over the entrances.

Walk up any stairway and, chances are, you might find yourself in an antique shop, an Aladdin's cave: silver lapis lazuli-embedded talismans hanging in the window; a stack of British Lee Enfields captured during the second Anglo-Afghan war gathering dust in one corner; bowls brimming with lockets from Turkestan; finely embroidered Afghan wedding dresses ...

Next door, there might be a carpet shop, like the one owned by my friend Mr 'Honest' Salim, packed to the ceiling with *kilims*, rugs and saddle bags. The colours and designs of oriental carpets are so subtle and sophisticated you find yourself staring at them, as if in a semi-hypnotic state, for hours. Trying to choose your favourite carpet is always difficult as the variety is overwhelming.

Peshawar's carpet dealers take pride in their wares and most are highly knowledgeable about their goods. 'Every rug has a story,' Mr Salim used to say and to simply ask 'how much?' is an insult to them, degrading the whole affair.

You could sit all day in the carpet bazaar, talking about all manner of things. And if, dozens of glasses of tea later, no one piece had caught your fancy above all the others, you were usually welcome to take a few home, or to your hotel, and consider the matter further. Sometimes this went on for weeks, perhaps months. And never was I asked for my telephone number or address, nor was I ever pressurised into buying.

The bazaars put the average department store to shame: you could buy anything and what you couldn't buy, you could have made. I once bumped into a Brazilian aid worker, leaving a shop, carrying an old-fashioned brass diving suit, like something straight out of *20,000 Leagues under the Sea*. It was a beautiful thing, so shiny and polished that it seemed to light up the whole bazaar. He told me that it had actually been made from his own design, right down to the metal grate over the glass window in the bell helmet. Of course, what a Brazilian would want with a brass diving suit in the middle of Peshawar is a question worth considering.

Leaving the Old City, I walked along the Jamrud Road, the main thoroughfare which runs past the beautiful Peshawar University and leads to the Khyber Pass.

Bedford trucks chugged by, painted a myriad colours, ornamented with glistening bells and beads. Piled high with sugar cane and scrap metal, livestock and fodder, these were the modern world's answer to the camel. They vied for space amongst the bicycles and mopeds, many overloaded with three or four passengers all sitting side saddle. Police in blue uniforms and berets tried to control the traffic, while truck drivers squatted by the side of the road drinking hot milky tea from saucers.

Being something of a romantic, I was looking for the old British cemetery. I hoped to find the resting place of some of those who fell during the three Anglo-Afghan wars. Perhaps there might even be some gravestones inscribed with heroic epitaphs.

Leaving the pollution and commotion behind, I walked amongst the white gravestones and the overgrown grass. Disappointingly, however, many of the British soldiers seemed to have died from cholera, typhoid and childhood viruses. The inscriptions were far from glorious. The first I found read, 'RUPERT BLUNDELL-SMYTHE. DIED 23 FROM MEASLES'.

* * *

Back at the hotel, the French doctor who had trained Abdul was waiting to take a few of us out to dinner at a local hotel. The mercenaries, the punk Muhjahid, Sean, the American war correspondent, and myself, joined him.

We stood in the spacious foyer of the Pearl Continental surrounded by bulky Afghan commanders meeting with foreign diplomats, khaki-clad Western tourists, snotty-looking hotel managers and wealthy Pakistani politicians with entourages of veiled women following dutifully behind.

The doctor introduced us to a middle-aged European lady, a nurse who was working in the refugee camps. We all shook hands, all except Abdul. He promptly refused, placing his right hand over his heart instead, and piously whispering, 'Muslim ... Muslim,' adopting what he thought correct Islamic etiquette.

Showing signs of confusion, the lady offered her hand a second time, but he still refused.

'Muslim ... Muslim,' he intoned.

Slowly, the woman's face lost all colour and she started stuttering. Now confused himself, Abdul again put his hand over his heart and bowed slightly.

She turned to the rest of us shouting in French: 'What is the meaning of this? Who is this person? Why is he with you? I don't want anything to do with him!'

And with that, she turned and ran away. We looked at one another in bewilderment.

'What's the mat-er with 'er?' complained the punk Muhjahid, 'I'm Muslim. I'm not suppos-a shake women's 'ands.'

Granted, Abdul was revolting to look at and I had never risked touching any part of him, but I had to agree that she had over-reacted and caused an unnecessary scene. I even felt sorry for Abdul who had no idea how repulsive he was perceived to be.

My sympathy was short-lived, however. The doctor, following the lady to seek an explanation, returned, having discovered the reason for her seemingly irrational behaviour. To our further astonishment, he explained that when Abdul had refused the handshake, a red swastika on the back of his right hand, another leftover from his punk days, was flashed up in front of her face.

The offended lady, a French Jew whose father had been murdered by the Nazis, reacted with understandable hostility.

* * *

I decided that, although life in the hotel was colourful, I needed somewhere to stay that was less frenetic where I could concentrate on my writing. I soon found a house which I decided to share with a group of journalists.

The last I heard about my acquaintances at the Quetta, Ali the hotel owner was alive, if only because his cousin was still in prison. Abdul contracted hepatitis and was deported back to the United Kingdom. The Welshman made it into Afghanistan, but was summarily kicked out; his friend was spotted eighteen months later wearing a Mother Teresa T-shirt. Apparently reformed, he was working for an aid organisation.

Towards the end of my stay in Peshawar, I bumped into Sean who lived permanently in the Quetta. He, too, was full of stories about the hotel and its guests. Only the day before, just outside the entrance, he had met a Westerner with henna-dyed hair and shredded clothes and bandages wrapped around his bleeding feet.

Curious to discover how this man had come to be in this condition, Sean bought him a meal and asked him where he was from. But when the war correspondent questioned him, he looked blank. Sean asked the same questions again and again, but there was no response. His guest just stared at the wall.

Finally, however, the stranger seemed to come to his senses. He suddenly looked at Sean and said, 'I'm going back to England – tonight. I've got a ticket.'

He produced the ticket and Sean examined it.

'But this plane leaves from Islamabad in three hours! How are you going to get there?' he asked.

The stranger looked surprised. 'What do ya mean?' he asked, rubbing at the itchy needle marks on his arms where he had injected himself over and over again with heroin. 'I thought this was Islamabad.'

EIGHT

The Pushtun
and the Perfect Murder

This has been the best day of my life! I sold my first article – to The Friday Times, *an English-language weekly here in Pakistan. When the editor called me to say he was publishing, I jumped up and down with joy for ten minutes. Couldn't stop singing all day. He's going to pay me, too. Fifty dollars. It's being published and I've got to send a copy to everyone ... Hopefully I can start writing for them every week ...*

Diary, 24 November 1989

The North-west Frontier was still a place where the locals preferred to settle their differences and arguments the old-fashioned way – with the sword, or rather with the Kalashnikov. Peshawar's thieves, unlike their counterparts elsewhere in the world, did not only carry flick knives and crowbars, they were also equipped with machine guns and grenade launchers.

Our house on Peshawar's Canal Road was surrounded by an immense twenty-foot high wall, topped with bails of rusty barbed wire and slivers of sharp, green glass. If, from the street, it looked more like a brigand's mountain retreat than somebody's home, that was the intention. The front door was made of reinforced steel and a ferocious dog that looked like a werewolf patrolled the courtyard and garden.

It came complete with an armed guard. Abdur Rahman was an Afghan Pushtun built like an ox who could knock a man unconscious with one blow. His parents had named him after the infamous king of Afghanistan, or the Iron Amir as he was known, who gave the British a run for their money during the latter part of the nineteenth century until he died in 1901, the same year as Queen Victoria.

Abdur Rahman looked older and more distinguished than his twenty-six years. He had a shiny hooked nose like a raven's beak, a noble philosopher's brow, and a black beard so thick that it would have made a comfortable nest for a bird. He looked after it with the care of a devoted gardener tending his roses; he had watched it grow and blossom, and I used to catch him combing methodically the bristly hairs, checking the effect in a small, cracked face mirror which he kept in a pocket at all times. Like all Pushtuns, he looked forward to the day when he might dye his beard a fiery orange henna colour.

A gentle and kind man, he had an infectious laugh. His green eyes sparkled behind the thick-rimmed glasses which he hated wearing, not being quite as devoid of vanity as he pretended. Yet, ever since he had taken a drink from a well poisoned by the Soviets in Afghanistan, his eyesight had weakened. He was fortunate to be alive, as he was the first to admit.

Abdur Rahman's story was as tragic as that of so many Afghans. He was only seventeen when, in December 1979, the highly mechanised Soviet army swept across his country. In those days, his family knew nothing of Communism, only that since the overthrow of King Zahir Shah in 1972, there were new problems in Kabul. But what was so extraordinary about that? As far back as anyone could remember, some individual or group had been scrambling for power in the capital. Abdur Rahman remembered the gripping stories told by his grandfather who had fought under the banner of the Royal Family in the bloody civil war of 1929. In that year alone, five or more kings and leaders had come and gone. Even the great Nadir Khan, who eventually brought relative peace to the country before ascending the throne, only reigned for three years, until his murderer's bullet found its mark.

But with the coming of the Russian Bear, Abdur Rahman and his countrymen soon learnt new lessons – they learnt about Communism, and they learnt about the Soviets.

The Russian invasion was more horrific than anything his country and people had experienced since Genghis Khan. Then the Mongol hordes had laid waste to the whole of Central Asia on horseback. This time, the destroyers swooped down out of the sky, dropping toy butterfly mines deliberately designed to maim rather than kill, machine-gunning whole herds of camels and sheep where they grazed, and dropping bombs which flattened entire villages.

'Suddenly the whole world seemed to have gone mad,' said the Pushtun.

Abdur Rahman's father, mother and three brothers were killed in one such raid. He and his sisters watched from the safety of the fields as their home was reduced to rubble. After that, it was not safe to remain in Afghanistan. And so, with just a few charred belongings and a little dried fruit and bread to share between them, they walked for two weeks over some of the toughest terrain in the world, across the border to Pakistan.

Amidst the confusion and the countless malnourished and miserable millions in the camps, they located an uncle and gave him the sad news of his sister's death. Without hesitation, he took them into the cramped tent where he and his immediate family were living. Then, Abdur Rahman, thirsting for revenge, decided to return to his homeland to fight the invaders. He rarely spoke of that time. But it seemed to haunt him.

After drinking from the poisoned well and developing temporary blindness, he returned to Peshawar, only to discover that his uncle had died from a combination of old age and dysentery. Now, Abdur Rahman looked after his remaining family.

His relentless will to keep going never ceased to amaze me. Despite the fact that the war had taken its toll upon him, Abdur Rahman was not bitter; he retained a sense of humour and never made excuses for himself. Life, to him, was a set of challenges to be faced and dealt with.

His commitment to his job as *chowkidor*, or guard, was absolute. Despite coming from a comparatively wealthy family and being well educated by the local teacher, he fulfilled each task, however menial or tedious, as if it were the most important in the world. I felt sure that if our Fort Knox-like house were ever attacked, he would lay down his life to protect us, not willingly, but because he was honour-bound.

Our *chowkidor* regarded all those who knocked on the gate with respect, but also caution until their identity was fully and unequivocally established. Consequently, our visitors often thought that he was a touch abrupt; in fact, Abdur Rahman was a trusted friend and reliable guard: just what was needed in the North-west Frontier.

Abdur Rahman was a Pushtun first and a Muslim second; his approach to Islam being a personal one, a part of his everyday life, so he would never have dreamt of preaching religion. He did, however, teach me about the *Pushtunwali*, or the way of the Pushtuns, which has been passed down from father to son, mother to daughter for centuries.

This chivalrous code of conduct takes precedence over any local or Islamic law. *Melmastia*, or hospitality, comes before all things. Without anticipation, it should be offered freely to all visitors – even enemies. If a KGB general were to knock on a Pushtun's door, he would have to be protected and cared for. Secondly, women must be protected, cherished, respected and honoured above all things, rape being the worst crime imaginable.

Thirdly, a Pushtun is required to defend the name of his family, tribe and people at all costs. Any slur or attack upon them must be avenged – in blood.

I once asked Abdur Rahman under what circumstances it was deemed necessary for a Pushtun to take *badal*, revenge. No sooner had this question been put to him, than his face grew dark and he led me outside to a secluded spot. There, he related a gripping story. It was one of revenge, of hatred – and the perfect murder.

'Two years earlier, my eldest sister, Aisha, married a boy who hailed from our neighbouring village in Afghanistan,' he said slowly. 'His name was Hamed. He came from a respectable family, one that was an old ally of our clan.'

For some months after the wedding, the couple appeared to be happy and content. Then rumours began circulating that Hamed drank and beat his wife, and even forced her to have sex when she was unwilling. Eventually, these whispers reached the ears of our *chowkidor*. When Abdur Rahman paid Aisha a visit, she refused to say anything against her husband, yet the bruises on her face told their own story.

'I became enraged like an animal,' said Abdur Rahman, spitting between his teeth. 'I thought I would go mad. I felt like ripping Hamed into little pieces. I knew that if I did so, a blood feud would begin between our two families that might last years, perhaps centuries.'

As Abdur Rahman spoke, the events seemed to grip him anew. He was seized with rage, his eyes ablaze. I was seeing a new side to the Pushtun's character.

Nothing was to be gained by talking to Hamed, so Abdur Rahman bided his time. He was sure that an opportunity would present itself in which he could avenge these abominable acts.

'I knew that Allah would show me a way,' he said.

Months passed. Then, one day, Hamed invited his brother-in-law to join him for a week of falconing in the mountains. 'Hamed was idle, a degenerate. He did nothing for Afghanistan. While many were dying, fighting the *Rouss*, the Soviets, he only hunted with his birds. He was a disgrace to all Pushtuns and I saw it as my duty to rid the world of him,' continued the *chowkidor*.

'Yet I was vexed. How could I kill Hamed without bringing about a feud? I knew that if I shot or strangled him, the body would be discovered. And even if it were not, then I would still have much explaining to do.

'We were walking through a mountain pass on the third day,' said Abdur Rahman. 'My heart was heavy with hatred for that man. I was being friendly, talking of our time growing up near Kandahar. Then we came to the top of a cliff.'

Hamed stood on the edge, looking down.

'I knew that this was my chance. I knew I might never get another one,' continued Abdur Rahman. 'Without really thinking, I ran and pushed him. It was like in a dream. One moment he was there and then he was not. There was no noise. When, at length, I looked over the edge, I could see Hamed on the rocks far below – dead.'

Abdur Rahman was breathing heavily through his mouth as he spoke.

'No one saw me, thanks be to Allah. We were in an isolated place ... It was not an honourable way to kill him. I am not proud of what I did except that I spared us all further suffering. We had all suffered enough.'

Dutifully, Abdur Rahman returned the body to Peshawar together with a story about how Hamed had tripped on a rock and fallen over the brink of a cliff. Nobody suspected him of any crime, not even his sister.

As Abdur Rahman finished speaking, he looked down at the crusty earth, still breathing heavily. Being a man of conscience, the events still weighed heavily on his mind and, no doubt, they always will.

I found that my throat was as dry as a bone. His words had been filled with such conviction and strength that I felt certain this was the first time he had told his story to another human being.

Nothing further needed to be added. Pushtun justice had been served – and my question answered concerning the nature of *badal*.

* * *

Those who have never been given an Afghan bear hug should count themselves fortunate. Imagine how a walnut feels when it is crushed in a nutcracker and you may have some idea of just how painful the experience can be.

Abdur Rahman was a renowned bear hugger. He had arms like a yeti. I once saw him almost hug someone to death: the unfortunate victim was Najam, the turbaned Punjabi taxi driver, who owned a clapped-out 1952 Buick.

One afternoon, Najam arrived at the house to take a guest to the airport. In truth, none of us was overly fond of Najam. He was a miserly sycophant who always smelt of camels and entrusted his money to no one, not even a bank, always keeping wads of notes tucked away in some secret inner pocket. If you required change after a journey, he would begrudgingly dip in amongst the filthy folds of his clothes, checking first to see if you were watching, and then dole out each grubby note as if he were parting with pieces of his own anatomy.

Even more annoying, was his habit of chewing *paan*, a concoction of betel nut and tobacco wrapped in a lime leaf. *Paan*-chewers are numerous throughout India and, unfortunately, the stuff also has its devotees in Pakistan. When chewed, it creates a volume of red liquid which taxi drivers like Najam spit from their moving cars.

The Afghans hate the stuff. They also consider anyone who hails from south of the Indus River to be an Indian – 'a curry eater'. And Abdur Rahman never lost any time in reminding Najam of this fact.

When the Punjabi arrived that afternoon, Abdur

118

Rahman welcomed him in true Afghan fashion, gripping him enthusiastically in a vice-like embrace. I smiled at the sight of the massive *chowkidor* picking up the terrified, whimpering driver from the ground, as if he were a mere stuffed toy. Half-smoked cigarettes, a few peanuts and a pair of dice dropped out of his pockets. Then, gradually, Najam's podgy face went puce, then purple as if he was being filled with prune juice; all his muscles tensed up like a body builder then, just as suddenly, he went limp.

Horrified, Abdur Rahman released his grip and laid the stricken Najam on the ground. He tried frantically to revive the driver, but to no avail. The Afghan shouted at me to bring some water which we splashed on the Punjabi's face. Neither Abdur Rahman nor I were aware that Najam had a weak heart.

Unable to revive him, we bundled Najam into his own taxi and I drove like a madman to the nearest hospital. Abdur Rahman sat on the back seat, pleading with Najam to wake up, massaging his chest, urging me to drive faster, intoning prayers. '*Bismillah rakhman a rahim ...*'.

At the hospital, we rushed him into the emergency ward where a doctor took charge. It was a drab place and full of the victims of a horrific accident earlier that day on the infamous Grand Trunk Highway. A Flying Coach, or Flying Coffin as we called them, had collided with a lorry carrying Pepsi bottles. The survivors were in shock, their faces filled with terror.

I sat in a nervous silence while Abdur Rahman paced and up and down, still intoning prayers, and cursing himself for being so foolish until, after nearly an hour, a doctor finally told us that we could see Najam. He was now in a stable condition, having passed out and experienced heart palpitations. We both breathed a sigh of relief.

Abdur Rahman and I entered the room and the Afghan sheepishly approached the bed to apologise.

As he did so, from beneath his blanket, the Punjabi quickly lifted a cocked pistol. He took aim at Abdur

Rahman, cursing him, and before I could say anything, pulled the trigger ...

It was fortunate for everyone that Najam was a poor shot. The bullet, even at such close range, whistled past its target and buried itself in the far wall. Before he could get off another round, I caught his arm and wrestled the weapon from him. Just then, a nurse and the doctor ran into the room, only to find me holding the gun while Abdur Rahman was sitting on their patient, pinning his arms down to the bed.

'What's going on?' shouted the doctor, 'Are you trying to kill him?'

'No,' replied Abdur Rahman, 'we're trying to defend ourselves!'

Calming everyone down, I handed the doctor the pistol and managed to explain what had happened, showing them the bullet hole in the wall.

Sadly, the matter did not end there. No sooner was Najam out of hospital than he arrived at our gate taking pot shots at Abdur Rahman as he left for home. This time the Punjabi got off three rounds; but his aim had fortunately not improved and again, I found myself struggling with him.

Once I had retrieved his gun, I forced Najam and Abdur Rahman to agree to a truce. Threatening to have the Punjabi thrown into prison if he refused, I then made them shake on it. But any future hugging was certainly out of the question.

* * *

Waking early one morning to the roar of the Pakistani fighter jets warming up their engines at the nearby airport, I staggered, bleary-eyed into the kitchen. As I opened the fridge, I felt something pecking at my foot and jumped back in surprise. There, with its head jutting back and forth like an old woman in a rocking chair, was a beautiful cockerel with fine brown and red plumage, a sharp beak and floppy red jowls.

Pecking around for scraps, it jumped inside the fridge and poked its head, somewhat ironically, into a chicken casserole. When I tried to pull the creature out, it bit my hand, so not quite knowing what to do with it, I shut the cockerel inside for a few minutes.

When I eventually opened the door, the bird burst out with a flurry of feathers, crowing furiously, and flapped around the kitchen making a mess on the floor. Abdur Rahman, hearing all the commotion, raced into the kitchen, speaking to me in Dari, Afghan Persian. My command of the language was, at best, minimal, although I was endeavouring to learn, and Abdur Rahman and I had agreed not to speak English that day.

The cockerel flapped on the floor at his feet. I wondered if this bird belonged to him, so drawing one finger across my throat and pointing at the cockerel, I tried to ask him whether he planned on eating it.

'*Khor!*' he said, the Persian for 'yes'. 'But why don't you kill it?' he seemed to say.

I declined, shaking my head. Smiling at my squeamishness, he carefully picked up the unfortunate fowl by the legs and, taking a Kabuli knife from a drawer, he headed off towards the courtyard. From outside, I heard the sounds of beating wings and a muffled squawk then, after a few minutes, Abdur Rahman appeared again with the cockerel's featherless carcass. Proud of his fast work, he placed it down next to the sink. I assumed that the hungry-looking Pushtun would now prepare a meal, perhaps even a delicious pilau, so I left him to it, adjourning to the sitting room.

Half an hour later, however, there was a sudden, piercing scream from the kitchen. I rushed in to find the cleaning lady, a look of horror on her face, holding the still uncooked, naked cockerel by her fingertips, as if it were a dirty nappy.

'What happened?' screamed the cleaning lady, who had just returned from the local bazaar.

Abdur Rahman turned to me and asked half-heartedly in English, 'Wasn't this your cockerel?'

'No, I thought it was yours!'

The cleaning lady burst into tears, pulling at her hair, emitting noises made at concerts by sopranos struggling with crescendoes. I thought this was overdoing it; after all it was only a cockerel. In between her interminable sobbing, however, we discovered that the bird was her husband's prize fighter. For some unknown reason, she had brought the creature into the house in a basket and placed it under the sink for safe keeping, but it had escaped.

Trying to suppress our laughter, we asked her how much the bird was worth. It wasn't cheap, but I compensated her well. Once she had gone home, appeased and sure that her husband would, in fact, be pleased with the money, Abdur Rahman and I licked our lips, broke out the rice, and the Pushtun prepared one of his famous pilaus which we shared together.

* * *

Abdur Rahman was to have another run-in with a bird – only this time one from the US.

During my time in the house, there were a number of Western military personnel in Peshawar who had been seconded to the UN in order to train Afghans to clear mines and defuse unexploded ordnance. One of them, an American engineer called Gary, rented a room in the house during his three-month tour of duty.

Gary was as culturally sensitive as a lager lout on the Costa del Sol. He divided his time between dreaming of his native Seattle, watching videos at the American Club and eating hamburgers and pizza because he 'couldn't stand the local shit'. He used to whine continually about the fact that there were open sewers in the city, considered anyone in a turban to be a 'fundamentalist just like those Ayatollahs in I-ran' and, when he saw the locals praying, would ask, 'What are those I-slam guys doin slammin' their heads against the floor again?'

Indeed, the only thing the Yank was really any good for was his contacts in the UN through whom he was able to get his hands on hard-to-get items: American goodies like cookies, peanut butter, chocolate and, of course, alcohol.

American Thanksgiving was fast approaching and Gary wanted to hold a party. The fellow journalists who shared my house raised no objection to the idea, especially when four cases of beer, four jars of cranberry sauce, a lettuce (the Pakistanis and the Afghans do not grow or eat lettuces) and one, pre-basted, butterball turkey appeared on our doorstep. Considering that we had all been living on the local diet, the arrival of these items was quite an occasion and we all gathered round to examine them like wartime spivs who had just got their hands on some black market merchandise.

The American beer was a special treat. For months, the only alcohol those of us who were not members of the American Club had tasted was the Pakistani stuff produced at an old British brewery in Murree, near Rawalpindi, or 'Pindi' as it was known.

The Murree rum was vaguely palatable if you mixed it with a lot of Coca Cola. The local beer, on the other hand, was rot-gut stuff. To make matters worse, in order to drink it, you were required to go to one of the Peshawar hotels' specially licensed drinking rooms. These were all located somewhere 'in the back', like gambling dens in American Western saloons, away from prying eyes. They were frequented by journalists and alcoholic tourists who had come to Pakistan for a holiday, not realising it was a 'dry' country.

The drinking room at the Pearl Continental was dingy

and smelt of sour milk. As you entered, the barmen reacted as if you were there to make a drugs deal: none of them ever looked directly at you and they spoke in whispers, clamming up and pretending to be busy if you looked in their direction. Eventually, one of them would shuffle over to the table and, without saying a word, covertly slip you some lengthy forms.

Anyone wanting a drink was required to fill these out in triplicate, detailing their life history and outlining any past convictions. You then had to present a foreign passport and a fistful of rupees. All these were then carried silently away into another room where they were given a thorough inspection, stamped and signed by an official. After the barman had scanned them and scratched his head, a copy was given back to each person. What happened to the others was always something of a mystery.

The beer was as warm as the Australian outback, yet it was generally recognised that Americans preferred to drink it cold. If there was an American present, he or she would be provided with a plastic bowl containing no more than three irregular-shaped chunks of ice. Putting these anywhere near your mouth was highly inadvisable as you never knew where they had been, nor for how long, and they usually brought on a speedy case of diarrhoea.

The drink tasted like mouldy water mixed with mud. There were only two familiar things about it: namely that it was faintly brownish, and that it had some discoloured froth on top that looked like the kind of scum which forms along the banks of a polluted river. Each sip made its way down the throat with difficulty. And after swallowing a quarter of the contents of one bottle, you felt sufficiently sick to swear that you would never touch another drop of alcohol again. Perhaps that was the idea.

Despite being in the middle of the North-west Frontier surrounded by millions of Afghan refugees and a great deal of misery, American Thanksgiving had suddenly become an event worth looking forward to. On the great day, the fresh-faced, crew-cut American was in the kitchen bright and early, washing, chopping, preparing for the feast with all the enthusiasm of a proud US patriot. At around ten o'clock, he stepped out to do some last-minute shopping and hunt down ingredients for stuffing. Meanwhile, unknown to any of us, Abdur Rahman, who was milling around as usual, went into the kitchen and took it upon himself to start preparing the food. Two hours later, the American reappeared, humming the tune 'Whistle While You Work' and entered the kitchen with his shopping.

Never before had a man looked so carefree one moment, and totally crushed the next.

The precious cranberries were still in the jar, but the prize lettuce – which Abdur Rahman thought to be spinach – was boiling away in a pot on the stove, having already taken on the consistency of stewed seaweed; the pre-basted butterball turkey sat on the counter, cut into perfect cubes ready to be kebabed.

The American dropped his shopping, said nothing and, defeated, retreated to his room.

Abdur Rahman had never heard of anyone cooking a roast. He was used to preparing meat on a spit or in a pilau, and was intrigued by the idea of cooking it in an oven when I explained that this had been the American's intention.

At last, however, the turkey was cooked over a barbecue on metal skewers. I wondered whether the Pilgrims would have really minded: it tasted just as good kebabed.

NINE

Going 'Inside'

Tomorrow I go into Afghanistan, Insh Allah.
Somehow I've put the fact that it's a war zone to
the back of my mind. Seems odd. Most people
usually want to steer clear of wars. Here I am
wanting to see one ... Have a feeling of trepidation
and excitement ... There were more accounts today
of heavy fighting around Jalalabad. Should have
lots to report ... Have left a note for Mum and Dad.
Hope they never have to be given it ...

Diary, 9 January 1990

Peshawar's resident journalists and aid workers went to extreme lengths to avoid mentioning, in public at least, the word 'Afghanistan'. Instead, they talked about being 'inside', travelling 'inside' and going – 'inside'.

In the American Club, anxious hacks would sidle up to you and ask, 'Psst ... how do I get "inside"?' Busybodies would enquire, 'Have you been "inside"?' And those who had actually travelled in Afghanistan were forever boasting about having 'just got back from "inside".'

The reasons for their secrecy were two-fold. Firstly, just about everyone in Peshawar fancied themselves as a suspicious character caught up in some sizzling plot straight out of an Ian Fleming novel and went to inordinate and often ridiculous lengths not to mention the Forbidden Word. 'The walls have ears!' they would confide, even when you were in the middle of nowhere.

Secondly, there was a genuine necessity to keep travel plans secret. The Pakistani authorities, who were naturally anxious to deter spies, arms dealers, drug runners and buccaneer adventurers from travelling in areas where they risked being killed or kidnapped, made it officially illegal for foreigners to cross over the border into Afghanistan.

Only UN personnel and those with 'strong ties' to Pakistan's secret service, Inter Services Intelligence, could move in and out of the country with any degree of ease. The rest of us had to rely on our ingenuity and cunning to get 'inside'. It was a challenge to test even the most seasoned hack. Those caught, faced instant arrest and eventual deportation.

Journalists, in particular, braved great obstacles trying to reach Afghanistan. Those with blond hair dyed it black and pale complexions were blemished orange-brown with henna. Passes were forged, officials bribed, documents counterfeited. Men grew beards or wore false ones, and travelled with camel trains disguised as nomads; some swam rivers and climbed mountains, while others crawled past checkpoints on all fours in the dead of night.

When Sean went to interview the renowned commander Ahmed Shah Masoud in the Panjshir Valley in eastern Afghanistan, he stowed away in a secret compartment affixed to the bottom of a truck. After being jostled around like a milk shake for six hours, and sitting bent double in his own vomit, he finally got his story.

A French TV crew were less successful. They tried crossing the border in *burkas*, disguised as women. As original as their disguise may have been, they failed to take into account that most Afghan women are nowhere near six feet tall and certainly wouldn't be seen dead wearing heavy, black Dr Marten boots.

Veronica Bottomley, an Oxford graduate who was determined to become the first woman journalist to travel covertly into Kabul, also disguised herself as an Afghan woman. She wore a *burka*, plastic shoes and no socks or underwear. Ms Bottomley had done little research into Afghan customs or Islamic traditions and her *burka* was too short. When the crucial moment arrived and she had to walk past a checkpoint, her ankles were exposed, an act deemed unseemly in an Afghan woman and a dead giveaway. She was immediately arrested.

I had advised Ms Bottomley to carry some form of identification, preferably her passport, so that if she were caught, at least the Pakistanis would precipitate her release. Instead, she chose to ignore my advice. It took me over a week to get her released from a cell which she had been sharing with a family of rodents. She was only freed on condition that she be immediately driven to Islamabad and put on a direct flight to London.

After her departure, I was accused by the Police Special Branch of having arranged her trip. My phone was bugged, I was interrogated on two occasions, and was followed by people other than the regular group of spies and ears who were always lurking around the last corner.

Getting 'inside' proved impossible for many journalists. A few, on the other hand, having become familiar with stories and gossip, were simply too lazy to leave the comfort of their hotel rooms. One Australian photojournalist who was supposed to be investigating the heroin trade, considered the whole affair to be far too dangerous. Instead, he gave his film and cameras to two Afghans who claimed to be photographers, paying them to take pictures of poppy fields on his behalf. When the Sydney-based journalist eventually had the pictures developed, the prints contained shots of the two Afghans and their friends standing in groups, together with a few shots of a particularly handsome donkey.

This is not the first time Westerners have had to move covertly around Central Asia. When the Imperial British and the Russian tsars vied for control of Afghanistan, spies or army officers, such as Colonel Charles Stoddart and Captain Arthur Conolly, posed periodically as Hindu

*A cow breathes its last: a wedding celebration at an
Afghan refugee camp, Peshawar, Pakistan.*

Victoria Terminus, Bombay, India.

*The elephant god, Ganesh, is paraded through
the streets of Bombay at night.*

The Bala Hisar Fort, built by the Sikhs in 1834, later modified by the British and illegal to photograph, Peshawar, Pakistan.

The Khyber Pass, west of Peshawar on the Afghan border, looking back towards Pakistan.

*One of the author's first 'wire' photographs
for the Associated Press, Peshawar, Pakistan.*

*Afghan refugees amongst the squalor of the camps, Peshawar, Pakistan,
In the late 1980s and early 1990s, they still made up the largest refugee
population in the world: 3.5 million plus.*

Goal! A champandaz *Buz-Kashi player puts one away,
Peshawar, Pakistan.*

*One of the giant Buddhas in Bamiyan, Afghanistan, dominating the
valley where they have stood for nearly two thousand years.*

*The mysterious Band-i-Amir lake which is embraced by huge walls,
damn-like in appearance, west of Bamiyan, central Afghanistan.*

A Khuchi nomad girl, Ghazni, Afghanistan.

*MiG deterrent: a captured Russian anti-aircraft gun,
on the western edge of Paghman, Afghanistan.*

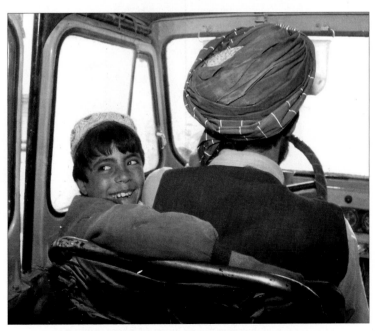

An Afghan boy squeezed into a jeep, Afghanistan.

Muhjahid in the ruins of a village near Jalalabad, Afghanistan.

A falconer exercises his bird as he travels on the back of a Bedford truck between Bamiyan and Ghazni, Afghanistan.

gurus and horse dealers, Tibetan wise men and dervish-
es; both officers were eventually executed by Emir
Nasrullah of Bokhara in June 1842. These were the men
who played the Great Game in the real life world of
Kipling's *Kim*.

Like many of those officers, with a fair amount of good
planning, I succeeded in making a series of journeys into
Afghanistan over an eighteen-month period. There was a
selection of border crossing points to choose from,
depending upon which part of Afghanistan you hoped to
reach, but it was unwise to enter the country without a
translator unless, of course, you were fluent in either Dari
or Pushtu. Once across, you had to know exactly where
you were going or you risked walking blindly into one of
the thousands of unmarked minefields, or losing your
way and wandering into an area controlled by the central
Communist Government. Those adventurers who blun-
dered in on their own, stood a good chance of coming to a
sticky end ... and many did.

Most hacks made their travel arrangements through
the semi-official Muhjahidin party offices in Peshawar.
The Afghans were eager to show journalists the destruction wrought by the Soviets, so they were usually accom-
modating, offering their full protection; many were willing
to act as guides.

My trips, however, were all organised through personal connections. Sean set up the first journey. One of
his contacts, speaking in broken English, instructed me
over the telephone to wait in Lalas Grill in Green's, the
Peshawar hotel which was frequently bombed because its
guests were mostly high-powered officials of one sort or
another.

I was in place at the pre-arranged time when a young
man approached and whispered further instructions.

'We leave within the next three days. Be ready.' The
conspiratorial informer mumbled lines straight out of a
spy adventure. 'Stay in your house and don't tell anyone

where you are going ...'

They phoned me two days later and my guide, who was called Jalil, came to the house where we laid our plans. Jalil was the son of a chieftain from the south-eastern city of Jalalabad, one of the first tribal leaders to call for the *jihad*, or holy war, against the Soviets and their puppet president, Babrak Karmal. Jalil spoke fluent Dari and Pushtu, fair Arabic and good German. He had learned English from a New England American while they shared a cell in Kabul's infamous Polycharki Prison. Consequently he spoke with a slight Bostonian twang, pronouncing words like car as 'caa'.

Like so many Afghans, Jalil was proficient in many skills. He was not, like the majority of Westerners, simply a specialist at just one thing. Indeed, he could turn his hand to almost anything. While blindfolded, he could take a Kalashnikov apart, clean it and put it back together; he cooked delicious *mantu*, the ravioli-style dish served with yogurt and kidney beans; he was a black belt at karate, could fire a Stinger missile, and fix a car engine – and he was an expert kite flier. In fact, just about the only thing that Jalil had never been able to master was swimming, but that was hardly surprising as he had grown up and lived in a land-locked country.

Jalil was quick to give me a new name. 'Turkun will never do,' he said. 'You must have a proper Afghan name.'

Names, as Jalil explained, have more significance in the Islamic world and their structure differs greatly to the Christian forename and surname system.

'I have heard many of you *Farangis*, many times making mistakes with our names,' said Jalil. 'You always shorten them and this is a mistake. Abdul-Haq cannot be shortened to just Abdul because Abdul means "servant" and Haq means "God", so the whole thing means "servant of God". By reducing it, you are calling someone a "servant" which will not do.

'Men in Afghanistan are given a single name of their

own, plus their father's name and the name of their town and sometimes tribe.'

At length Jalil named me 'Hazrat Gul': '"Hazrat" means "nice person" and "Gul" is a flower,' he said.

Not overjoyed about being called a flower, I set out with Jalil on a cold January morning shortly after the call to prayer. I had decided on a disguise – a long grey and black striped turban with the end wrapped around my neck, an olive-green *shalwor kameez* tucked into thick camel-hair socks, a Saudi Arabian army jacket with camouflage design, and new black leather boots which I had scraped against a concrete post to make them look old.

I had carefully applied some brown boot polish to my face and hands, and grown as much of a beard as I could manage. As we crept through the shadows of Peshawar's back streets on our way to the bus station, Jalil instructed me not to talk to anyone. I felt like the explorer and adventurer Sir Richard Burton on his way to Mecca.

* * *

We boarded a minibus which would take us through the Khyber Pass to the closest border crossing with Afghanistan. It trundled though the Tribal Territories, a no man's land where anarchy rules, the sort of place where tourists go and are sometimes never seen again. It was because the British found it too costly to control and administer these wild border areas during their rule of India that the Tribal Territories were established. The Pakistanis inherited them during the 1947 partition of India, and today visitors must carry special travel permits in many parts of western Pakistan. The areas are administered by political agents, each of whom control a small army. They have limited power, however, and can only officially take action when crimes are committed on the main roads.

The Pakistani Government endeavours to deter

tourists from travelling into these areas. Just days before I made my first trip, an English girl was shot dead when she was caught in the crossfire of an inter-tribal war. A few days later, a Scottish priest was kidnapped near the same spot while visiting some ancient Buddhist *stupas*, or shrines.

'I was kept in a cave for days on end,' the unfortunate padre told me in Peshawar after his release. 'The fellow who captured me carried more weapons than a band of mercenaries and he even picked his teeth with the end of his bayonet. But he was a proper gentleman, I'll give him that.'

The Scot passed the time of day in prayer and meditation. 'Finally, I think he became so impressed by my strong faith in God that he let me go. In fact, I'm sure it was that, because by the end of my captivity, he seemed to revere me to a certain extent.'

The minibus crawled under the cliffs and around the curves of the Khyber Pass. We passed in the shadows of small hill-top towers with slit windows and ramparts from where British red coats once guarded the approach to India. Jalil scanned the craggy slopes for any sign of movement, reminding me that at any moment a bullet might drill the driver through the head and we could be set upon by bloodthirsty brigands.

Fortunately, however, we reached the border without incident. The minibus dropped us off in the middle of a busy market and we started to walk towards the final and most crucial checkpoint. It was located in the middle of a shallow gully, groups of police positioned on either side. Afghans were crossing the border in both directions, many of them refugees. Some were returning to the villages and towns which now lay within 'the zones of tranquillity' as the UN called the liberated areas of Afghanistan; others were fleeing from the cities which were under seige by the Muhjahidin, trying to oust the last remnants of the Communist regime.

Men squatted by the wayside glaring into the Sun, thin blankets draped over them, listening to loud Punjabi music blaring from a smuggled Japanese radio. A water buffalo was being killed nearby, its throat cut, blood frothing up onto the road like a raspberry milk shake. Bullock carts and haughty camels laden down with bulging canvas bags sauntered past Waziri nomads; a butcher crouched on a block of wood was cutting meat by drawing it against a blade which he held firmly between his toes.

Jalil pressed a rosary into my hand and took my camera bag. 'Walk with your arms behind your back. Hold the rosary and keep your head stooped forwards,' he instructed. 'If there's any trouble, say nothing and leave everything to me.'

I swallowed hard on the lump in my throat and followed Jalil through the opening in the barbed-wire barricade. I was three, perhaps four, steps from setting foot on Afghan soil.

Suddenly, someone to my left shouted, 'Hello!' Instinctively, I turned my head in the direction from which the voice had come. I looked for no more than half a second – yet it was half a second too long. Standing there, beaming at me like an evil vizier, was a sharp-eyed Pakistani guard.

Saying nothing, I kept on walking. But it was too late. Two men grabbed me by the arms.

Standing in front of the guard, Jalil and I babbled at one another in pigeon Dari. A Pakistani policeman slapped the Afghan across the face. Jalil glared at him as if to say, 'This is your moment. Mine is yet to come.'

'Who are you? Where are you going?' growled the official.

I refused to answer any of their questions, and soon I was pushed before the desk of the local head of police. He looked uncannily like the late Pakistani President Zia Al-Haq, a portrait of whom hung on one wall.

'I recognise all you people,' the chief bellowed in my ear before I could utter a word. 'I know French, Japanese, Germans, Australians, Americans – and I know British. You ... you are British ... BRITISH!' he repeated.

He clutched my chin between powerful fingers and squeezed, looking deeply into my eyes like a head hunter inspecting his quarry. 'You look very young. How old are you?'

'Twenty,' I said.

His look terrified me. I thought that at any moment he might have me dragged away and thrown me into a dark, damp cell, the key to which he would misplace for a very long time.

'Why are you attempting to cross into Afghanistan?' he asked.

I was ready for this question and had my answer prepared. 'I want to become a Muslim,' I told him, 'and I want to fight in the *jihad*.'

He let go of my jaw. He tittered for a moment. The titter turned into a giggle. The giggle turned into laughter. The laughter into a Dracula-like cackle. I relaxed my shoulders.

'A Muslim!' he roared suddenly, grabbing me again, this time by the throat. 'You want to be a Muslim! Do you realise the consequences facing those who lie?'

'It's true,' I croaked, gasping for breath, 'really.'

I could see him weighing up the facts in his mind. The picture of Zia Al-Haq stared down at me from the wall. Finally, his expression changed.

'Most excellent boy,' he bawled, like a proud father, inviting me to take a seat in front of him. 'There are far better holy wars than this sideshow. The Afghans are not good: they are dirty. We tolerate them in Pakistan for one reason and one reason only: they are Muslims – of a kind. Go to Kashmir. There you can take part in a real *jihad* and one that is worth while. I will arrange it!'

He shouted for tea: '*Chai*!' Feet scurried on the wooden veranda outside his office. A tray was soon carried in holding a plate with a surprisingly large selection of Pakistani pastries and savouries.

'Would you like Earl Grey or Lapsang?' he asked.

After we had drunk several cups with buffalo milk, discussed a little politics, and he had reminisced on his time in Manchester, the head of police invited me to visit him at any time. He then released me, saying that I should return to Peshawar. 'If you do not,' he said, his voice returning to its former, less than cordial tone, 'you will be jailed as an agent of the CIA! For life!'

He then hugged me like a brother, smiled and waved Jalil and me on our way.

But I had come too far to give up now. The risk of being captured again seemed unimportant, trivial. The challenge of getting 'inside' had me in its grip. By this time, Jalil was recounting – omitting no detail – the story of our recent encounter with the Pakistanis to some friends of his in the shanty town on the border. He then took me to a Muhjahidin safe house. We waited there until dark and then doubled back, avoiding the border crossing, and climbed for five long hours over the tortuous, rock-strewn mountains, dodging the Pakistani patrols.

* * *

It was a warm night and we felt lucky. But as we emerged from a narrow pass, our luck ran out. Without warning, we were caught in a strong beam of light. We stood quite still. Once again, I imagined myself being dragged away to prison. We could hear footsteps coming towards us in the darkness. The beam grew more and more powerful. I strained my eyes. We could hear voices.

At last, to my relief, two young boys stood before us, both probably no more than fourteen years old. One carried a torch, the other a rifle, a British Lee Enfield, doubtless a replica produced at Darra. He pointed it at me threateningly.

'Who are you and where are you going?' the taller one demanded in the rough Pushtu dialect of the border land.

'He is my guest,' explained Jalil.

The boys, who had vivid imaginations, seemed eager to believe that I was a Russian and were anxious to learn how Jalil had captured me and, more importantly, how he was planning on disposing of me. I saw myself being used for target practice by these two young ruffians and began to regret not having taken up the police chief's offer of a trip to Kashmir.

Jalil tried to explain: 'No, no. You don't understand, brothers. He is here to fight. He is a friend.' They still didn't seem convinced.

Just then, I remembered that I had some coloured cigarettes with gold filters in my bag. I gave them each a red one and they beamed at me as they lit up. Still pointing the torch in our direction, they invited us to spend the night at their house. It was a tempting offer as we were tired. But Jalil and I were anxious to press on, so we shook hands and said goodbye. Trying to hide their disappointment, they disappeared back into the night.

My companion and I walked on. It was now pitch dark, as if the Moon had been swallowed by a black hole. Soon we noticed that the air, which had been hot and dusty in the Khyber Pass, had changed. It was now cold and sweet. Without passing through an actual border post, or crossing over a painted line, we had moved from one country to another. Never before or since have I sensed such a genuine change in the air and environment.

We had moved from the Indian sub-continent into Central Asia. We had arrived in Afghanistan ...

TEN

The Giant Buddhas

... a plane dropped a bomb a few hundred yards from where we were riding. It was too far away to harm us. It frightened the horses ... We rode through what must have once been a lake bed. The dust was so fine it got into everything: my eyes, ears, nose, mouth, cameras ... Gave a Muj who was returning to Peshawar my article on the de-mining programme to post to The Friday Times *...*

Diary, 12 July 1990

A monster is said to lurk within the depths of the mysterious Band-i-Amir lake in central Afghanistan. The ancient Afghan bards, who can spin yarns as tall as trees, describe the creature as being half seahorse and half dragon.

'They say it has talons as sharp as razors, long purple tentacles with powerful suckers, and green eyes,' Jalil told me. 'Its screech has scared men to death and it is said to be so ugly that it refrains from looking at its own reflection in the water.'

Many a mischievous Afghan girl and boy have been put to bed at night with a warning that should they misbehave, the monster will carry them off to its underwater lair and devour them. The legend of Band-i-Amir is as famous in Central Asia as the Scottish Loch Ness Monster in the West; so much so that during the early 1970s, a team of French scientists ventured here to conduct research. Yet they found nothing, and Band-i-Amir's submarinal resident remains an enigma, like its Caledonian cousin, feared by the natives and sought by the curious.

I had journeyed to Band-i-Amir in search of one of the rarely seen wonders of the God Gifted Realm, as the Afghans call their country. Eight months had passed since my first trip 'inside' which had begun with so much trouble on the Khyber Pass border. That trip lasted ten days, spent mainly around the eastern city of Jalalabad where the Communist forces and Muhjahidin were dug in on a long front.

Since then, I had made five other forays into the country, of which this, the sixth, was proving the longest. I was now thoroughly familiar with Afghan affairs and politics, and was reporting for the BBC Farsi and Pushtu language services, and occasionally for the press agency Reuter, as well as continuing to take photographs for the Associated Press. I had been covering the ongoing war between the Muhjahidin and the Soviet-backed central Government in Kabul.

As Jalil waited nearby, I peered into the still water, searching for the faintest streak of fin or tail. For a second, I thought something moved far below, but just then the wind caused ripples on the surface and by the time the lake grew calm again, the something had vanished. Perhaps, it had simply been a shoal of fish – or maybe the sunlight catching on a clutch of rocks.

I was looking into the water once more when, without warning, an Afghan boy wearing an embroidered prayer cap leapt out from the boulders behind me, swinging his arms in a frenzied, windmill-like action. Apparently terrified, he shrieked, '*Bus* (stop)! It's dangerous!' He quickly tugged me away by the arm and we retreated behind some rocks, watching the surface of the lake with trepidation, as if the Thing was about to rise up and roast us alive in a breath of fire.

In my broken Dari, I asked the blushing urchin whether he had ever seen the monster and if so, what it looked like. Without a word, obviously frightened, he ran helter skelter to his herd of fat-tailed Karakul sheep, repeatedly glancing back over his shoulder at the lake.

During the 1960s, Band-i-Amir was one of the main stopping off points on the old Hippy Trail to India. The long-haired peace-lovers who came from as far afield as Haight Ashbury and Earls Court travelled in converted Volkswagen vans, each loaded down with bags of hashish. They stayed in a small inn, now destroyed by bombs, near the lake and divided their time between smoking water pipes and swimming naked in the cool waters, much to the amazement of the Afghans.

The hippies believed that Band-i-Amir had magical properties. They may not have been far wrong. The water is crystal clear and its surface mirrors the sky's brilliant blue, creating an intense and striking colour like a piece of lapis lazuli. When I first spotted the lake, lodged between the iridescent purple-coloured hills and pinkish scrubland, I thought I must have been hallucinating. It was like discovering a concrete swimming pool in the middle of the Colorado desert.

What's more, Band-i-Amir, which is fed by subterranean springs, is contained within a thirty or forty-foot high wall, dam-like in appearance. Unlike any other dam, the wall does not bridge the sides of a narrow valley or pass. Instead, it protrudes into the middle of a valley floor forming a large blue tongue.

I examined the sides of this strange structure, pulling away the superficial covering of mosses and shallow-rooted plants. Underneath, I found the interwoven surface was not made of brick, nor of concrete, but of smooth limestone that appeared to rise out of the earth. Had it formed when mineral deposits in the water gradually solidified, like a giant stalagmite? Or was it constructed thousands of years ago by some long-forgotten civilisation? One expert has suggested that it may have formed when a quantity of lava spilled out onto the Earth's surface during some prehistoric eruption. I was to learn from a Pakistani geographer, whom I met a few months later, that there is no conclusive evidence which proves its origins.

'Come! It is not safe here! There are thieves!' shouted Jalil anxiously. He flung a shawl around his shoulders, thereby concealing his Kalashnikov.

Ever since we had arrived at the lake, Jalil had been agitating to leave, keeping his distance from the water's edge, behaving nervously. It hardly seemed possible that he should be scared of the monster: Jalil never showed any fear of anything. Even when part of his left foot had been blown off by a butterfly mine four months earlier, he had defied the doctors and started walking again within a matter of days. I had even spotted him speeding down Peshawar's dangerous Jamrud Road on his ancient Matchless motorbike, wearing his customary Soviet fighter pilot's helmet with its tinted visor down.

I asked him if he believed in the monster's existence. He fidgeted in his saddle.

'We have a saying in Afghanistan ... "Flight is two-thirds of valour".' So saying he turned Burak, his chestnut-coloured horse, and galloped off along the dusty trail towards the valley of Bamiyan. Perhaps Jalil had listened to the storytellers just once too often?

Over the months, Jalil had become a trusted travelling companion and a good friend. It was true that I paid him for his services as guide and translator, but he always accepted the money reluctantly. At times we had been in dangerous spots, sometimes coming under fire, yet Jalil never crumbled, saying only that it was his sworn duty to protect me.

I continued to be fascinated by his ability to learn almost any skill or task. His latest interest was photography, the basics of which I had taught him. Having grasped the technical side, he still had little idea of what made a good picture, preferring to take photographs of groups of his friends.

As Jalil and I made our way along the eastward trail, I reflected that although to my Western eyes the country seemed backward, Afghanistan has been the major cross-roads of Asia for thousands of years. Trade and ideas followed in the footsteps of imperial armies and nomadic tribes. Alexander the Great occupied much of Afghanistan on his march towards India three hundred years before Christ, and scholars have identified at least twenty-five different ruling dynasties during the past two thousand five hundred years. Each new invasion or migration left behind its own ethnic deposit, creating a cultural mosaic of bewildering complexity.

Islam was firmly established as the region's predominant religion by Turkish and Persian adventurers who overthrew the last Hindu kings four centuries after the death of the Prophet. Two hundred and fifty years ago, a branch of the powerful Durrani Pushtun clan effectively established itself as the Afghan Royal Family and the concept of a State was realised. Their rule was terminated, however, by the Communists in 1978 who initiated the Soviet invasion resulting in a decade of war, the devastating effects of which were evident all around me.

We were on our way to Bamiyan, the provincial capital of the Hazarajat, the central area of Afghanistan populated by Shi'ah Hazaras, thought to be descendants of the hordes of Genghis Khan. Bamiyan had been liberated from the Communists one year earlier and life had returned to the villages and the land. The ancient bazaar with its spacious caravanserai, which once housed affluent traders moving along the silk route, had been rebuilt: shell holes filled in, roofs replaced, homes repaired. Life remained a struggle, however. There was little medicine available; staple foodstuffs such as sugar and rice were in short supply; and the UN World Food Programme, whose staff knew little about Afghanistan, its culture and traditions, had flooded the bazaar with emergency grain rations. Thus, they undermined local prices and deterred farmers from sowing their land with anything other than poppy.

Dusk was falling as we arrived in the town. The main street was deserted by all but the desert rats and jerbils. They scurried under our horses' hooves as we clipped our way past a mosque with a turquoise-coloured minaret. A *muezzin*, a mullah or imam who summons people to prayer, sang out the shrill Shi'ah call to the faithful. Lights flickered in glassless windows and smoke billowed out of small chimneys near to where doves perched and cooed on flat rooftops. Up on the hill over the town loomed the silhouette of the burned out Soviet military base, now roofless and open to the sky.

In the distance, the snow caps of the Hindu Kush rose like phantoms above the threatening black mountains. The silence was eerie. I felt a sense of great anticipation. Near the end of the bazaar, Jalil stopped Burak and pointed to a mile-long sandstone cliff that stretched out to our left like the wall of a mighty fortress. As my eyes strained in the darkness, I could just make out a towering figure carved in a deep alcove, like a gigantic mute being. It was the larger of the two giant Buddhas of Bamiyan, standing fifty-eight yards high above the valley which it has dominated for nearly two thousand years.

Mesmerised, I urged my horse on. Nothing could have prepared me for this sight, made all the more magical by the eerie silver moonlight.

I thought of a few lines by the Scottish writer, Morag Murray, who married an Afghan during World War One and spent much of her life travelling in the Middle East and Asia. In her memoirs, entitled *The Valley of the Giant Buddhas*[1], she describes the statues as being, 'so striking that they far overshadow such sights as the Pyramids and Sphinx in Egypt or the rose-red city of Petra in Jordan. The scene was, and still is, something unexcelled in Asia.'

A path led through the fields to the second of the two

[1] 'The Valley of the Giant Buddhas', Morag Murray Abdullah, The Octagon Press, London.

142

giant Buddhas, a towering, faceless, armless colossus draped in a stone robe or toga with ears like merry-go-rounds. Dismounting and grabbing a torch from my rucksack, I ran up to its feet. Worn at the toes, they were as large as railway carriages. Gazing up, I imagined that the giant was about to squash me like a bug and stride off into the valley.

Jalil lingered behind me. He wanted us to wait to explore the Buddhas in the morning. I ignored him, such was my excitement. There was an opening in the cliff, an archway; I entered, urging the Afghan to follow.

We started up a carved, spiral staircase alongside the Buddha. The steps were narrow and worn, some crumbling at the edges. The curved walls felt rough in places and smooth in others, like sandpaper that had been half used; narrow openings or windows cut from the stone looked out onto the immense body.

Short of breath, we reached the top of the stairs and stepped out onto the flat-top head, thirty-eight yards above the ground. Looking out in the moonlight, we could just make out the landscape below; Jalil shone the torch at our horses where they stood tethered. Resting only briefly, we crept on through a maze of passages. Tunnels led into honeycomb cells which led into assembly halls and catacombs with hundreds of niches in the walls. They formed an ant-like city in the rock, where noises fuelled the imagination: sounds of dripping water seemed to emanate from everywhere and our footsteps echoed and re-echoed around us as if we were being followed by an invisible army.

Just as Jalil was protesting that we should return to the horses, the torch flickered out. We were thrown into complete darkness. The batteries were dead.

'Now look what has happened,' grumbled the Afghan. 'We are probably going to have to stay here all night.'

But as our eyes adjusted to the darkness, we noticed a faint light coming from the opening at the far end of a tunnel. Drawn to it, we stumbled over loose stones and, as we edged closer, we could hear a voice murmuring like an old man sleep-talking. We crept silently towards the opening. Water dripped from the wall above us and ran down my back. We peered inside.

On the floor of the octagonal cell, whose walls and roof were wet with moisture, squatted an old man wearing a white camel-hair robe and a hat with floppy ear flaps. He had a far-off look in his eyes that suggested he was in a semi-hypnotic state. His ghostly features shimmered in the light of a kerosene lamp which burnt with a brilliant white flame and in front of him stood, within a circle drawn in the sandy floor, a small brass peacock.

He stared up at us as if we were expected and without standing, introduced himself in English as Baba Ibrahim. He bore an Islamic name, but was a Yezidi Kurd, a high priest of a cult about which Jalil and I knew nothing.

To the Turks, Syrians, Iraqis and Iranians, and many people in the Middle East, the Yezidis are devil worshippers. Yet their cult, as I later discovered, is far more mysterious and complex than is generally assumed. Essentially, their religion is an indiscernible mix of other systems, principally Zoroastrian and Sufic in origin. The Yezidis believe that by recognising Satan, humanity increases his power on Earth. Therefore, they seek to pacify the devil, worshipping his representative, the Peacock Angel.

'Come, come,' the Kurd said, motioning us towards him. 'Come and sit with me.'

Hesitating, we crouched beside him, facing his peacock. Jalil, who was always ready to learn something new, was now eager to stay. Once we were settled, Baba Ibrahim began telling us about his many adventures.

'I left Mosul, in Iraq, sixteen whole years ago. It feels like a lifetime,' he began in a voice that was barely audible. 'Why did I come to Afghanistan? Because this country is the source of all spirituality.'

144

Baba Ibrahim leaned backwards, one hand cupped over his right knee. The kerosene spat and hissed and, for a moment, it seemed as if it might go out. However, the Kurd turned a knob on the side and the flame grew bigger, as he continued. 'So many religions have their roots and origins here,' he told us. 'Zoroaster was born and lived somewhere in the west of Afghanistan and the Vhedas, the holy books of Hinduism, are said to have been written here as well. Long after Buddhism died out in India, it flourished in Afghanistan before moving into Nepal, Tibet and China ... Rumi, the Sufi mystic, was born in Balkh, the mother of cities. Some even say that humanity's secret guides have their base hidden in the depths of the Hindu Kush. Those are the people I am searching for ...'

In the tradition of the wandering dervish, Baba Ibrahim had travelled on foot across the Middle East to reach Bamiyan and, upon arrival, he decided to make the caves his home. The locals thought that he was mad, but in accordance with tradition, they had fed, clothed and humoured him. Since then, he had left only periodically to travel back to Iraq to visit the Yezidis' holy shrines, and to Kabul to read about the Buddhist culture that thrived in Bamiyan for five hundred years.

I asked him about the giant Buddhas. Who had carved them and how?

'It took highly skilled and dedicated Buddhist monks four or five hundred years to sculpt the gigantic monuments and the city of caves and passages. The monks erected an ingenious form of wooden scaffolding which allowed them to carve and paint their way to the top,' said the Kurd.

'The Chinese pilgrim Hsan-Ysang, seeking the roots of his faith, journeyed here fourteen hundred years ago,' continued Baba Ibrahim. 'He found the effigies covered in brilliant, shimmering gold and red paint. Even today, there are still remnants of sophisticated frescoes and designs. You'll see some tomorrow in the daylight. Interestingly, unlike the contemporary Buddhist images, the faces are those of Europeans. This highlights the Macedonian Alexandrian influence on ancient Afghanistan.'

As much as we wanted to continue our Bamiyan history lesson, by this time, Jalil and I were exhausted. The kerosene lamp, together with the hypnotic effect of the Kurd's soft voice, were plunging us ever deeper into drowsiness. Baba Ibrahim stopped speaking and offered to guide us back down to our horses by the light of the lamp, realising we were too tired to listen any further.

* * *

The next day, when we were refreshed, Baba Ibrahim took me on a guided tour of his city in the rock. In the labyrinth of silent cells, I could picture the monks cross-legged, meditating; their flickering candles left carbon deposits still visible on the ceilings. The walls were painted with frescoes of the life of Buddha, dancing girls, singers playing on harps, and landscapes.

'This was all executed by the artist-monks with great delicacy and amazing detail,' Baba Ibrahim said. 'The loose, draped garment, ribbons and the three golden crescents which form the crowns on each Buddha became the model and style for designs appearing on virtually all Chinese and Japanese cloth, pottery and other objects made after that time.'

I was still confused as to how Buddhists had come to be in central Afghanistan. 'For at least a thousand years, Bamiyan was the world centre of Buddhism,' explained the Kurd, as we sat on the head of the smaller of the two giants. 'Due to overwhelming Hindu opposition in India, it was forced to re-establish itself in Afghanistan in about 500 BC.'

The word 'Buddha' is a title meaning 'to wake'. The

first Buddha, an Indian prince, was born about 560 BC in the region of the Gangetic Plain just below the Himalayan foothills. His real name was Sakyamuni, the Sage of the Sadyas. At the age of twenty-nine, he renounced the orthodox influences of his Hindu childhood. The young prince believed that humanity could free itself from earthly restrictions and fulfil its destiny through inner peace, harmony and self-knowledge.

Research by eminent archaeologists shows that the Giant Buddhas were probably carved in the first to third centuries AD by the Kushans, a unique mix of the Yue-chi people of Persian Sasanian stock and Greek Bactrian Afghans, descendants of Alexander the Great. The Kushans, the most powerful rulers of their time, converted to Buddhism and spread their new religion via fervent missionaries who travelled as far as China, Mongolia, Korea, Japan and beyond.

'An exotic festival was held in Bamiyan every five years,' continued the Kurd. 'Eighty thousand monk converts drawn from the local community and five hundred Greeks joined the throngs of Chinese pilgrims and others who came from all over the Buddhist world. They paid to have paintings of the giants done for them, although the most expensive prize was to have a portrait painted of oneself in the style of a Bamiyan Buddha.'

From ancient times, Bamiyan was strategically important as it lay along the trade and caravan routes between China and the West, India and Central Asia. Because of its geographical position, the valley fell victim to Genghis Khan and his Mongol hordes who swept through northern Afghanistan in the thirteenth century. Some historians say that it was the Khan's men who destroyed the Buddhas' faces.

'Lamentably, once again, Bamiyan was occupied in 1979, this time by the Russians,' Baba Ibrahim told me. 'They took advantage of the caves, using them to store armaments and weapons, a criminal act when you consider that one explosion would have destroyed the cliff. The Soviet military was also negligent for not ensuring that the Buddhas were properly cared for. A drainage channel at the top of the cliff was destroyed, and for over a decade, water has poured down the cliff-face, eroding the sandstone at an alarming rate.'

Baba Ibrahim, who remained in Bamiyan during the entire occupation, had tried to dig a new channel, although his efforts had proved futile. 'Now, with the Soviets gone, there is renewed hope,' he said.

Borrowing money from myself and the local UN officer, Baba Ibrahim set off to Pakistan. There, he aimed to raise money to save the Buddhas and the city of caves that had become his home.

ELEVEN

The Roughest Game
in the World

*... I haven't seen another Westerner for more than
a month ... while I miss having a conversation with
someone in English, it is very refreshing to be
completely away from it all. I could be living in the
Middle Ages. People here, despite their troubles,
seem more comfortable with their culture and
history ... The runs aren't letting up. I've lost a lot
of weight and am still taking oral rehydration
salts. I'm running on adrenalin.*

Diary, 20 August 1990

Jalil and I spent over a week in Bamiyan. I photographed
the Buddhas and visited two newly established schools,
sat in the bazaar, and interviewed local politicians and
military leaders. We were making preparations to move
further east when we were told about the possibility of
seeing the Afghan sport of Buz-kashi, a cross between
polo and American football, played with the headless carcass of a goat or cow. This was one of the first times in
over ten years that it had been played inside Afghanistan.

Over four consecutive days, Jalil and I went to the
same field in the hope of seeing a match, only to be disappointed each time. On the fifth day, we bumped into
one of Jalil's local contacts, a man who, like so many men
in Asia, whiled away his day in the bazaar, collecting
information. After the customary hugs, greetings and tea
drinking, I tactfully asked whether there would be a Buz-
kashi game that day.

He replied, 'Why not?'

Now, to the English, the question, 'why not?' means, 'of course there is' or 'why shouldn't there be?'. But to Afghans, it has become a way of saying, 'I don't really have any idea, but I don't want to say no.'

The Afghans, who avoid giving direct answers whenever possible, have the makings of first-rate diplomats. This man was no exception. When I needled him with further questions, he was as equally evasive.

'Don't you know if there is a game today?' I asked.

'Yes!' he said.

'Yes you know, or yes, there will be a game?'

'Yes, Buz-kashi has been known to be played here.'

'Will there be a game today?' I pressed him.

'They usually play on Fridays and Saturdays.'

'And today is Saturday.'

'Yes,' he agreed.

'But is there a game today?'

'It depends on the weather ...'

'... Good, it's a fine day ...' I interrupted.

'... and the will of Allah,' he added quickly.

I was beginning to think I was up against Nasruddin, the humorous wise fool who appears in many guises in the Islamic world and never gives a straight answer.

Our contact led us to the field in which Buz-kashi was 'usually played'. To my amazement and delight, a game was about to begin. Near the centre of the pitch, ferocious-looking Afghans sat hunched astride magnificent Central Asian steeds; younger men glaring; leather whips held firmly between strong teeth. Older, self-assured men with sagging stomachs protruding from sheepskin jackets and brightly embroidered waistcoats, were waiting for the arrival of the referee.

The enthusiastic riders began warming up their horses by galloping around the pitch. Hooves dug into the loose soil. Cascades of dust rose into the air, pierced by shafts of light. The decorated bridles, reins, stirrups and woven carpet-like saddles added to the pageantry of the occasion. These were the renowned horseman of Central Asia about to start a game of their national sport which they inherited from the Mongols.

Perched on a rickety stand surrounding the pitch sat dozens of Afghan spectators, their apricot complexions glowing under the rolled woollen hats from Nuristan in eastern Afghanistan which had become the emblem of the Muhjahidin. The assortment of beards was bewildering: henna-coloured, grey, long, short and bushy. The referee, a jovial character dressed in a scarlet corduroy jacket, dragged a beheaded calf into the centre of the arena and announced that the game was about to begin.

Jalil introduced me to the local commander who invited us to sit with his other guests. He was a slight, brown-bearded man, who could easily have passed for a European. Like many Afghan leaders, he wore baggy trousers and a military tunic. I found it difficult to believe that this serene, gentle man was a renowned commander among a race of warriors.

As the game was beginning, I asked my host to explain the rules. 'There are few!' His reply came as no surprise. I had come to realise that Afghan people are individualists with little interest in, or regard for, conformity and codification. On the other hand, during the eighteen months I spent amongst them, I observed an impressively high degree of teamwork and service. Indeed, Buz-kashi typifies the Afghan temperament. The game seems to be a brawl in which every player is out for himself; in reality, there are two teams whose players work together.

The object of the game is to scoop up the calf's headless carcass from the ground, ride it around a post at the opposite end of the pitch, then ride it back, and finally dump it in a circle drawn at the other end of the field, thereby scoring a point. With the exception of whipping or hitting each other, the players are allowed to ride in any manner, often only just managing to stay on their steeds in order to gain possession of the calf. They may, however, with moderation, whip each others' horses or charge into one another, bumper-car fashion.

There is no limit to the size of the pitch – Afghan friends described matches in the days before the Soviet invasion where entire valleys were marked out. Neither is there a limit to the number of players, and it was not uncommon to watch Buz-kashi games in which hundreds of horsemen participated at one time. As for the duration of the game, they play until the animal has been torn apart.

The match was now in full swing. A Turkoman Afghan, wearing a deep-blue coat with a dashing crimson band around his waist, plunged his arm down his horse's left flank and, with stupendous strength, pulled the calf up to his saddle. Gripping a whip between his yellowing teeth, he held onto one limb of the calf and hooked his foot under the stomach. He galloped to the other end, went around the post and prepared to make his charge. The opposition were thundering towards him.

Into the fray he crashed, his horse rearing up open mouthed. The commander assured me that the horses are rarely injured and are extremely well treated – even spoiled – by their owners. Buz-kashi horses are bred and trained for the game, not unlike polo ponies.

Meanwhile, the valiant Turkoman had lost his grip on the calf and the carcass had fallen to the ground. Team-mates were calling instructions to one another. A younger and inexperienced horseman made a play for the carcass, but dust was kicked into his face by a flying hoof. He retreated from the pack, his eyes bloodshot, tears streaming down his hairy cheeks.

The commander's commentary helped me follow the game. As with American football, players from both sides repulse their opposite number while the best and strongest players scratch in the dirt for a hold of the calf. During the match, several players leant heavily to one side and disappeared from view. I held my breath while they struggled back into their saddles. Occasionally, they fell and crawled away to regain their composure.

As the dust cloud grew, a Hazara pulled the battered beast to waist height. The others clawed and snatched at it, bashing into him. He managed to manoeuvre away from the pack and, once firmly in control of the calf, rode towards the circle. A fellow team-mate wedged in behind and seized one of the calf's limbs. The carcass was now suspended between the two leaders as the pack stampeded past. They left us coughing and spluttering, straining to see the outcome. Some riders were unable to stop and rode into the crowd, scattering people in all directions.

'This is what you might call a spectator sport,' laughed Jalil.

Triumphant, the Hazara and his friend breached the gap between the opposition and reached the circle. They dropped the calf unceremoniously. The crowd rose as one and roared praise and cheers in Dari. Many tossed their hats in the air. Cut and bruised, the now exhausted horseman accepted their praise humbly.

'He is a *champandaz*! A champion! A master player!' cried the commander. 'He used to play in Kabul at the Royal Games and was praised by our former king, Zahir Shah.'

The winners moved forwards and, as is the custom, they were given money by a group of elders. This reward was for the upkeep of the horses.

'Nowadays, these horses eat better food than most of their owners,' sighed the commander. The expression on his face changed. It was the sort of daydreaming look which shows contemplative reflection in a person's mind.

While we peeled hard-boiled, henna-dyed eggs and munched on popcorn, the *champandaz* rode around the field accepting money from admirers.

He did not have long to enjoy his glory. A competitor whisked the calf to the other of the pitch. The pack galloped after him, punching their fists in the air.

'God is great!' they shouted. 'Long live Afghanistan!'

TWELVE

East Towards Kabul

*... woke up this morning thinking of home. It seems
like a long way away from where I sit writing in
this tea house near Kabul. If people could see me
now! ... I don't like to be shot at. I've discovered
that much ... Guess I've also seen what a
responsibility journalists have in a situation like
this. We become the eyes and ears for the rest of
the world when no one else has access ...*

Diary, 3 September 1990

'Who is the king of Germany?' asked the yellow-skinned
Hazara as he recklessly steered his captured Russian jeep
around a hairpin bend. A faded picture of Lenin stared
out at me from the dashboard. Underneath it was written
one of the most colourful Afghan insults which translates
as: 'Son of a noseless mother'.

'Do you mean Chancellor Kohl?' I asked, glancing nervously down the sheer drop to our right.

'No, no! Not Kohl,' cried my new friend, a Genghis
Khan lookalike, right down to his jet-black moustache,
oriental eyes and stubby legs, 'the man who calls himself
Hit-lair.'

'Oh, you mean Hitler. Adolf Hitler. The leader of the
Third Reich, World War Two ...'

'Very good man! Very good man!' shouted the Hazara.

I was shocked that anyone other than a Nazi skinhead should be describing the Führer in such favourable
terms. I tried to put him right on this point.

'Hitler wasn't a good man. He was a mass murderer.

154

He killed millions of ...'

'... Yes! Killed millions of Russians! Very good man! Very good man!'

The Hazara slapped my thigh and laughed a ho-ho-ho kind of laugh like Father Christmas, navigating the jeep down a hill and through a gurgling stream.

Jalil and I were heading east. Our intended destination was a secret mountain base near Kabul where we hoped to find a Muhjahidin group who were training in urban guerilla tactics.

As usual, my guides, including Jalil, were vague about how long it would take to get there. Shrugging their shoulders, I was informed that the timing depended on the number of burst and flat tyres; how often we came under fire; how frequently we broke down. Of most concern to me, however, were the excessive number of tea stops at local caravanserais. At best, we might reach the camp in 'one to five days, *Insh Allah*' – but only if we managed to escape being attacked by brigands and if our driver decided against a lengthy detour to the north where he wanted to watch the winter Buz-kashi matches and visit his extended family.

When travelling in Afghanistan, there seemed little point in making assumptions or forming plans and schedules. Just when you were counting your chickens, your host's eldest son might decide to marry and insist that you stay for a month of celebrations. Without warning, three feet of snow might fall overnight and you would get stuck in a remote valley. And there was also the constant threat of a tribal blood feud, sparking off or being rekindled, making it hazardous to travel along any given route.

For these reasons and a myriad more, journeys that should have taken only a few days, frequently stretched on for weeks, sometimes months. For newcomers to Afghanistan, and especially Westerners like myself, this concept of time can drive you to distraction. While we demand to know where we will be from one day to the next, the average Afghan thinks little of spending a week waiting by the roadside for a truck hopefully heading in his direction.

The Afghans, sensing my impatience, lost little time in teasing me. Often, upon our arrival in a village, I would ask when we would be pressing on. Jalil was always deliberately vague. On one occasion, he replied, 'We will probably have to remain here for the winter.'

'The winter!' I exclaimed, tearing at my hair. 'The whole winter? But I have to be back in Peshawar in a week!'

'Why not stay here,' he said, coolly, 'the apricots are delicious.'

'The apricots! The apricots! I have to get my stories to the BBC!'

Jalil raised and then lowered his broad shoulders and sighed deeply. Then, after just half an hour, he stood up abruptly from where he was sitting and said, 'Let us go! Take your bags and hurry.'

'But you said we would have to stay here for the winter!'

'I have changed my mind. It may be dangerous to linger here too long. And besides, these people are running low on tea.'

There was little doubt in my mind that it was this kind of behaviour and attitude which had won the Afghans the war against the Soviets. The Russians were faced with a force of hillsmen who were totally unpredictable. The Muhjahidin might pop up at any time, at any place. No amount of KGB intelligence helped the Soviet invader because the Afghans seemed to be so disorganised. It was difficult to know who were the real leaders, as there were so many in different places. What's more, two groups a mile apart from each other rarely knew what the other was planning or thinking.

To make travelling in Afghanistan even more challenging, there was no longer a system of paved roads. The all-weather highway built by the Soviets during the 1960s and 1970s to connect the cities of Kandahar, Herat and

Mazar Sharif with the capital, Kabul, had been bombed and mined. The Kabul-to-Kandahar Highway, as it is known, was now little more than a pitted track full of gaping craters. Afghanistan was also without a rail system. The prospect of tunnelling through the mighty Hindu Kush – which makes the Alps look like a mere set of mole hills – was not deemed feasible by Russian engineers, even if the astronomical costs involved could ever be met.

The Afghans moved around the country in a collection of raggle-taggle vehicles, anything from mopeds and bicycles, to makeshift buses constructed from bits and bodies of shattered Soviet transport helicopters. Moving at agonisingly slow speeds, they followed the old caravan routes: rock-strewn river beds, passes and rough tracks which have been used for countless millennia by silk and spice traders, smugglers and invading armies marching south to India. At the end of the day, it was quicker to travel by horse, donkey, camel – or simply walk.

When Jalil and I needed to cover long distances, we hitched lifts on trucks, paying our way with vitamins and aspirin tablets. The trucks were mostly old British Bedfords bought in Pakistan, but occasionally you would come across an ancient American monster with a converted Japanese engine. Their cabs were plastered with tatty stickers of Country and Western singers, and the original licence plates, still in place, hailed from such places as California, 'the sunshine state'.

The Hazara treasured his jeep, which was flimsy and shook like a dinghy in a ferocious storm. 'It belonged to an officer of the Red Army,' he boasted. 'I slit his throat – the son of a dog – and stole it. Then I sneaked it out of the city by bribing the Russian checkpoint guards with half a bottle of watered-down Chinese whisky.'

The jeep was now packed full of eager young Muhjahidin. Seven men were squashed onto the back seat like the folds of an accordion. If the two sitting next to the windows moved, they squeezed their neighbours and, one after another, let out a series of grunts and groans; when repeated rapidly, this sounded like a short tune. Two boys sat on the driver's seat along with the Hazara. Three sacks bulging with juicy red pomegranates bounced about on the roof, and four hitchhikers clung to the back door. I was forced to share my seat with a man aptly known as 'the Ox'. When he wasn't busy fighting Communists, he was an arm wrestler and had the biceps to prove it.

He also had an ammunition box on his lap. 'What is inside that?' I asked him as he sat with one arm over my shoulder clutching the head rest.

'R – P – G,' he said sternly.

'Rocket propelled grenades,' I mused. 'Hmmm. How many – exactly?'

'Enough,' he replied.

Enough for what? I asked myself. Enough to kill us if we hit a mine? Certainly enough to cause more than a few headaches in Kabul.

As the jeep trundled on, the young Afghans in the back started firing dozens of questions at me. What little they knew about the West, they had picked up in the tea houses; their information was collected from gossip and rumour.

'Is it true that you can have sex before you marry?' asked a young man, gaping at me as he awaited my answer.

'Yes. It is true.'

The occupants of the back seat all nudged one another as if this was the most incredible thing they had ever heard.

'Is it true that you burn your bodies after death like the Hindu Indians?'

'Yes, it is sometimes true,' I replied.

Again there was much nudging.

'Is it true you keep dogs in your homes?'

'Yes, that is also true.'

This time my answer brought about a high-pitched chorus of laughter.

The Hazara was munching on a bag of walnuts and *toot*, dried mulberries. A few had fallen from his mouth and, as the jeep rocked and jolted, they danced up and down on his lap.

'Do you like Afghani music?' he asked, giving me a look that pleaded for me to answer in the affirmative.

'Can't get enough of it,' I said, half-heartedly.

With a satisfied walnut-filled grin, he slipped his short stubby fingers into a pocket of his warm, woolly sheepskin coat and produced a tape. He asked me to rewind it by spinning it around my index finger; this done, he jammed the tape into the cassette player.

The music began with a grunt, like the sound made by a camel as it wakes in the morning. An up-tempo, high-pitched screeching voice then reverberated from the speakers, backed up by a wailing chorus. It sounded like a cross between music from a Greek tragedy and a bad performance by a heavy metal band. This was *jihad* music played in the arabesque style with acoustic instruments. The lyrics told of the war and the *shaheeds*, the men and women who had died fighting the Soviets.

The Afghans sang and hummed, glancing out the windows with sad expressions. The jeep rolled on ...

* * *

Half a day later, as I was rewinding the tape for the umpteenth time and nursing a throbbing headache, the jeep came to a grinding halt. Before us, up on a low ridge, lay the ruins of a village which looked as if it had been struck violently by a giant fist. Across a square mile, not one house remained intact, not one room, not one roof. Thick oak doors which had been splintered like matchsticks, lay amongst the rubble. The few remaining mud walls left standing had been eroded to almost nothing, like sand castles in the rising tide.

The only objects which were still standing above eye level were a number of tall posts which the local Afghans had placed at the heads of their graves. At the top of these, waving like flags, hung scraps of dyed fabrics, placed there to scare away evil spirits.

The rays of the Sun did not warm this place. It was cold and lifeless, like empty school corridors during the holidays. There were no happy children running along the lanes; no people in the fields; no proud men returning from the bazaars; just the whispering wind in the nearby trees which seemed to warn us to keep away. With good reason: butterfly mines had been scattered about, booby traps left for the innocent, wells poisoned. You could almost hear the dead calling to us for vengeance.

As if the tragedy had just occurred, we found a dazed old man sifting through the rubble, apparently still searching for his loved ones. Draped in a flowing baggy shirt that hung from his arms like bat wings, and with a turquoise ring on one finger, he had a look that I had seen on a thousand Afghan faces: a distant, glazed stare – reflecting the horrors of a world turned upside down, and yet his determined air was that of a man who believed, reluctantly, in destiny.

Gesticulating with his arms, his long, bony fingers pointing to the sky like leafless twigs, the old man described how, three years earlier, during Gorbachev's last ditch attempt to control Afghanistan, the invaders had destroyed his village.

'It was during the day when the evil ones came down from the sky in their great beasts,' he told Jalil and me. 'There was great noise, its claws seemed to grab at the air, stirring the very ground beneath us. Then it spat out death. I watched helplessly as many people ran. I saw our people killed, butchered as if they were insects. The evil ones destroyed everything and then they left as they had come – the sons of Sheitan.'

Before the war, many Afghans living in remote villages in near medieval conditions had no contact with the outside world. Few owned radios, and knowledge of any modern technology was very limited. When the fearsome Soviet helicopter gunships swooped over villages making terrifying whirring noises, the locals often imagined them to be dragons, straight out of a fairy tale. It was difficult for me to grasp just how terrifying this must have been. I tried to imagine what it would be like if alien spaceships suddenly appeared in the skies over London firing laser beams.

'I had seen the destruction in a terrible dream many years before,' continued the villager. 'It came to me three times and I saw all our homes destroyed. A voice told me to make preparations.'

The old man shook his head solemnly. 'Many did not listen, but my family and those who believed spent seven years digging caves in the nearby hills.'

The old man pointed to a hill to the east.

'Time passed and we carried on with our lives. When they came, we moved our belongings and lived like rabbits in our warrens.'

Since the Soviet withdrawal, he explained, the survivors had come down from the hills and started building new homes on a site not far from the old village. Although their materials and resources were limited, they were making progress. Their experiences, however, had so scarred the villagers that, as they worked, they continually looked up at the skies.

'We will never trust the *Rouss*. They say they have left Afghanistan. They can come back and we will be ready.'

* * *

The further east we drove, the more it felt like the forces of chaos had taken over. Even though the Russians had withdrawn in February 1989, the remnants of the regime and the Muhjahidin were still locked in bitter combat. As a result, the local economy was in a shambles and the Afghan currency was virtually worthless.

Scrap metal was the only commodity of any real value: it lay about in the bazaars like piles of unwanted modern art. Grey-coloured tail-fins from unexploded bombs, a rudder from a downed helicopter gunship, the tracks of a T-72 Russian-made tank, spent anti-aircraft cartridges, defused mortars, a burnt-out anti-personnel carrier. Dealers weighed out the twisted pieces of iron and steel on makeshift scales, the weights themselves just lumps of fused metal.

Drivers, stopping at ad hoc petrol stations by the side of the 'road', filled their vehicles with diesel from dented barrels using hand pumps. Not a drop was wasted, so precious was this black liquid; it was as if the oil wells of the world had finally dried up. Wood was also in short supply and children with muddy faces, eyelashes darkened with *kohl*, sparkling yet fretful eyes, were selling piles of dead branches, twigs collected from the rivers, anything they could lay their hands on.

In places, refugees were living in rusty American shipping containers, an incongruous sight in Afghanistan, especially when positioned near an ancient Sufi tomb. Yet to the homeless, they were a welcome form of shelter. It was distressing to see human beings in these extreme circumstances; men and women eking out a sparse existence in the middle of disorder and discord.

But in many areas, Afghans carried on relatively normal day-to-day lives in spite of the civil war raging all around them. Nowhere did I see this more clearly than in a valley between Bamiyan and Kabul where a group of Muhjahidin controlled the mountains to the west, the Government forces held the high ground to the east, and hundreds of civilians were caught in no man's land smack in the middle. All day, every day, stopping only for tea, the two sides pounded one another with shells. You could watch and hear the missiles as they passed overhead like flocks of migrating iron geese. Children would peer up at the sky, point and smile: 'Look! Look!'

The valley was stunning: lush green and light yellow, and well irrigated. Willow trees grew in abundance, and when the sun shone you wondered how, on such a beautiful day, people could be so determined to kill each other. There was a small bazaar stocked with essentials such as oil, soap and sugar, although at a pinch you could get your hands on anything – from a Stinger missile to smuggled Japanese cigarettes – provided you were pre-pared to pay the black market rates. Men were farming their land, sheep were grazing on sweet grass, families were being raised – there was even a tea house where old men gathered in the traditional way to tell stories.

The Hazara and his band stopped in the valley for two days and some of the locals took me swimming in a near-by stream. The water was cold and clear and sharply refreshing, and we took a quick dip before sitting on the sandy banks.

As we talked, we could hear the background din of shells whistling back and forth.

One of my hosts produced some raw lumps of plastic explosive from a knapsack and, having set the fuses, threw them into the stream. The resulting watery erup-tions stunned dozens of fish which flipped into the air. Some lay on the surface and floated away. A string of men stood further down stream to pick out the slippery catch with their bare hands while we collected up the ones which had fallen on the bank.

A single shell whizzed overhead.

Our hosts took us on another walk along the shaded river bank, past the remains of a schoolhouse, to a mud fort that had been recently rebuilt. There the Hazara, who loved fish, grilled our catch with juicy tomatoes and fresh onions and we devoured them ravenously. We moved on for dessert to a command post where a Muhjahid, who spoke a smattering of French, provided us with plates of blood-red water melon, pomegranates and mounds of walnuts. There was an abundance of food in this valley thanks to the rich farmland and orchards, and this Eden in the wilderness was a tremendous treat despite the shells. As we gorged ourselves once more, we listened to the village fool tease the children and tell stories and jokes. Lazily we registered the noise of a distant, far-off explosion.

We went for another walk later on that afternoon, picking our way through the fields, admiring the wild flowers and the gnarled, twisted mulberry trees.

Suddenly, we heard a loud whining noise.

After just two days in the paradise valley, I had become unmindful of the fighting; the sound of this latest shell caught my attention, however. It seemed to be uncomfortably close, although I could not judge from which direction it was coming.

Panic seized me. Every part of my body moved in a different direction: my right foot went left, my left foot went right, my left arm reached behind, the other in front. I fell over. The Muhjahidin stood around me in a circle, pointing and laughing. The shell exploded several hundred yards away. My hosts hardly flinched; they had become so sensitised to their hazardous surroundings that in the few split seconds before the shell's impact, they had judged themselves not to be in any danger. Most of them didn't even turn to look at the small mushroom cloud that rose in a nearby field.

As I picked myself up, a girl and a boy ran out of a neighbouring house carrying a heavy shovel between them. They pointed enthusiastically to the cloud and ran towards it. I followed, my two Nikon cameras bouncing on my chest. The shell was still smouldering in the earth when we reached the spot and the children dug energetically at the hot metal like a couple of foxes making a den. Later, no doubt, they hoped to take the scrap metal to the bazaar and sell it for a few pitiful *afghanis*.

As I was taking photographs, it dawned on me that another shell might land in or around the same spot. Jalil was shouting for us to come back. Sure enough, seconds later, the same sound reverberated through the air, tearing at my eardrums like the sound of nails drawn across a blackboard. The boy immediately dropped to the ground and lay as flat as he could, hugging himself to the dirt, wishing he could melt into it. I picked up the girl, ran and jumped over a wall, smashing a lens and grazing my head.

The bomb exploded, sending an invisible ghost-like force rushing through my body, threatening to lift me off the ground. When the noise had subsided, together with the pitter patter of earth landing all about us, we stood up behind the wall. The little boy was kneeling, surrounded by a cloud of dust and smoke. He seemed trapped in time, his mouth stretched open, but he emitted no noise. Two of his left fingers had been blown off and the rest of his hand was smashed, covered in flowing blood, the knuckles mangled. The little girl began crying. She ran over to her brother and tried to help him. But it took Jalil to stop the bleeding, and later the boy was taken to a nearby clinic where his hand was stitched up and bandaged.

This incident left me feeling dazed and with a strange sense of displaced time and space which I experienced several times in Afghanistan. One moment we had been admiring the countryside, aware that there was a war around us but somehow blanking it out; then suddenly, the bomb had exploded and the boy was bleeding.

After a further three-day drive, we reached the Muhjahidin base. The Hazara and the band of men in the jeep were anxious to press on to take part in a major operation against the military airport at Baghram. Jalil off-loaded my bags and we said goodbye to the Muhjahidin. The Hazara tried to give me a hug but, being so short, he only managed to get his arms around my waist.

'Remember!' he said as he released me, 'Afghanistan is your home too! Treat it as such!'

So saying, he, the Ox, and the others squeezed back into the jeep. Not looking back, they drove off in the direction of Kabul, the *jihad* music blaring out from the old stereo.

* * *

The training base was cleverly hidden within a series of caves and heavily camouflaged bunkers. It was in a narrow valley surrounded by a fortress of mountains with sheer cliffs. Each snow-capped summit was crowned with an anti-aircraft position manned throughout the year by groups of three or four men. Bit by bit, these heavy, cumbersome weapons had been carried thousands of feet up the mountains and then re-assembled. There were eight in all, acting as a formidable deterrent against MiG fighters, seeking to bomb positions on the valley floor below.

Jalil and I were led along a path patrolled by guards wearing green fatigues. Passing each one, they whispered, 'May you never be tired,' their hands over their hearts. Dozens of Muhjahidin lined the top of one gorge, shooting their Kalashnikovs into the air in the form of a salute. They scared the crows in the trees, the sound of beating wings mixing with the echo and re-echo of machine-gun fire.

After a short climb, we were led inside a man-made cave furnished with *kilims* and cushions. At one end, there was a stand holding an open copy of the Koran; on the floor, a stack of tomes written in French on the history of guerilla warfare. Stretched out on a table, I spotted a map of Kabul, certain roads and buildings marked with red circles and lines; hanging on the wall was a poster printed with the outline of Afghanistan, a cartoon of blood dripping from the bottom.

The entrance to the cave was soon filled by the frame

of a stocky man dressed in US army combat gear, a black submachine gun complete with silencer slung neatly over one shoulder. He looked like Blackbeard the Pirate without the patch and the parrot. This was one of the greatest Afghan commanders, Jan Fishan.

Hundreds of men were directly under his control, men who regarded him as a legend. He had fought innumerable battles, survived many assassination attempts and plagued the Soviets by regularly attacking their supply lines. The stories of his deeds resounded from one end of Afghanistan to the other. Jan Fishan, named after the legendary nineteenth-century Afghan warrior and philosopher, offered me his hospitality and protection and called to his guards outside the cave for *chai siar*, dark tea, and boiled sweets.

From the day the Soviets had stormed into his country in December 1979, the commander had fought them, organising guerilla attacks on targets in Kabul. Proudly, he took me to another part of his cave where his men had set up a small printing press which produced a weekly newspaper, and where we also found a colour television and video recorder powered by a diesel generator. A helper played us candid camera-like videos showing his meticulously planned attacks on Kabul's political, military and logistical centres that had secretly been taken by Jan Fishan's operatives.

Jan Fishan was the most successful Muhjahid commander I had met. I asked him what had really motivated his people against the Russians. Why had they sacrificed so many lives?

'We are a proud people,' he began, his voice rumbling through the cave like the sound of an avalanche searing down a mountain. 'We knew little of these Russians before they came. Suddenly they were attacking us, killing our children and our women. It was our duty to fight.'

Did he consider himself to be a fundamentalist?

He smiled and played with the edge of a *kilim* upon

which Jalil, Jan Fishan and I now sat cross-legged. 'If you, in your country, were suddenly attacked for no reason that you knew of,' he answered, 'wouldn't you fight, perhaps even give your life? And if you did, wouldn't you consider yourself to be a patriot rather than a fanatic?'

Jan Fishan, who was remarkably well informed and listened every day to the BBC World Service, saw further trouble brewing on the horizon. He was distrustful of the Muhjahidin leaders in Peshawar who claimed to represent the Afghan people.

'When the invaders descended upon our great country, we started fighting with nothing. All we had were these,' he said, lifting his hands in the air, stretching his thick fingers into two wide fans. 'The *Rouss* were well equipped and our Lee Enfield rifles were as nothing against their armour. We desperately needed modern weapons, so we went to Pakistan in search of them.

'The Pakistanis allowed our families to stay in their country and for that I am grateful. May the blessings of Allah, the merciful, rain down upon them!'

But the Pakistani Government was only able to provide the growing resistance movement with limited numbers and types of weapons. Desperate to prevent the Soviets from advancing any further into Asia, the CIA began a covert operation to supply the Muhjahidin. Arms were brought into Pakistan and it was then left to the Pakistanis to distribute the mainly Egyptian and Chinese weapons to the Afghans.

This was a difficult task as most of the commanders were inside Afghanistan fighting. The Pakistanis were also wary of supplying pro-royalist Afghan groups. So they hit upon a plan of allowing seven or so exiled political and religious figures – men of whom the majority of Afghans had never heard – to form the so-called Muhjahidin parties.

'We were then told we had to join one of these groups,' said Jan Fishan. 'We joined a party, depending upon our tribal allegiances. That was the only way to receive supplies. In the eyes of the world, those seven political parties and the leaders soon came to represent the Afghan people struggling for independence. It was the greatest tragedy to our cause, because they did not represent us at all.'

* * *

We spent a week at the mountain base, making excursions into Paghman and Parwan provinces and watching the Muhjahidin training on assault courses, experimenting with explosive devices, and practising martial arts. Jan Fishan offered to sneak us into Kabul where he was planning another daring attack. The offer was a tempting one, but Jalil was anxious to push on south as his family was expecting him in Pakistan. And as much as I had enjoyed seeing the country west of Kabul, we had been on the road for over six weeks; I too was already overdue in Peshawar and friends would be worried about my safety.

On telling Jan Fishan that we wished to leave, he looked dejected, as is the Afghan custom. When, for the third time, I implored him to let us take our leave, saying that we had important business to attend to, he gave Jalil and me his blessing, placing us in the care of God. Quickly summoning two of his men, he instructed them to find places on a suitable truck heading for Ghazni in the south.

The men searched for a truck but we had to wait a day or two. Eventually, one was found, but we were unable to secure seats in the cab as it was already occupied by several women passengers; a mother and her two daughters. Draped in black cloaks and scarves, jewellery and jangling trinkets, they struggled to keep their faces covered from prying eyes. Jalil explained firmly that it would be improper for strangers such as ourselves to be in such close proximity to women, so we sat in the back.

Jan Fishan came to say goodbye, giving us both mighty bear hugs. We settled in amongst sacks packed with pine nuts and pungent-smelling onions. As we drew away, the commander stood amidst a group of Kalashnikov-toting troops, giving the orders for his latest operation to begin in Kabul.

When the base was out of sight, Jalil placed a package in my hand. 'It is a gift from Jan Fishan himself,' he said. Wrapped inside a piece of soft leather was a square object made of copper with elaborate Arabic inscriptions around the edges. It was like something from the cave of Ali Baba's forty thieves. It had a turquoise stone embedded in the centre and a chain attached to the top.

'It is a talisman,' whispered Jalil, looking at me mysteriously. 'If you are a man who has faith in what is to be and what is not, this will always protect you, no matter what happens. Wear it always.'

I was astonished and at the same time upset that I hadn't been able to thank the commander personally, nor had I given him a present in return. 'But why didn't he give this to me himself?' I spluttered.

'He practises a true kind of generosity,' continued Jalil, 'and does not wish to feel any self-satisfaction for giving this to you.'

I wasn't sure that I understood exactly what he meant, but all the same, I promptly hung the talisman around my neck.

The truck laboured south through copper-streaked hills which gave way to limitless seas of sand where only the black-haired goats stood out against the surroundings. From time to time, in the middle of a great void of desert, naturally camouflaged amongst the light-brown sandy earth, we would spot a fortified mud-walled stronghold with twenty-five foot high walls, squat turrets and long battlements. Each one was like something from the pages of *The Tales of King Arthur* with spacious courtyards full of lovingly watered flower beds, greenery and blossoms. When I spotted one of these magnificent structures, I half expected to see a troop of warriors clad in shining armour come galloping out to challenge us on their Central Asian steeds.

The hills, the very foothills of the mighty Hindu Kush, undulated like a giant quilt on a bed. Each time we came to the crest of one, we held our breath, praying that we had reached the plains near Ghazni. But days passed and still we were trapped in a monotonous lunar landscape that took the truck up and down, up and down, up and down ...

There was hardly a soul to be seen along the 'road', only caravans of Khuchis, nomads leading their herds of sheep and camels. Clad in flowing robes, the Khuchi women, who are permitted to have their faces unveiled, were colourfully adorned with necklaces strung with rare coins and lapis lazuli. They walked for days through the roughest and most arid country, land avoided by even the hardiest Muhjahidin.

Our fellow male passengers were a cheerful group and a colourful sight in their turbans and furry Uzbek hats. Most of them were heading for Parachinar in Pakistan. Amongst them was a falconer, a Tajik, from the north, with a burnt-orange hue to his skin like a native American Indian. He had a falcon that perched on a piece of coarse leather wrapped firmly around his left arm. The bird's plumage was as soft to the touch as a baby's face. Its wings were mauve coloured, its eyes black and bulging, its beak yellow, and its talons golden. Caught somewhere in the Hindu Kush, where the falconer also hunted snow leopards, the bird was destined for the bazaars of Peshawar.

'Perhaps one of the rich Arab sheikhs will buy it from my pitiful and undeserving self – by the grace of Allah,' he told Jalil humbly.

The Tajik exercised his falcon four times a day, removing its blindfold; with a string tied to its legs, he let it ride on the breeze. The bird would move its graceful wings up and down majestically, keeping its body straight and proud, squawking fiercely.

Sitting opposite me was a man who had the features and complexion of a European – blond hair and blue eyes. I thought at first that he must have been Danish or Scandinavian but I was to discover that he was from Nuristan, an easterly part of Afghanistan and home to a mysterious mountain people.

Prior to the 1890s, the Nuristanis were known as the *Kafirs*, or unbelievers. They worshipped pagan gods and effigies. It was not only their religious beliefs that remained at odds with their Islamic surroundings; also certain other practices, such as burying their dead in coffins and eating at tables, practices which have done much to fuel the theory that the Kafirs have anthropological and historical links with Europe.

Indeed, some say that the Nuristanis are descended from Alexander the Great's army; others that they are the original Aryans. Having heard something of these legends, Adolf Hitler sent a deputation to Kabul before the Second World War, to forge links with what he saw as the original master race. But the Afghan officials and people gave the Nazi contingent a lukewarm reception and, since then, little further research has been done on this subject.

The Nuristani spoke Dari, as well as his own dialect, so we were able to communicate with him. He carried a coarse goat-hair saddle bag decorated with woven designs and tassels. Dipping his hand inside, he brought out a selection of uncut gemstones which he hoped to sell in Pakistan. He had mined them himself in the mountains near the Panjshir valley, the site of the largest lapis mines in the world. He also had other bits and bobs for sale which he spilled out onto his lap.

I picked out what looked like a small coin encrusted in mud. Covering it in saliva, I started to rub, and soon the surface became visible. I had picked out an ancient

Greek or Bactrian coin. It had a horseman on the back, and on the front the head of a warrior king, his sword raised aloft. The Nuristani told me that it dated back to the time of Christ. I tried to pay for it, but he refused to accept any money.

'You are a guest in our country,' he said, 'and I cannot accept money for something of mine which you desire. It would not be honourable.'

* * *

Day after day, the truck trundled on. At night we slept on the floors of tea houses and survived on what little and unvaried food was available in that part of Afghanistan. Nearly all our meals consisted of greasy soup and stale bread. An onion became a delicacy and in my dreams I was haunted by visions of cheeseburgers, tuna fish sandwiches, succulent steaks with crisp salads, smothered in snappy vinaigrette ... meals I had enjoyed at the diner in New York with Barb and friends ...

Two broken axles, fourteen punctures, a dilapidated motorcycle, two exhausted horses and ten days later, we arrived at Moqor in Ghazni. It was dawn and we were exhausted. We found a tea house. We collapsed on the dirty boards only to be woken by shouts of panic a few hours later.

I hobbled out into the sunlight. The villagers were running around as if they were on Speed. Jalil grabbed my rucksack and another man my cameras and both ran in opposite directions, shouting, 'Follow me!'

Another burly Muhjahid pushed me to the ground. My eardrums throbbed at the sound of a shrill whistle and a thundering boom which shook the ground. A missile fired by a lone MiG fighter overhead shot through the open door of another tea house across the street, sending debris and shrapnel hurtling over our heads. The fortunate but dazed proprietor emerged through a cloud of dust, brushing himself down.

The Muhjahid grabbed my shirt and wrenched me to my feet. Together we ran helter skelter towards Jalil who was cowering on a nearby hill.

An hour or so later, we ventured back into the town. Having not eaten a solid meal for ten days, our stomachs, now tender to the touch, growled and grumbled from hunger. Not surprisingly, since leaving Peshawar, I had lost nearly a third of my total body weight and even Jalil was looking frail. To our relief, Moqor was thriving with life and the markets were full of fresh and delicious food: shiny apples, purple aubergines and cauliflowers piled high on trestle tables. Vendors kebabed great chunks of meat and bakers produced sponge cakes and fresh bread.

* * *

Jalil and I spent three days just eating and resting. On the fourth day, we were introduced to the local commander who invited us to his home for a feast. It happened that his elderly father was returning after twelve years spent in Peshawar. It promised to be a spectacular celebration.

Afghans are known for their unremitting hospitality and it is practically a blasphemy not to accept. They are also famous for their absolute ruthlessness, as the British and the Russians have found to their cost over the last two hundred years; fortunately, the British have been forgiven.

We drove to the commander's fort and were ushered into a room where a hundred men sat facing inwards, their backs against the walls. They all rose as we entered. I made my way around the room greeting them and shaking each one by the hand. Afghan introductions are often lengthy. Sometimes, two men will spend all of ten minutes greeting one other, speaking rapidly, asking after families and friends. I heard Jalil greet one man with whom he had been at a school:

'*Salam-alaik-um* (peace be upon you),' said Jalil.

'*Wa-laik-um-a-salam* (and peace be upon you),' said the second man. They hugged for a minute.

'Hello, how are you by Allah?' asked Jalil.

'I am well, by the grace of the Almighty. How are you?'

'I am well, thanks to Him. You are well?'

'Yes, well, thank you, by the Great One. How is your health?'

'My health is good, thanks to divine Providence. How is yours?'

'My health is good, thank you. How is your family?'

'My family prospers ...' And so on.

It took Jalil well over twenty minutes to make his way around the room and it was only after he finished that everyone was able to sit down. The commander then instructed a young boy to inform his mother and sisters that all the guests had arrived. This was not a signal for the meal to begin as the food was not yet ready. Indeed, the chickens and calf which were destined for our bellies were still very much alive.

Jalil explained: 'The food is not prepared or even bought at the bazaar until the guests are in place.'

'Why? Doesn't that make your guests impatient?' I asked.

'First of all, as I have demonstrated to you many times, we are far more patient that you *Farangis*.' Jalil always called me a *Farangi*, a European, when I showed some Western trait or characteristic of which he disapproved.

'Secondly, there is some logic behind this. You can never be sure even on which day your guests will turn up. When we Afghans invite each other for a feast, we rarely, if ever, set a date or time. That would be most rude,' he said.

'You mean you just wait around for hours, sometimes days?' I replied, once again amazed by the Afghans' blasé approach to time.

'Exactly.'

Jalil and I were both poured glasses of tea laced with spoonfuls of sugar. I asked the commander who the men were in the pictures up on the wall.

'They are my sons,' he said proudly, his voice creaking like a cedar tree in the wind. 'All three of them died fighting the curse of humanity. They died fighting bravely, all three of them in different battles. One of them was captured, but he told them nothing. Now they are in the gardens of paradise with their mother, blessings be upon them all.' As the commander spoke, the guests all looked down at the ground.

The Muhjahid sitting next to me, who had been flown to London some years earlier to have an operation performed on his leg, was at the feast with his youngest son. The boy crouched next to his father, listening to his every word, absorbing and imitating the Afghan trait of rugged individualism which is instilled into all youngsters. Then, during a lull in the conversation, the young boy piped up and began to tell a tale about a journey he had made to Pakistan. I was surprised to see how the other older Afghans listened, concentrated even, for ten minutes without interruption. When the boy had finished, another man spoke and again they listened, engrossed.

At length, the tea glasses were cleared away and the food carried in. Fatty chunks of mutton, plates of aromatic chicken, platters heaped with steaming pilau, sour yogurt and juicy pomegranates were placed before us. Many of the guests had never been in the presence of a Westerner before and they watched me discreetly, curious to see how I would behave.

Fortunately, having made the odd gaffe in the past, I was now familiar with Afghan etiquette and sat with my legs crossed. To point my feet outwards and show the bottom of the soles would have been discourteous. A servant boy brought a bowl of water in which we washed our hands. I was careful not to flick my fingers dry, holding them up in the air for several minutes. No one had yet touched the food. They sat patiently waiting for me to start. As soon as I broke a piece of bread, they began to eat. I found these oriental Afghan customs very civilised.

When they can, Afghans devour enormous meals. I have seen individuals consume substantial mounds of rice which would feed an entire London household. They do this with their hands, which I always found extremely difficult, always managing to drop grain after greasy grain in my lap. Discreetly, Jalil pushed a spoon in my direction.

'Eat!' said the commander, helping himself to a whole chicken, 'you never know when you may get another meal. That's what I always say ...'

After stuffing ourselves for over an hour, I thought my stomach would burst; however I knew that when I stopped, the feast would end and this would make me very unpopular, so I ate slowly and precisely. Once all the food was finished, we washed our hands again and our host said a prayer, his arms propped on his knees, his hands held in the air. Not being a Muslim, I simply lowered my head. Never in all the time I spent in Afghanistan was I pressurised into becoming a Muslim; nor was I made to feel ill at ease because I am a Christian from the West.

We then drank yet more tea, and afterwards the commander led us outside where we inspected his stable of fine horses. I made the mistake of admiring one of them.

'You shall have it! It is yours to take away!' said our host without a moment's hesitation.

Embarrassingly, I had forgotten my Afghan etiquette: because I had admired something that belonged to our host, he felt obliged to give it to me. This was a tight spot and one that I would have to manoeuvre out of with care.

'Commander that is too kind,' I said, 'but I am not worthy of any gift, let alone your horse.'

'You shall have it!' he repeated, instructing the stable

boy to bring a saddle.

'I would value it more than anything in the world-commander, however I cannot ride,' I lied.

'Then you shall learn!' he replied, slapping me on the back.

I was not doing very well and looked around for Jalil. Fortunately, he came to my rescue, avoiding further embarrassment by explaining that I would soon be returning to England; he joked that it would be impractical to take a horse on board a passenger aircraft.

'I will keep it for you then,' said the commander who led us towards an awaiting jeep.

And for all I know, the horse is waiting for me still.

* * *

We returned to the tea house in Moqor where we were staying. Spreading out our sleeping bags, we settled down on the hard, wooden floor amongst the twenty or so other guests, who were by this time snoring in unison like a group of pensioners in a rest home. I found that after eating such excessive amounts of food that day, my system was full of gas which I was barely able to control; I nudged Jalil who was just dozing off and explained my problem.

'Go outside and relieve yourself,' he advised. 'Whatever you do, do not make a smell or noise in here. It is the worst insult you could pay these people.'

'Is it really as bad as that?' I asked. 'After all it is only gas.'

Jalil, smiling ever so slightly, leaned up on his elbow as he lay under his blanket. 'Don't you know the story of the woodcutter who farted?' he asked.

'No,' I replied.

'Then I'll tell it to you ... Once,' continued Jalil, 'there was a woodcutter from Herat who used to work in the forest in the morning and sell his wood in the bazaar in the afternoon.

'He was a generous man, well respected, and had a good wife and small children. Everyone liked him, but then one day, as he was selling his wood in the bazaar, he leaned over to pick up a coin that had fallen on the ground. It was then that the most unfortunate thing happened. He let out an enormous fart!

'Now, of course, every one in the bazaar heard this noise. They all started laughing and jeering at him. And the woodcutter was so ashamed that he ran out of the town and kept on going and going until he was many, many miles away.

'Now several years passed and the woodcutter found work in a far-off forest where he was happy enough, but he missed his own village and his wife and wondered about his children.

'One day, he decided to return home. Surely by now the people would have forgotten about the unfortunate fart?

'As he walked through the forest where he had spent his best years cutting wood, he spotted his home on the hill side and approached.

'Soon he hoped to be reunited with his family. But just as he was nearing the front door, he heard his wife scolding one of his children. "What have you done? You've broken my best pot, idiot child!" she shouted. "Oh! I know you for what you are! You are indeed a useless, imbecile – and a son of a farter!"

'And with that,' said Jalil, 'the woodcutter turned wearily once again and left his home village — never to return.'

Jalil rolled over and went to sleep.

Hearing this story, I decided to step outside to a secluded spot in order to relieve myself in private. I might never return to Moqor. Nevertheless, I recalled the saying, 'a reputation can be a terrible thing'.

* * *

The city of Khost lies in Afghanistan's eastern Paktia province, a stone's throw from the Pakistan border. It guards one of the few southerly routes from Afghanistan, a strategic position which the British, and more recently the Soviets, long sought to control. The Russians proved somewhat more successful at holding the city than their predecessors, having done so throughout their ten-year occupation. However, in February 1989, when the Red Army withdrew back across the Amu Darya or Oxus River, Khost's freedom seemed assured along with the rest of the country. The CIA and press corps predicted that within a matter of weeks the entire country would fall under Muhjahidin control.

In the event, they were wrong. The Muhjahidin, commanded by a disorganised band of Pakistani army intelligence officers, bungled the 1989 spring offensive on Jalalabad. Consequently, President Najibullah's forces failed to surrender in the numbers which had been expected and Gorbachev continued to prop up the fragile regime with hundreds of millions of dollars in aid and weapons.

Meanwhile, Najibullah's army dug itself in and the Muhjahidin, whose hit-and-run tactics had proved extremely effective against the mechanised Soviet forces, suddenly found themselves trying to fight a conventional war, a task to which they were ill-suited.

The battle for Khost raged on and the BBC Pushtu language service and Reuter had asked me to visit the area to report on the ongoing siege. To reach the Muhjahidin lines, Jalil and I had to travel through Government-held areas. Setting out in the light of a full Moon with a group of seven guards, we spent the night dodging through narrow valleys, clambering on all fours over rocky slopes, and stopping regularly to listen out for the roar of tank and weapon convoys moving through the night.

We marched in silence, never speaking in anything

above a whisper. One loud noise would have alerted the Government forces to our presence – most of whom were conscripts, press-ganged into the army. They were reluctant fighters; however they would not have refrained from shooting us. Being miserable and frightened, they had itchy trigger fingers. Somehow, though, the thought of being shot was not as terrifying as the prospect of tripping over a booby trap or stepping on a land mine in the dark. Afghanistan had been littered with an estimated ten million mines and, bearing in mind that the country is roughly the size of Texas, I followed cautiously in the footsteps of the man ahead of me like King Wencelas' faithful page.

At dawn, we reached the headquarters of Jalalidin Haqqani, the supreme regional commander of the Muhjahidin's Khost forces. His base comprised a series of tents, with mud and stone bunkers, nestled into the side of a narrow gully. Guarding this was a trackless T-64 tank with a green Islamic flag tied to the turret, and a rusting corrugated-iron sentry post.

Exhausted and thirsty, we stopped and sat down on some rocks under a dead tree. A depressing atmosphere hung over the place. The earth was stained with black patches of oil, the still air was heavy with the rancid smell of unwashed men and dirty bed clothes, and the river was littered with the refuse of war. Discarded lengths of bandage clung to rocks. Defused plastic mines lay submerged in little pools of stagnant water. Spent shell cases jutted out from the sand.

Haqqani's Muhjahidin were emerging from their tents and caves to have some refreshing Afghan tea, being prepared over a small wood fire, after yet another night of uneasy sleep. Two teenagers were inspecting an unexploded bomb that had been dropped during the night. I took some pictures of a line of older barefooted men; kneeling on blankets, they faced towards Mecca and repeated their prayers and fingered their rosaries while brushing away the thirsty black flies which clung to lips and fingers like flying leeches.

A sentry provided us with a bottle of cloudy water and, as we were ushered towards a tent, we drank from it gratefully. Inside, our reception was cordial but not enthusiastic, for Haqqani's forces were shell-shocked and fatigued. Many of these men, who were in their late twenties, had been fighting for ten long years. They looked old.

Even Haqqani, who was the archetypal Pushtun tribal leader, appeared frustrated when we talked to him. No matter how hard he tried, he was unable to capture Khost. The reason for this, he said, was because Najibullah's forces enjoyed air support and continued to be supplied with food and weapons by the Soviets via Kabul.

Haqqani's nearest position to the city lay on a steep hill two to three miles to the south of Khost. A carefully planned and co-ordinated offensive would almost certainly have met with success as his men outnumbered the opposition by ten to one. Time after time, however, the Muhjahidin had proved that they were incapable of pulling off such a conventional operation.

* * *

Haqqani, who relied heavily on support from wealthy patrons in the Middle East, needed all the good press coverage he could get and he arranged for Jalil and me to be taken to the front. We travelled in the back of a Toyota pick-up packed with sixteen men. We sped along a narrow river valley which was shielded from Khost's artillery by the hills in between.

Amongst our group sat five Middle Easterners and North Africans. The two wearing red and white patterned head gear were from Damascus and Beirut respectively; their three tall companions, who were darker-skinned, hailed from northern Sudan. Like hundreds of young

Muslims from as far afield as Sarawak and Algeria, they had come to Afghanistan seeking military training and a *jihad*. When they discovered that I was a Christian, they spat and cursed. Hatred evident on their faces, they called me 'a dog' and 'the son of Sheitan', or the devil. They berated the Afghans for permitting my 'unclean' self to sit amongst them.

'What's the matter?' I asked Jalil, pretending that I didn't understand what was going on.

'They say you are a *kaffir*, a non-believer, and that you should embrace Islam or die like a dog.'

The Syrian was glaring at me with the eyes of a psychopath. One of the Sudanese cursed again, spitting at me and gritting his crooked teeth. The man from Beirut, who was dressed in white, toyed with his Kalashnikov. For the first time during my travels in Afghanistan, I felt that I was in peril. These men, who were poor representatives of the Islamic world, were true fanatics. Many of them had come to Afghanistan to die on the battlefield, believing that in this way they would earn a place in paradise. A few had even dug their own graves before going into battle. They would certainly have no qualms about killing a Westerner.

I asked Jalil what he thought we should do.

'Don't worry,' he said, placing one hand on mine as if to say, keep calm. 'If they kill you, I will kill them.'

At these comforting words, the outraged Afghan driver stopped the Toyota and ordered the foreigners to get out. They had, he said, committed the worst of crimes – that of insulting a guest. The fanatics stood up, reaching for their guns while cursing the Afghans as heretics.

I could see that if these Arabs had their way, some of us were not going to live to see another sunset. Before the situation escalated any further, however, a Pushtun who was missing most of his front teeth, grabbed one of the Sudanese by the throat.

'By Allah,' he bellowed like a bull, 'if any harm comes

to the *Farangi*, the ground will run red with your blood!'

Cursing even more, the fanatics climbed down from the Toyota and we sped off, leaving them standing by the river bed, fuming.

'Those men, donkey men,' shouted one of the Afghans, 'they come to our country and tell us how to be good Muslims. Donkey men ...'

The scene at the front line was one of total chaos. If Haqqani had ever set up an effective line of command, it had long since disintegrated. Anyone who could get their hands on a walkie-talkie was giving orders. Ill-disciplined groups of young Muhjahidin were launching their own mini-strikes on the city.

Close to the main command post stood a long cannon, pointing over the hills in the general direction of Khost. Every twenty seconds, it was loaded and fired; as far as I could see, there was no co-ordination between the spotters on the hills and those operating the cannon – for all they knew, the shells were hitting friendly positions.

Jalil was sickened by the scene at the front. 'This war has gone on far too long,' he said. 'I am weary of this madness.'

What medical facilities we found were as disorganised: three of the five ambulances had been commandeered as troop transports, anaesthetic was in short supply and all the bandages had been stolen and used by men with only blistered feet. There was not even a field clinic, let alone a doctor; as a result two male nurses had to amputate a Syrian Muhjahid's leg in the back of a truck without anaesthetic. The unfortunate man was unconscious through loss of blood, his skin pasty and his lips pale.

We rested in a moth-eaten tent half-flooded with rain water. Once we had regained our energy and eaten a little bread, we made our way to the main position on a near-by hill.

A path wound its way up the steep approach and,

with a sprightly old man guiding us, we picked our way through the piles of haphazardly stacked ammunition boxes, and began the hard climb. The sun beat down on us like a hammer striking an anvil. With sweat dripping from his brow, Jalil wondered out loud how the Muhjahidin had ever captured this position, for the 'hill' was more of a small mountain with vertical cliffs on one side and an easily defended summit.

The old man boasted proudly that he had taken part in the operation. He re-enacted the battle with his hands, adding sound effects and pointing out where groups of Muhjahidin had been cut to pieces by the enemy machine guns. Time and time again, he said, they had launched suicide runs through the minefields and in the end, the army troops had run out of ammunition. The old man smiled a toothless smile, savouring the thought of that victory.

The crest of the hill provided a bird's eye view of the entire battle ground. A ten mile long oval plain stretched out to the west, surrounded by mountains and stony hills, pockmarked with bomb craters, and hundreds of feet below, blurred by the haze of heat, we could make out a vehicle and a line of men crawling over the sandy terrain. They were moving towards a group of half-destroyed buildings where Haqqani's forces were attempting to set up mortar positions.

But where was Khost? I asked myself while taking in the view.

'Welcome! Welcome!' shouted a man with a scar on his right cheek. He was standing with a dozen other Muhjahidin in a trench which ran along the ridge of the hill.

'Where is Khost?' I asked him, still taking in the spectacular scenery.

'There! There!' he shouted.

As I looked in the direction in which he was pointing, a feeling of utter disillusionment and disappointment swept over me. After all the commotion down below, after all the hysteria, after all the energy which we had seen being put into this offensive, I had somehow expected the city to be a gleaming prize. But it seemed Khost was little more than an airstrip and a collection of flat-roofed mud buildings and bombed-out warehouses. How many more lives were going to have to be sacrificed over this insignificant little outpost?

Before I could think further, with a thundering of engines, a MiG fighter shot over my head, so low it felt as if it was brushing my hair. I clasped my hands over my ears as the supersonic jet tore down into the valley like a huge bird of prey. As we watched it dive below us, we could see the tops of its wings and the blaze of its tail engine. Banking right in a breathtaking manoeuvre, it dived over a Muhjahidin position and released a cluster of incendiary bombs. A split second later these exploded, sending columns of fiery napalm shooting up into the sky like ignited oil wells.

'Allah! Allah!' roared the Muhjahidin jumping up and down in their trench, impressed by this stroke of flying genius. '*Allah! Bismillah!*'

'A mad Afghan in a MiG,' pondered Jalil, watching the jet soar off to the east, 'that is a deadly combination.'

Nervous that the daring pilot might come round for a second run, Jalil, the old man and myself clambered down into the trench. The commander of the position, who had strapped on plastic goggles and a pair of furry ear muffs, gave the order to fire. Like a gang of trigger-happy teenagers, the Muhjahidin opened up with everything they had. Mortars, heavy field artillery, even an anti-aircraft gun, spat out a deadly hail of ordnance. Thick, grey clouds of cordite drifted over the trench as the commander grinned at me and laughed like a maniac. 'Boom! Boom!' he shouted, punching his two fists in front of him. 'Very loud! Yes?'

I switched on my tape recorder to record some actuality which might come in useful for one of my BBC reports. Khost replied by firing a series of missiles which ripped into the top of the hill, the explosions sending chunks of rock hurtling through the air. The commander ordered his field gun to respond. This pattern of bombardment and counter bombardment continued for nearly an hour. Thousands of rounds were fired with no apparent effect. The whole thing seemed so pointless.

The afternoon was drawing on. During a pause in the firing, as the commander of the position screamed abuse down the radio at his opposite number in Khost, and with the old man leading, Jalil and I began our descent to the valley below. But as we were half-way down, the MiG appeared once again overhead. This time it was higher, like an annoying fly out of reach of the swatter. It was too late to return to the trench at the top of the hill. We were now without adequate cover. 'Run!' shouted Jalil, 'Run! Run! RUN!'

We raced down the hill like devils out of hell and at the bottom, we took a flying leap feet first into a shallow stream bed. With my heart beating and my head spinning, I sank waist deep in mud, pressing myself against the bank.

As we waited, a sudden silence fell over the entire area. Even the birds in the trees stopped chirping. All I could hear was the thumping in my chest. 'Please,' I thought to myself, 'Not us. Please.'

The unnerving sound of the jet's sonic boom came first, then the whistle of the bombs falling and, shortly afterwards, the explosions. The first was poorly aimed. However, the second and third landed not thirty feet up the slope from where we lay. Shrapnel shot over our heads, tearing at the leaves on the small trees and sending a cascade of rocks bounding down the hill in an avalanche. Terrified, I kept down, my hands locked tight over my head.

When we looked up, the MiG seemed to have disappeared. We waited in the stream just to make sure.

Shortly afterwards, Jalil gave the all clear signal. But looking up, I noticed another plane in the sky. 'There's another one,' I shouted as we all crouched down again. It was only then that Jalil noticed that it was a passenger airliner cruising at approximately thirty thousand feet.

Inside, tanned tourists were probably watching a film while being served hot food, sublimely oblivious to the skirmishes of the protracted thirteen-year-old war that continued to rage below them.

Jalil turned towards me, his head went back and, for the first time since I had known him, he started to laugh – really laugh. This laugh was not just a chuckle at some passing joke, it came from deep down. Like someone on laughing gas, I joined in, unable to control myself, and then the smiling old man joined in laughing as well. Standing waste deep in mud in the middle of the Afghan war, we three laughed and laughed and laughed until the tears rolled down our dirty faces and our sides hurt.

* * *

It was not many weeks later before I, too, was reclining in the seat of a jumbo jet. I was destined for Kenya via the Gulf. Far below, the Indus River wound across the plains of the North-west Frontier as we passed over the Afghan border. The powerful jumbo droned on.

I felt myself becoming drowsy, idly wondering if I would ever return to the God Gifted Realm and what the future held for this vastly beautiful, resource-rich country and its extraordinary people.

As I dropped into sleep, the Afghan proverb 'Migurazad' flashed across my mind: 'This too will pass'.

Part Three

Africa

THIRTEEN

Aboard the Lunatic Express

*... I heard from Pete. He's half way through his
third year at Bristol. He's still enjoying it and
talking about coming out to Africa this summer, if
I'm still here ... I've been thinking hard lately about
whether I'm getting more out of these years than if
I had stayed at university. Today, I think a
Canadian answered the question for me. I was
telling him about what I had been up to and he
said, 'Wish I had done something like that when I
had the chance ...'*

Diary, 7 March 1991

'*Allahu Akbar!* God is great. Come to prayer!' cried the
muezzin through a loudspeaker positioned just a few feet
from my hotel window. 'Prayer is better than sleep!'

Lying in bed listening to the call to the faithful, I
thought for a few drowsy moments that I was back in
Peshawar. The sticky humidity was familiar, as were the
green geckos with their bulging black eyes, which crawled
across the walls and ceilings in search of prey. Yet, as I
stirred from slumber and began to focus on my
surroundings, it dawned on me that I was in fact many,
many miles from the North-west Frontier of Pakistan: it
was the second Thursday in March, and here I was in
Mombasa ...

It had been nothing short. of traumatic leaving
Peshawar. Unfortunately the place offered few further
journalistic challenges. Sadly, Fleet Street considered
Afghanistan to be a 'dead story', and with only eighteen

months remaining of the four years I had set myself to become a journalist, I badly needed to break into the mainstream British press. Peshawar was clearly not the place to do it.

I had chosen to move to Africa principally because of the influence of my godmother, Pat Williams, a South African. During my schoolboy years, she had given me a number of extraordinary books written by explorers and travellers, such as Burton and Livingstone, Huxley and Van de Post. Now, I wanted to see the continent which they had written about with such affection and awe.

East Africa, especially, seemed to be a part of the world continually making headlines, so when I wrote to all the national British newspapers explaining my intention to base myself in Nairobi, several showed interest, particularly the *Daily Mail* – although none was prepared to pay me a retainer, they would take material on a freelance 'stringer' basis.

Arriving in Nairobi, I headed to the Kenyan coast. Here, I had been recuperating from a dose of Afghani amoebic dysentery which had caused me no end of discomfort. Finally, nearly two weeks later, my strength had returned and I decided to explore Mombasa, Kenya's alternative capital.

Mombasa Island has been dramatically influenced by arabic culture. The Old Town, with its whitewashed stone buildings complete with wooden shutters, elegantly carved balconies and hanging plants, is reminiscent of Moorish Spain. The minarets of twenty mosques rise up above the narrow alleyways, and in the harbour, *dhows*, with their characteristic triangular sails, continually load and off-load wares and passengers.

The local people, known as the *Swahili*, a word derived from the Arabic plural of *sahel*, meaning coast, are a mix of African and Arab peoples. They have a distinctive, noble look with brownish skin; and although they are a small tribe by African standards, their language, Kiswahili, has developed into the lingua franca of Kenya and much of East Africa. The Swahili's Middle Eastern ancestors began establishing trade routes and centres on the Kenyan coast from the ninth century onwards. Trading in gold and ivory, they developed Mombasa into a thriving commercial centre and so prosperous did the city become that the Portuguese spent nearly a century endeavouring to capture it, finally seizing their prize in 1593.

Mass tourism has inevitably brought irreversible changes to the Kenyan coastline, and with the ever diminishing volume of trade between Mombasa and the Middle East, the locals have entered into tourism-related business. Nowadays, Mombasa's streets are cluttered with curio sellers, safari tour shops and on the beaches between Mwabungu and Malindi, dozens of boat-hire companies offer scuba diving instruction.

Each morning, I had been waking late due to the humidity and relaxed environment. The people seemed sluggish and laid back, taking long siestas during the afternoon and only really becoming active at night when the bars and night clubs were open into the early hours.

Once washed and dressed, I donned my sunglasses and, taking a bottle of mineral water and a camera loaded with a fresh roll of film, I went for a walk in the Old Town.

The streets were not busy; donkeys stood in the shade tethered to posts; Western tourists sweltered along the pavement, wiping the sweat from their brows, as if lost in time and space; shop owners sprinkled water on the ground in front of their shops to stop the dust rising.

Plump housewives, wearing bright yellows, reds, greens and blues, stood about, gossiping and munching on pieces of roasted maize, sold by a nearby vendor. Schoolgirls in short brown skirts and lemon-coloured shirts, exercise books under their arms, waited in a group at a bus stop, recalling in loud voices a scene from a television show which they had watched the night before.

Opposite, a street barber, who doubled as a shoe shiner, was giving a young man a trim and shave. A sign in front of his stand read, 'Shaving, cutting and more'.

I was still getting used to being the only white person amidst a sea of black faces, but I was not made to feel uncomfortable. Indeed, as I stood outside one shop, a young girl, evidently fascinated by my white skin, glared up at me and giggled when I made a funny face.

'Which country? Which country?' asked a young man who said he worked in the local branch of the Kenya National Bank.

'England,' I said. 'I'm from England, London.'

'Ah, Britannia. Yes. Very good! Margaret That-cher!' He surveyed me for a few moments, smiling all the time. 'First time in Kenya?' he asked.

'Yes,' I replied.

'Welcome to our very, very FINE country. Nice time. I have an engagement,' he said with some pride, 'so good-bye. Nice time.' He crossed the street, walking on his toes.

As I moved along the uneven pavement, trying to stay in the shade, I stopped for a moment to admire a building which had a carved wooden façade and a doorway covered in cracked turquoise tiles. Standing there lost in thought, staring at the attractive architecture, a Kenyan waif sidled up to me. Before I knew it, he had his hand in my pocket and was running down the street with my wallet.

'Hey! Stop! Come back!' I shouted, attempting to run after him with the bottle of mineral water in one hand and the Nikon camera dangling awkwardly from my neck.

'Stop him!' I called out, pointing to the young boy who was making for a crowded market.

My calls for help were received with blank expressions from the locals on the street. Only a helpful curio seller joined in the chase. He jumped out from behind his stand, almost grabbing the young boy; but amongst the confusion of the crowds and traffic, we lost him. I threw the bottle of water to the ground, trying to catch my breath, cursing my misfortune.

One man pushing a wooden wheelbarrow filled with fish stopped for a moment to watch my temper tantrum. I cursed and kicked at the ground and clenched my fists. Nonchalantly, the man continued on, leaving only a small pool of water at the spot where his wheelbarrow had stopped.

'I had fifty pounds in that wallet!' I shouted. 'Fifty pounds, damn it!'

The Kenyan curio seller who had helped give chase stood in the road next to me, biting his lip, not quite sure how to comfort me. At length, he said: 'Don't worry mister. Worse things happen. Last year, someone burnt down my friend's house.'

'Yes, I'm sure,' I said, hardly in the mood for consolation of any sort. 'Anyhow, thanks for your help.'

We shook hands. 'No problem,' he replied, 'come and have a papaya juice. It's so nice.'

Giving one last glance down the street, just to check that the pickpocket had not been struck by guilt and decided to return my property, I followed the curio seller to the nearest juice stand. We sat sipping the delicious drink. My new friend introduced himself. 'My name's Brush. My father was a decorator. He gave me the name.'

Brush had a nose shaped like the tail of a trout and a gentle and inquisitive personality. His clothes reminded me of the fashion worn in the 1960s by my uncle: tight, pink trousers, psychedelic tie and red shoes with frayed string for shoe laces. Brush spent his days hawking carved wooden giraffes to the droves of heat-exhausted tourists arriving in Mombasa. As reasonably priced as his wares seemed, competition in the carved wooden giraffe business was fierce, so to make ends meet, Brush also worked as a gigolo.

'My clients are mostly German women,' he laughed. 'They have, how do you say, large bodies and large wallets.' He outlined the figure of a big woman in the air with his hands. 'During the day,' he continued, 'they lie about on the beach like whales. But at night, they want some action – isn't it?' Brush often used the question 'isn't it?' to qualify a statement.

With his young, athletic frame, the Kenyan was just what the German women were looking for to liven up their visit to Kenya. His Maasai warrior outfit, including loin cloth, spear and orange paint, proved particularly popular and, as he strode down the beaches, his ostrich feathers quivering in the light Indian Ocean breeze, his admirers tittered, 'He's a varrior, you know! A varrior!'

In actual fact, Brush was no more Maasai than myself. 'I'm the youngest of four brothers, from the Abiluyer, or Luyer, tribe, from the hills of Kakamega near Lake Victoria,' Brush told me in confidence. 'I left home shortly after finishing school and ventured to Nairobi to seek my fortune.'

There, he landed a job as a sales 'rep' for Coca Cola and settled down, finding himself a wife. Two years later, however, the company made him redundant and he was forced to leave his wife, moving to the coast to work for a friend's uncle who owned three clapped-out taxis and side-lined in carved wooden giraffes.

Like many young Kenyans, Brush had a sound education but no real prospects. What he needed was an opportunity to develop. Somewhat disillusioned with the corruption of his country, he wanted to improve himself and work his way 'to the top'. That, at least, was where his eldest brother was heading. He had a secure and lucrative position as a fund-raiser for the Government. The job came with a car and prestige.

'Put it this way,' said Brush, underlining his brother's success, 'He's not carrying his own briefcase – isn't it?'

Finishing the papaya juice, I continued my walk through the Old City and Brush, who was doing little business that day, chose to join me. As we walked, he asked me questions about London: was it true that the

English ate snails?

'Sometimes,' I said, 'but it's mainly the French. They love them.'

Brush scrunched up his nose in disgust. 'Have you ever eaten snails?' he asked.

I shook my head, more interested in hearing about his life as a gigolo. Surprisingly, he enjoyed the work.

'Fat women are the best – isn't it? The fatter the better, he said. 'You should try it some time.'

We returned to his stand and I looked over his carved wooden giraffes. They came in a number of sizes, as large as six feet tall. He asked me how long I planned on staying in Kenya. I explained my plan and the timescale; he smiled a knowing smile, his pearly-white teeth highlighted against his healthy dark skin. 'Then you'll need someone to work for you – isn't it? Translation work?'

'Maybe. I ...'

'... I can work for you – isn't it?' said Brush, 'I speak NICE Ki-Swahili,' he continued, 'NICE English. Even a little Somali. And I know many people. I'll work for you.'

I continued along the sun-drenched pavement, unsure whether I really needed a helper. Brush seemed set on the idea. 'Money's not a problem. I'll find you a place to live. Please boss. I really need a job, a good job. You can teach me things, bwana. I can help you – isn't it?'

From that moment, Brush clung to me. Although I liked him and thought that I might indeed need an assistant eventually, I just couldn't be sure at that time whether or not I could afford to hire him. There was no discouraging him, however. Brush would not take no for an answer. During the rest of my stay on the Kenyan coast, he was never far from sight. In the morning, I would find him asleep on a cart outside the hotel; during the day, he would insist on showing me around; at night, he would have papaya juice sent up to my room. Even his uncle paid me a visit, brought me enough beer to start my own bar, and pointed out that Brush badly needed a job.

After a few more days, I decided to head to Nairobi by train. At the station, backpackers wearing shorts and sandals, their pockets bulging with Lonely Planet guide books, mingled with the porters pushing green barrows piled high with luggage. Swahilis in their becoming white prayer caps were selling mangoes and shifty touts peddled black market train tickets for exorbitant rates.

I arrived on the platform in time to catch the overnight train. The station master was already blowing his whistle and calling all the passengers to board. Brush, who had come to see me off, now realised that although I admired his persistence, I couldn't afford to hire him. Despondently, he wrote down the number of the public phone box outside his uncle's shop and handed it to me, wishing me luck and shaking my hand.

The diesel locomotive, which was painted Kenya's national colours – black, red, green and white – grunted like a boar. The wheels spun round on the tracks in rapid succession and with a strain, it pulled the carriages out of the station like a mother dragging a reluctant child to school. Brush waved to me from the platform and, with some regret, I wondered whether I would ever see him again.

* * *

My compartment was located in one of the second-class carriages. A Mombasa concierge had informed me that these were older and more comfortable than their modern first-class equivalents. Although rather cramped, there were two bunks made up with freshly starched, beautifully ironed white sheets. The pillows were like the ones you find in five-star hotels, feather-soft and puffy.

Each bunk had a leather guard strapped across it to prevent passengers from rolling off their beds, and a reading light that flickered as the carriage jolted over the narrow gauge. In one corner, there was a triangular basin and a face mirror with the initials EAR, East Africa Railways, etched into the lower right-hand corner. The same letters were also printed on the faded green blind which snapped open with a sound like a whip cracking each time the train shuddered to a stop.

I shared the compartment with Justin Omwanza, a Kenyan wheeler-dealer who was buying and selling gold on the world market. His English was impeccable and he proved to be well-informed about the affairs of his country. Justin, who smoked Sportsman cigarettes, a Kenyan brand, was hell-bent on getting into politics and saw himself, together with a new generation of educated Kenyans, leading the country into the twenty-first century.

After proper introductions, we made our way through the train to the dining car. The restaurant was dimly lit with lanterns, the tables laid with pretty white china and tropical flowers in pottery vases. Well disciplined, uniformed waiters served passengers ostrich stew with rice from polished platters. A bar steward saw to it that glasses were always full. Overhead fans buzzed like bees.

'Mee friends, mee friends. Join mee,' called out an elderly African who was sitting on his own. 'Forgive mee for not gettin' up. Mee bones, you know. Not strong. Not strong at all. Mee name's Thomas – like dhee tank engine.'

Thomas was a charming, elderly Ugandan with greying stubble on his face which grew in clumps like heather. I recognised him as the man working in the corridor whom I had passed earlier, singing tribal songs in a high-pitched voice and punching the train tickets. He offered us some rum from a bottle which, he confessed, he kept under his bunk and got out for special occasions.

'Mee, I've been workin' dhees railway for dhirty years today,' he began, leaning back in his seat. He was proud of his country's past. 'Dhirty years. Can you bel-ee-ve dhat, mee friends?'

Justin and I toasted his health. Thomas, who reminded me of a New Orleans jazz musician, had a passion for train travel. Afflicted by a constant desire to be on the move, a trait rare in most Africans who generally prefer to stay put, he loved nothing better than to sit in his carriage and listen to the rumbling rollers running over the tracks.

He proved to be one of those great African storytellers whose natural wisdom shone through his love of a tale.

'Dhey call dhees line dee Lunateec Exprees. Dee Lunateec Exprees,' said Thomas, who often repeated himself and began his sentences slowly, suddenly speeding up at the ends, rather like the trains he rode. 'You know why it's called dhat? I'll tell you. Oh yes! Dhey call it dhat bee-cause anyone wishin' to build a line through Keenya must have been a lunateec ... you see, mee friends.

'Dee British ... Dee ... British. Dhey came to Mombasa. And dhey gazed in land, dhey did, into the inteeree-or ... into the inteeree-or ....' Thomas moved his extended arm through the air gazing into infinity, the rum slowly warming him and the drama of his storytelling. 'Dhey said, "Let's build us a railway. Let's build a railway".'

Justin emptied the last drops of rum into Thomas's glass, making a plink-plonk sound.

'... Who would have been theenkeeng such a theeng? Lunateecs. You see mee friends dhey had to be lunateecs to have even theenk of eet. Only dee British, you seee. Dhey just started building into dee middle of nowhere ...'

Thomas started singing: 'Mad dogs and dee Engleeshmarn. Dhey go out in dee mid deey sun ...'

Strangely, at the time of the railway's construction, nobody in England or Mombasa seemed to have a clear idea why it was being built. No Europeans had yet settled in Kenya, apart from the few on the coast, and for the British Empire, which already controlled India, trading prospects were minimal.

One radical British politician, Henry Labouchère, frequently scoffed at the whole idea, writing at the time:

'What is the use of it none can conjecture:

What it will carry there's none can define:

And in spite of George Curzon's superior lecture,
It is clearly naught but a lunatic line.'

Even after the railway's completion, Sir Charles Eliot, one of Nairobi's first British administrators, wrote: 'It is a curious confession, but I do not know why the Uganda Railway was built, and I think many people in East Africa share my ignorance.'

However, the construction of the Mombasa to Uganda line proved to be an engineering miracle. When work began in 1896, its architects were faced with the bewildering prospect of crossing desert and thorn savannah, the Great Rift Valley and, finally, malarial swamps. It was territory inhabited by hostile tribes and wild animals. What's more, it was territory through which only a handful of white men had travelled and survived. To construct the railway, thousands of labourers were shipped to Kenya from India. Conditions were, at best, dangerous, and along the route the workers were continuously attacked by tribesmen who looted the telegraph wire to make bracelets and pulled up the tracks to make spears.

Inevitably, hundreds died along the way. Some contracted untreatable equatorial diseases, and many others were eaten alive by the infamous man-eating lions of Tsavo who, in the middle of the night, would carry off men from their tents. Half-way to Lake Victoria, on the edge of the Rift Valley, work temporarily halted and a shanty town sprang up, quickly attracting gentlemen of fortune, prostitutes and merchants. As the railway continued north-westwards, the settlement expanded, and today it is called Nairobi, from its Maasai name, *Nyrobi* – 'Place of the cool waters'.

The Mombasa to Uganda line took a further two and a half years to complete. It remains one of the world's greatest railways, crossing the equator at nine thousand feet before descending to the shores of Lake Victoria – over six hundred miles all told. Yet the Lunatic Express is much more than just an engineering marvel.

201

'Dee railway creea-ted dhis land ... creea-ted Keenya,' said the conductor. 'Beefore, dee land was tribes. Many, many tribes. Dhen, suddeenly, dhere was a train line. It creea-ted a countree. A whole countree. Incred-ee-ble!'

* * *

That night, I slept on the top bunk. Steadily, the train chugged and puffed its way up onto the Nairobi plateau where the climate was cooler, a welcome change from the oppressive humidity of the coast. When I awoke, my feet were cold and the blind was open, and as I looked out the window, I could see wildebeest grazing near the track.

Slowly, I dressed and woke Justin, as the train moved on through the suburbs of Kenya's capital, Nairobi.

The Mombasa to Uganda railway is, apart from the Blue Train in South Africa, probably the only transport system in the whole of sub-Saharan Africa that runs on time. We pulled into Nairobi station on the dot.

As Justin and I made our way to the exit, I heard a voice call out my name. Spinning round, amazed, I saw Brush walking towards me.

'*Karibu*! Welcome!' he said.

I couldn't believe my eyes. 'What on earth are you doing here? How ...?'

'I took the night bus – isn't it?' said Brush. 'It left an hour after you, but got here TOO fast. Besides, the train is SO expensive.' I said nothing and there followed a few seconds of awkward silence. 'I decided to return to Nairobi,' he continued, 'I might find a job here – isn't it?'

He reached for one of my bags. And, after a pause, I let him take them.

'I know a nice hotel. It's owned by my cousin's friend,' said Brush.

'OK, let's go,' I said. Slinging my camera bag over one shoulder, we headed off into downtown Nairobi.

FOURTEEN

Nairobi Days

... Kenya seems to be deeply divided along tribal lines ... if President Moi dies, many people think the country will pull itself apart ... There is no effective common language and even when Moi travels around his own country, he has difficulty communicating in almost every district ... a hundred years ago, there wasn't even a country here ... and now the West wants to force feed it democracy ... A diplomat was telling me that he thought that if the Americans continued imposing democracy on Kenya, it would end in disaster ...

Diary, 2 April 1991

It didn't take me long to make the disappointing discovery that many more foreign correspondents were representing the broadsheet British press in Nairobi than I had ever expected. The only way to compete was to work on major scoops and exclusives, but these were few and far between and required considerable time and resources. Otherwise, I was left with the option of writing for the tabloids, but this, too, was a limited market.

'We've had enough of bloody famines,' the foreign editor of one rag told me when I called to say that I had arrived in Nairobi. 'Civil wars, too – unless we're talking about a body count. What we want is Brits-abroad stories. If a Brit gets hacked to death, get on it. If a Brit parachutes off Kilimanjaro, get on it. If a Brit fornicates with a goat, get on it. Otherwise, we don't want to know ...'

A few weeks later, an editor of one of the more upmarket papers called me at four in the morning.

'We're getting reports that there's been a riot at a school near Mount Kenya and a whole load of girls have been raped and killed,' he said. 'Do you know anything about it?'

'No,' I replied. 'I'm afraid I don't.'

'Well get on it. And find out if any white people have been murdered or raped. We're only interested if they're white.'

Further investigation proved that there were no white people anywhere near the area. I called the foreign desk to give them the 'bad' news.

'Not interested!'

Six weeks into my stay in Kenya, it was obvious that I was not going to be able to survive by selling foreign news to British newspapers – not for the moment, at least. In fact, my plans suddenly seemed to be on the rocks and, although it pained me to think about it, I began to wonder if I should return home and go to university. In desperation, I called New York and talked with Frank Renard, the journalist whom I had met in America. I explained my position.

'Don't give up now,' he said. 'You've come so far, I'm sure you can accomplish what you set out to do.'

'But, Frank,' I argued, 'I can't sell a damn thing to London and I don't have a penny to my name.'

'Then don't push it with the foreign editors at the moment. Try writing for the feature pages and Sunday magazine supplements,' he advised.

The next day, after some thought, I left my hotel and visited the British Council in downtown Nairobi, found a copy of *The Writers' and Artists' Year Book*, and wrote down a number of publications that I thought might be interested in articles from Africa. Amongst them was *Horse Review*, a relatively new bi-monthly. I called the editor in Oxford and asked him if he would consider taking a light feature story about racing in Nairobi.

'Love one,' he said in his public school accent. 'Wonderful course, if my memory serves me rightly. Superb country for racing, as well. Naturally, we haven't been there since the Mau Mau. Nasty little rebellion that ... Yes, nothing too technical. General stuff, plenty of colour. Give me fifteen hundred words, why don't you?'

How much would he be prepared to pay?

'Not much, old chap. Haven't got the circulation – not yet, anyhow. You know how it is. Shall we say two hundred and fifty? Plus pix. Let's call it three hundred? Paid on acceptance, of course.'

Three hundred pounds was enough to live on in Kenya for a whole month, as long as I kept my costs to a minimum. I told the editor that I would have a story for him by his next deadline.

'Jolly good. Look forward to hearing from you.'

* * *

That weekend, Brush and I visited the Ngong race course. A few miles outside Nairobi, it was surrounded by woods and fields, with a long tarmac drive leading up to the main stand. Within the enclosure, we found European and Asian settlers, Kenyans and tourists, all well dressed for a grand day out, standing against the impeccable white fencing waiting for a race to begin.

At the sound of the starter's pistol, a group of horses lunged out of their gates and headed down the first leg of the course.

'Come on Foxy Lad,' yelled a colonial youngster with neat pigtails. 'Move your bloomin' arse.' Her mother blushed and by way of an excuse, explained to those of us within earshot that the child had recently seen *My Fair Lady*.

As the thunder of hooves pounded down the finishing stretch, those in the stands sprang to their feet. The cheers of encouragement reached a deafening crescendo as the horses charged over the finishing line. A photo finish was ordered and the eager spectators hurried to the winners' enclosure for the results. Others sat in deck-chairs on the lawn in front of the stands. Parents kicked off their shoes and soaked in the warm sunshine, while their children giggled and romped on the grass. Finally, it was announced that Party Pooper had clinched the race. Some ripped up their tickets; other smiling people headed off to collect their winnings.

One of Ngong's many attractions was its beautiful flowering Bombax trees. These softwood trees have clusters of scarlet and white blooms; they grow particularly well in the rich well-manured loam thrown up from the race track. Brush headed off to lay a bet on the next race. I stood in the shade of one of the Bombax trees where I met Sammy McDougall, a jovial Irish character who had ridden for Sir Jock Jarvis in England back in the late fifties.

'This is a very intimate place,' he said, 'everyone knows each other. Kenya has probably one of the smallest racing communities in the world.'

Sammy took me up into his private box to watch the next race, pointing out some of the names of Jockey Club members, painted in black against the whitewashed walls. Among them was Delamere, a surname as synonymous with East Africa as Burton, Livingstone and Stanley. Sammy had worked for Tom Cholmondeley, the fourth Baron Delamere for eighteen years. The family owned forty-nine thousand acres in the Rift Valley and Aberdare mountains – known in the 1930s and 1940s as the White Highlands.

'Horses were his life and he loved to bet,' said Sammy nostalgically. 'He was a grand and generous man and used to throw parties with baths filled with Champagne.'

Tom Cholmondeley's father, Hugh, third Baron Delamere, was the pioneer leader of the settlers and the first to buy land at the turn of the century in this wild and mysterious country astride the equator. The British railway engineers who supervised the construction of the Mombasa to Uganda railway brought ponies from Somalia and soon they were staging informal races. Eventually, they decided to build a course at Ngong.

'The chaps who constructed the course came from Newmarket,' Sammy told me. 'It was bloody awful terrain – thickly wooded, with lions, zebra, buffalo and giraffe roaming about. But in January 1954, the Ngong officials staged the first races.'

After the next race, we walked back towards the track. Pretty young colonial girls with perfect tans, some wearing boaters, cotton summer dresses and sunglasses, mingled with the eligible young men. In their midst, I met 'the Mad Duchess', as Sammy called her.

At forty-nine, the elegant lady cut a fine figure in riding boots and jodhpurs. 'I grew up in Egypt and Abyssinia,' she told me, sipping a gin and tonic with lemon. 'At the age of fifteen I became a jockey for the Emperor Haile Selassie who owned six hundred horses. They were all at my disposal.

'And this country, well, it's not without its hazards, you know, darling. Take the Siafu ants for instance. They march in columns, and if you are in their way, an army of them will go straight up your trousers. Several times, I've seen jockeys, loaders and stewards frantically tearing off their clothes. Of course, the horses go wild, too. Those things can really bite ... and as for the baboons!'

The day at Ngong drew to a close. The locals made their way home across the fields and through the bush. The bookies calculated their profits. In the car park, Asians and Europeans bundled into their Range Rovers and Land Cruisers which have replaced the Model T Fords, Rolls-Royces and Bugattis of Kenya's colonial heyday.

Sammy took Brush and me to visit the British cemetery which was nearby. As we walked, I reflected upon what a young nation Kenya is – barely one hundred years old. After all, some of the colonials I had met were only the third or even second generation offspring of pioneers who forged new frontiers and farmed this dark and often dangerous continent.

Before the arrival of the settlers, indigenous Kenyans had been living the same way of life for thousands of years. Now, they were talking in English and wearing suits. Their culture has been irreversibly altered and, in many ways, this seemed a pity.

I asked Sammy how the newcomers and the Africans managed to live side by side.

'There are a lot of barriers between us and the natives,' said Sammy, who employed over forty Kenyans, 'but I consider myself to be a Kenyan as much as any African. After all,' he continued, 'we're all the same on the turf, as we are under it.'

* * *

Horse Review bought my article on Kenyan racing – my first British sale – and, following this, I wrote a number of other stories for specialised publications and the feature pages in Britain's broadsheets. They seemed only too glad to receive something out of the ordinary and quirky from Africa.

In the meantime, Brush showed me around Nairobi. We were standing at the Westlands roundabout when a *matatu*, or private minibus, pulled up. It was painted in rainbow stripes, like a fairground on wheels. The *manamba*, or bus conductor, jumped down and paced backwards and forwards on the pavement, gesticulating with his hands like a rap performer, shouting, 'River Road! River Road!' – the *matatu*'s destination.

The driver revved the engines as we clambered inside. '*Haraka! Haraka!* (faster! faster!)' shouted the *manamba*. '*Haraka mzungu* (hurry white man)!' I was always amazed to see how many people could be packed into a *matatu*. Each time you think that one is full to capacity, the *manambas* surprise you by squeezing in another dozen or so people. We pushed in with the other passengers. The windscreen and dashboard were decorated with flashing disco lights. Above the door, a speaker pumped out rap music so loudly that I could feel the beat pulsating through my chest.

With a sudden acceleration, the driver shot off down the road and the *manamba* ran alongside. Just as we pulled into third gear, he jumped on board, hanging by one hand.

'Faster! Faster!'

Nairobi's utilities may be broken and dilapidated, the public telephones rarely work, the pavements may be cracked and uneven, the roads rutted and dusty; but this shabbiness somehow gives the place character. Nairobi has all the unsettled attributes of a busy frontier town. Three hundred miles inland from Mombasa and the Indian Ocean, it is the point at which the modern world encroaches upon the old Africa.

An enormous capital by sub-Saharan African standards, Nairobi has continued to grow and expand since the first railway engineers established a shanty town here on their way to Uganda. Today, the downtown streets are lined with 1950s-style office blocks, together with brownstone, colonial-style administrative buildings, Ionic pillars embellishing the façades.

Recently, a staggering number of skyscrapers and four and five-star hotels have been put up by major international developers, construction workers toil on site round the clock; the city's slums continue to spread out along the Mathare Valley, and every month, it seems, work begins on some new shopping mall.

Once off the *matatu*, Brush and I walked across to the other side of the city. Outside the Khoja Mosque, Ismaili shop keepers, followers of the Agha Khan, stood in groups fretting that the country might be going the way of Uganda under Idi Amin. A group of protesting students marched out of Nairobi University watched by the riot police. A colonial farmer drove down Kenyatta Avenue in his mud-splattered Land Rover, doubtless on his way to the Muthaiga Club, the last real bastion of colonialism in Kenya. At the open-air Thorn Tree Café, tourists and young travellers sat writing postcards, describing the highlights of their safaris. And a few blocks away, at the Country Bus Station, dozens of coaches were arriving from rural areas unloading job seekers carrying bundles of belongings.

Brush took me to his regular bar, the Oasis, where he hoped to meet up with some friends. The Oasis served alcohol twenty-four hours a day. Whatever your fancy, whether it be a Bloody Mary at 8.30 a.m. or a nightcap at two in the morning, attentive staff were always on hand: it was the alcoholic's idea of paradise.

Males of any age were ill-advised to enter through the swinging doors without firmly taking their own groins in hand. The 'Nairobi handshake', the local prostitutes' intimate greeting, was a painful salutation, awkward to disengage from, and one that did little to impress protective girlfriends or wives.

The inside of the Oasis looked like something straight out of a Tarzan film, the sort of sleazy den of iniquity on the edge of the jungle where the evil explorers hole up while they satisfy their passions with the local girls, burn off their leeches, and drink whisky straight out of bottles.

The walls and ceilings were overgrown with creepers and vines, the floor lay thick with sawdust, and fluorescent blue light bulbs flickered from the ceiling, highlighting the permanent layer of cigarette smoke suspended just above head level. Scantily clad women paraded around the rectangular bar and anyone glancing in their direction soon found themselves being propositioned.

During the day, the Oasis was frequented by a number of regulars. These were not 'regulars' in quite the usual sense of the word, however; these were men who regarded the bar as their work place. On weekdays, as others would arrive at their offices on the dot of nine, the regulars would arrive at the Oasis. Rarely talking, they would sit at the bar for eight hours, sipping the local Tusker beer like professional tasters.

At five, they would look at their watches and then stagger out to the bus stop to join the other commuters on their way home. During the weekends, they were nowhere to be seen, but come Monday morning, they would appear once again and get down to the serious business of drinking.

The Oasis, I became convinced, was a front for the white slave trade or an ivory smuggling outfit, or something else equally illegal and shameful. It was Brush's favourite haunt. As we walked through the car park, we spotted two pairs of wriggling legs jutting out of the window of a pick-up. A pair of women's knickers hung from one ankle. The vehicle was rocking back and forth like a skyscraper in an earthquake. A group of drunken Australians cheered from the steps of the bar like football fans supporting their best striker.

'Get stuck in mate! Give 'er one!'

They raised their bottles of Tusker beer with a 'Yes!', toasting their friend's stamina.

Brush had arranged to meet his friends inside. They were standing at one corner of the bar, Tusker Exports in hand. They offered to buy us 'a drink'.

I soon learnt that when these men talked about having 'a drink' they weren't talking about consuming just one or two. I shook hands with Kamau, Brush's best friend. He had swollen cheeks like a boxer and wore a flat tweed cap and a red tartan waistcoat.

'I'm distantly related to Jomo Kenyatta, Kenya's first president,' Kamau told me. 'I'm interested in politics myself and follow what's going on in Kenya pretty closely, but my family steers clear of that world nowadays. It's too dangerous.'

Whenever I saw Kamau, who had spent time in Liverpool and spoke with a hint of a Scouse accent, he was always with a new woman. Tall or short, slim or fat, he didn't seem fussy as long as they were up for a good time. After I got to know him better, I asked him, as we stood once again at the bar, how relationships worked in Africa.

A former long-distance runner who had almost qualified for the Kenyan Olympic team, Kamau took me aside like a father telling his son about the birds and the bees: 'Sex, my friend, is more casual here,' he said. 'I can walk up to a lady on the street and engage her in conversation and if she agrees to have a drink with me, then she's saying she wants to go to bed. We're much more honest in our relations. It's more natural.'

Kamau turned towards his friends, seeking approval.

'Yes, but wives are forbidden from having affairs,' said Brush. 'Ask Elimo.'

Everyone looked at Elimo, who was a bellboy at the Nairobi Hilton. They all started laughing. I gathered that Elimo had recently found his wife in bed with another man.

'She shamed me, you know,' he said. 'I could have killed both of them, you know. But I didn't, you know. Instead, I forced them to get into a cupboard, you know. Then I locked the door and carried it with my brother and put it in the back of a truck and drove to her parent's house, you know.' He stopped talking and took a sip of beer.

'So what happened next?' I asked.

'Well, we unloaded the cupboard, you know. We put it by the door, rang the doorbell and drove off. She got a sound beating from her father, you know. She won't be marrying again. No man will ever have her for his wife ...'

As Elimo drained his fifth bottle of beer, another of

Brush's friends, Mungo, walked into the bar. Mungo, was a plain clothes policeman. Later in the evening, he told me that Kenya's legal system is corrupt to the core and criminals are able to bribe their way out of practically any situation.

'There's no point arresting no one,' said Mungo, who carried a Smith and Wesson revolver. 'I tried that a few times, but the crooks were all out on the streets as soon as they could raise enough money for the judge. Now, if I come across them committing a crime, I shoot to kill.'

Mungo was not boasting. Hours earlier, he had shot dead four Somali gun runners on the Quarry Road.

Most Kenyans consider theft to be the most serious of crimes and they have traditional ways of dealing with offenders. Once, as I sat on the balcony of Trattoria, an Italian restaurant in Nairobi, a teenager in the street below attempted to steal someone's hub caps. He was immediately apprehended and knocked over the head with a tyre iron. Two anonymous men then bundled him into the trunk of a car and he was driven away – probably never to be seen or heard of again.

'In most countries, you're innocent until proven guilty,' said Mungo. 'In Nairobi, if you get caught by a bent cop, you get off. If you get caught by me, you're dead.'

* * *

I had explained to Brush's friends that I was looking for a place to live and a few days later, Mungo called me to say that his brother, Chege, had a spare room in his house. 'The only thing is that he lives outside town,' said Mungo. 'But I think you're going to like it.'

After meeting Chege and seeing his home, I moved in. A long, bumpy driveway led up to the house. It was thirty minutes outside Nairobi, near Kiambu. The driveway passed a serpentine lake where the local dogs cooled themselves, and then cut through coffee fields where workers were often busy harvesting and drying Arabica beans. Chege's garden was dominated by a jacaranda tree with violet blossom and a rockery where two cats called Fred and Ginge – named after Fred Astaire and Ginger Rogers – sunned themselves.

The flower beds never lacked colour thanks to Nairobi's unique equatorial climate which provided plentiful rain and sunshine all year round. Chege's pride and joy were the two bougainvillaeas, with their electric purple petals, and a white and yellow frangipane emitting a powerful scent. In a corner of the garden stood two four-foot ant hills which, from a distance, looked like high piles of pancakes, and in another corner grew a collection of banana and papaya trees.

Mischievous monkeys, who lived in the nearby woods, would venture into the garden from time to time and swing from the avocado trees, trying to steal the fruit. Sometimes, when the monkeys climbed onto the roof, Johnston, the gardener, would throw them the odd banana; these were skinned and eaten and then, if the monkeys were in a playful mood, the peels were thrown at anyone who happened to be standing on the lawn.

Chege had bought the house from Major Dillon Thomas, an old colonial 'boy' who had been in a prisoner of war camp during World War Two and had emigrated to 'Keenyar' in 1950. Due to his good relations with the 'native fellas', Major Thomas, who wore shorts and light brown rugby socks pulled up to his knees, had managed to keep possession of his farm during the land redistributions which took place during Kenya's independence. He lived in another house at the top of the hill with his wife and three German Shepherd dogs.

Chege's house had been built by Italian prisoners of war held in Kenya during World War Two. It was typical of Kenya's colonial architecture with a long veranda, small metal-framed windows, brown stone walls and a red tiled roof. From the front it looked like a tiny cottage, but this was misleading, since there were four bedrooms, a spacious sitting room, two bathrooms, a kitchen and a walk-in larder.

At the back of the house, I had my own self-contained room and bathroom. On one wall hung a picture of a white man shooting a rhino and next to it a poster of Superman. At night, giant moths flew around the security lights mounted on the outside wall, beating their wings against my window.

Chege's wife had died seven years earlier in childbirth and he now lived with his son and two daughters. Although Chege knew a great deal about his tribal heritage, his children took little interest in such matters, which was hardly surprising as they had enjoyed a privileged upbringing and were more interested in what modern Kenya had to offer them. Mary, the eldest, was a great beauty with amber skin, full red lips and a slim figure. She wanted desperately to become a model. Paul, her brother, hoped to enter the air force, and Tanya, who sang in the local choir, wanted to raise her own family.

We played games, watched TV, went for walks in the nearby plantation, trying to salvage as many avocados as we could from the monkeys. In the evenings, we talked and sat around the fire drinking mellow Kenyan tea. Despite their fascination with everything modern, the whole family was deeply superstitious. They were always asking their aunts, who often visited after church each Sunday, to tell their fortunes. The whole family was afraid of dogs because they believed they were evil spirits in disguise. And Mary was so afraid of ghosts that she refused to stay alone in the house.

Chege was a successful businessman and always went out of his way to help me. He was a Nandi, from the same tribe as the president, and was close to many leading politicians and men of influence in Kenya.

'My grandfather was a cattle owner in the Nandi Hills,' Chege told me one morning soon after I moved in. 'He and his father before him and his father before him lived a quiet life on the land. Life was uncomplicated, you know, but then we began to prosper.'

With the coming of the Lunatic Express, the lifestyle of his tribe changed forever. The Nandi soon found that they could not survive simply as pastoralists in the new Kenya and started working on the tobacco and tea plantations.

'You Europeans are a strange people,' said Chege, who respected much the West had to offer, particularly the technology and mass education systems, but was worried that Kenya was losing too many of its ancient traditions. 'You came here and took over our country, but you never gave much thought to our wishes.'

Having fallen on hard times, Chege's father had moved to Nairobi after World War Two, looking for work. Eventually, he found a job in a margarine factory but it provided little money, which meant Chege grew up in the slums.

One morning, Chege, who owned a Range Rover, drove me into the slums to show me his childhood home. Along the way, we passed thousands of people trekking into the city like pilgrims.

'They're too destitute even to pay for the bus which costs just a few shillings,' said Chege quietly. 'The divide between rich and poor in my country is really terrible, but what can you do?'

The Range Rover inched its way down a muddy, evil-smelling lane where open sewage mixed with piles of festering rubbish. Scavenger children, or *cukuras*, played in the dirt, seemingly oblivious to the flies swarming around their heads.

The people whom we passed looked in through the Rover's windows, their expressions soured by life. Chege stopped to talk to some of them in *sheng*, the Nairobi gutter speak which he had picked up as a boy. Many to whom we spoke, unexpectedly complained that rampant inflation had been caused 'by Saddam Hussein and before him Gadaffi' but ultimately they laid the blame on their own politicians.

The actual shack where Chege had grown up had been bulldozed by the Government some years before and a new one stood in its place strung together with pieces of plastic bags, waxed rope and bits of old wood and some corrugated iron.

I could tell that this was an emotional moment for Chege.

'This is where I grew up,' he said, 'in this place, eating rubbish from dustbins and listening at night to women next door prostituting themselves.

'When I was a teenager, I decided that I was going to get out. I knew I had to. I knew I wouldn't survive here, so I started a business.

'When I was fourteen, I borrowed a few shillings from a money lender. It was not much and he charged a great deal of interest, and he told me that if I didn't pay it back within a month, I would have to steal for him. It was a risk, but I decided to take it.

'For those weeks, I got up every morning at five and I went to the butchers and the meat market and bought up as many chicken heads as I could. Then I cooked them and stuffed them with mashed potato, then I sold them outside bars.'

After four weeks in business, Chege had earned enough to pay the money lender all his interest, plus the loan – then he took out another. He kept his chicken head business going until he eventually opened a soup kitchen; from this he earned enough to set up his own garage.

'By the time I was thirty,' continued Chege, 'I was running my own private bus company and, from there, I went into all sorts of things.'

Chege was now extremely rich, a Kenyan success story. He wore finely tailored suits made in London, had a spacious office in a glass skyscraper and owned a fleet of cars; yet he had never forgotten his origins and did his best to try and help the slum dwellers, having set up various schools and given generously to charities.

Chege drove me back into downtown Nairobi and took me up into his office, which was furnished with thick carpets, new desks and chairs. One window looked over the city and the surrounding countryside and plains to snow-capped Mount Kenya in the distance. Chege pointed out towards the mountain, traditionally home to the Kikuyu god, Ngai.

'That mountain typifies our relationship with the rest of the world,' he said.

I asked him what he meant.

'When the first European travellers in Africa returned to Europe and told people that they had seen that mountain with ice on the equator, no one believed them. All the experts insisted that it wasn't possible.'

I still didn't understand what he was getting at.

'The point is,' continued Chege, 'that people always think they understand Africa, although they don't. Now people assume that because we have problems, we are finished.

'I always try to remember that this place has great potential,' he said. 'Yes, we have problems. Yes, we have corruption. Yes, we have terrible tribal divisions. But one hundred years ago, there was nothing but marsh where we are standing. Now look ...' He pointed in the direction of Nairobi's other skyscrapers and modern buildings.

'Look out there. Now that, my friend, that is progress.'

FIFTEEN

The Women Who Marry Women

... am beginning to get commissions from major magazines and papers. Just got one from Marie Claire *to do a full photo-feature. Had to talk the editor into letting me do the pictures ... The* Sunday Express *has me working on the corruption story ... My writing seems to be making progress. Find now that I recognise and value good writing more than I used to. I can't think of anything more satisfying than producing a piece that's readable ...*

Diary, 26 February 1992

At the back of the round straw hut, next to a collection of bulbous gourds, stood a wide, wooden chair with a seat made from the bottom of a tea chest. On the chair, sat an elderly, dignified woman with thick, swollen ankles, and sagging earlobes which drooped down to her shoulders.

The hut was in semi-darkness; from the faint light filtering in through the door and gaps in the roof, I could just make out the figures of three younger women crouching on the floor. One was breastfeeding a baby and the others were grinding dried maize between two stones.

The fourth and youngest woman rose as I entered with Fred, my translator, and gestured to us to sit down on two empty cans of cooking oil. She then lit a lantern which she hung from a stick suspended between the sides of the hut and, in the flickering light, my eyes met those of the old woman.

I could make out her face more clearly now. It was lined with age and it had a fatherly look about it. The old

219

woman, whose name was Sabina, gave instructions to the younger women, who appeared to be her daughters, or perhaps even granddaughters. As we sat there, now in silence, I wondered what would happen next. I still had little idea what to expect; all I knew was that it had taken me many months to find this old woman. My quest had involved weeks of research and days of travelling and walking. At times, I had wondered whether Sabina and her kind existed at all.

My quest had begun soon after my arrival in Kenya when I had heard rumours about the mysterious 'women who marry women'.

It was Brush who first mentioned them. 'They live near Tanzania, at the end of Kenya,' he told me. 'They have great power. They are witches who toy with men and capture their souls. Then they make them into slaves forever ...'

Brush's friends at the Oasis said they were lesbians, and other Kenyans I talked to were convinced they were hermaphrodites. When I had mentioned to Brush the idea of trying to track them down, he looked horrified and backed away: 'When you meet those women, you don't survive,' he said. 'They have too much power – isn't it?'

Despite his warnings, I had continued my research, suspecting that the supersitious Kenyans had blown the legend of the 'women who marry women' out of all pro-portion. There was little written about the women's tribe called the Kuria. I asked everyone I met if they had heard about them; yet few people, it seemed, had travelled to their homeland in the very south-west corner of Kenya. Many refused even to discuss the subject, professing that the women were evil.

Due to deadlines for other stories, I was unable to leave Nairobi, so I paid a local photographer called Paul to track them down. He didn't seem concerned about contending with witches, lesbians or hermaphrodites. However, on the weekend when he was supposed to be travelling to the south-west, I spotted him in a bar where he and his friends were drinking away my money.

Some months passed, and I had almost forgotten about the whole idea when, in the middle of a Nairobi riot, as I ducked into an alleyway to re-load my cameras, I chanced upon a philosophy student called Hezekiah.

Hez had a gouge in the top of his head where, in an earlier riot, a policeman had cracked his skull with a baton. In spite of this, his faculties seemed in place. As we crouched down on a rooftop, talking Kenyan politics and waiting for the tear gas to clear, he mentioned his time in south-west Kenya. I asked him if he had heard of the 'women who marry women'. He had – and what's more, his best friend had once met one of the elusive women.

'They sound most amazing,' said Hez. 'I think they are difficult to meet. It might be possible with a little help from the Lord above.'

This was my first and only lead. I asked Hez to take me to south-west Kenya and he agreed. Persuading Brush to come was no easy task, however. Even the thought of trying to find the women terrified my friend.

'I cannot come. It is bad luck,' he told me.

'You won't have to meet them face to face. All you have to do is help me with my equipment, then you can go back to Nairobi,' I assured him.

'Not even see them from a distance?'

'Not even from a distance.'

'And what about you? What if they put a curse on you – isn't it?'

'I'll be OK,' I assured him.

Brush considered my proposition and called me at home that evening. 'I'll come. Be warned though, if you become possessed, I'll have to take you to a tribal doctor,' he said.

I quite liked the sound of this. 'And what would that entail exactly?' I asked Brush.

'He'll have to bury you alive with a goat to take away

the spirit – isn't it?'

'Bury me alive with a goat?'

'Yes, that is what they do when people become possessed. It happens SO often. It's the only way.'

* * *

We set out in a coach that had been cannibalised from four sections of other coaches, written off during accidents. The windows were smaller than their frames and they shook and rattled like maracas. Near Lake Naivasha, the rear window suddenly dropped out onto the road and shattered into thousands of pieces. When it started raining, those of us at the back got soaked. Few of the seats were screwed down securely and each time the driver turned sharply round a bend, a row would come loose, sending passengers plunging down the aisle and over the tops of other seats.

The driver, who made even Pakistani bus drivers look restrained and law-abiding, only drove at one speed – seventy miles an hour. He, like so many Kenyan drivers, suffered from a kamikaze syndrome which gave him the uncontrollable urge to immediately pass any vehicle that appeared in front of him, whether on the edge of a precipice or stuck in heavy traffic on Nairobi's Haile Selassie Avenue.

This was illustrated graphically when we tore through a village near Nakuru, where he ploughed straight into a herd of goats. A few of the unfortunate creatures were hurled into the air and, looking back, we could see them lying on their backs in the middle of the road, legs wobbling feebly in the air.

He only slowed down if the police were after him – and only then because he knew they had faster vehicles. As we approached the town of Kericho, we were pulled over to a road block. An officer, who apparently knew our driver by reputation, discovered two human fingers lodged into the grate at the front of the coach. It was possible that they had belonged to a local witch doctor whom the driver had allegedly driven over the day before.

Instead of simply arresting the offender, however, the coach was impounded, together with all the passengers. Spotting me at the back, the officer offered his apologies. But he seemed more concerned that the driver had not stopped at the accident the day before than about his having killed someone.

'This is a serious business, I'm afraid,' he said, straightening his uniform. 'We can't have people running off after they've run over someone.'

We were driven to the nearest police station and told that if we wanted to continue on our journey, we would all have to chip in for the bribe. This was a strange turn of events, but we had little choice, so we paid up. The driver, having gained his liberty at our expense, set out once more along the road to western Kenya like a competitor in a demolition derby.

Our fellow passengers were mainly women returning to the countryside after visiting their families in Nairobi. They ate sausages and chips wrapped in greasy newspaper. In the overhead luggage rack, live chickens clucked and flapped about. Hez read a dog-eared, second-hand paperback copy of *The Silence of the Lambs* which he had swapped with another passenger for the brand new Bic biro I had given him. Brush listened to his favourite Swahili music tape on my Walkman. Meanwhile, I talked to a boy who was the grandson of a man with sixty-two wives.

'The *mzee*, the old man, he has more children than he can remember. He's always forgetting the names of most of his wives. You should come and meet him.'

'Perhaps later,' I said, explaining. 'We are going to look for the women who marry women.'

'They are devils,' he exclaimed, shrinking back from me. 'They will skin you.' He crept to the front of the coach and ignored us for the rest of the journey.

Driving over rolling hills neatly planted with tea bushes, we reached Kissi, home of the Gusii people who carve the local soap stone into smooth sculptures and figures. We later moved on through terrain bristling with banana trees, thick, green grassland and small *shambas*, or fields. The state of the road grew progressively worse. Now, the driver was zig-zagging around the craters; we were all tossed about like clothes in a washing machine.

Towards dusk, we finally entered Kurialand, a part of Kenya which is particularly well watered, yet inhabited by a poor people, a minority rural group in a tribal culture. Few of them seek work in the towns or cities. Radios, motor transport and Western clothes are the only traces of twentieth-century life. The majority of Kurias choose to live deep in the bush far away from the road, continuing a life their ancestors have led for generations.

The coach pulled up in Isibania on the Tanzanian border, a stopping-off point for smugglers taking stolen cars from Nairobi to Tanzania and, in return, bringing radios and other electronic items back for sale in Kenya. Isibania is a one-road town with lopsided kiosks and shacks on either side which all sell soft drinks and cigarettes and bunches of green bananas. A sign over the doorway to Odinga's Hospitality Hotel read 'All Parts Welcome'.

'Hotel' was hardly the word I would have used to describe Odinga's, which was no more than a bar with a room at the back where prostitutes entertained passing truck drivers. The concrete floor in the room was stained with vomit and the sheets on the two beds looked as if they had been used to mop up after childbirth. The owner, Odinga, a man with a permanent expression that said, 'I'm recovering from a hangover', sat behind a counter lazily perusing the sports pages of *The Kenya Times*. Hanging above his head was a torn poster encouraging the use of condoms. Brush, who was hungry, asked if he

224

Samburu boys watching a camel race, Maralal, Kenya.

Running the bulls: villagers accompany their champion home after a vicious encounter, Kakamega, Kenya.

Kenyatta Avenue, downtown Nairobi, Kenya.

In the Nairobi slums: a Dutch priest, Father Grol,
amidst a gang of street children.

Black mixes with white: a colonial woman and a Kenyan boy at the Ngong race course, Nairobi, Kenya.

Emma McCune with her husband, the southern Sudanese guerrilla commander Riek Machar, in Nasir town, southern Sudan.

Displaced Sudanese refugees brace themselves in the first few moments of a heavy rain storm, east of Nasir, southern Sudan.

Just two of tens of thousands of malnourished Sudanese, southern Sudan.

*Somali children cling to the remains of
a Ferris wheel, Mogadishu, Somalia.*

At a Save the Children feeding centre in Mogadishu, Somalia.

A gang of Technicals cruise the streets of Mogadishu, Somalia.

Family portrait: a group of 'women who marry women'
from the Kuria tribe near Isabania, Kenya.

A group of Kuria dancers demonstrating their
traditional wedding dance, Nairobi, Kenya.

*The view from behind Wilfred Thesiger's
home on the edge of Maralal, Kenya.*

*Relaxing in the sun room: the last great explorer,
Wilfred Thesiger, with a member of his adopted Kenyan family,
'the Little Horror', Maralal, Kenya.*

was serving any food.

'I only have tartar sauce.'

'Nothing else?'

'So sorry.'

'How about some water?' asked Brush.

'Only beer. Water's cut off.' He shook his head, look-ing at me. 'Life's not easy in Africa, boss.'

We asked Odinga if there was anywhere else to stay. There was another hotel, he said, but it was twenty miles back along the road from where we had just come. Odinga smiled, confident in the fact that we would be occupying his room for the night, vomit stain or no vomit stain.

We spent an hour sluicing out the room with some water bought from the soft drinks seller across the road. Washing ourselves as best we could, and exhausted from the hot bumpy journey, we bedded down for a fitful night's sleep.

* * *

In the morning, we asked Odinga if he knew any of the Kuria women.

'Aren't you here to tell us about Jesus?' he asked.

'What do you mean?'

'I like to hear about Jesus. You know Jesus, the Son of God. He's going to save us.'

'Well,' I said, somewhat surprised by this request, 'I don't really know what to tell you. Um, perhaps later ...'

'I like those stories so much, so much. Don't you know the one about the bread and the fish and the meal?'

'Yes,' I said, 'that's a famous story, but I really want to see the women.'

It was only then that I realised that Odinga had mistaken me for a missionary. After all, the few whites who came down to south-western Kenya were generally missionaries.

'OK', he continued, 'if you tell me the story of the

bread and the fish and the meal, then I'll help you.'

Reluctantly I agreed and cleared my throat: 'The miracle of the Feeding of the Five Thousand ...'

I hoped that no one would come in and overhear us; the last thing I wanted to be mistaken for was a missionary.

Odinga seemed satisfied with my rendition, and once I had finished he closed his establishment and took us to meet the local school teacher, Fred, who invited us all to his house for 'a drink'. Fred had never actually met any of the women; however he did know of a tribal dancer living over the Tanzanian border whom he believed might be able to help. Fred also warned us that in order to endear ourselves to the women, we might have to give them a radio cassette which they used as part of their wedding ceremonies.

'I know a man who could sell you one for two hundred shillings – only,' he said. 'It has flashing lights around the speaker. It's nice. I have one.'

We bought a radio cassette recorder – for quite a bit more than two hundred shillings – and Hez, Brush, Odinga, Fred and I set out to find the tribal dancer. Along the way, we met a boy on a brand new Chinese bicycle who knew Fred and insisted on being our guide. The boy, in turn, brought along a friend who wanted to be a drummer in a rock band. At last, we found the tribal dancer who promised to take us to meet an old man who knew some of the 'women who marry women'. For this service, he required five bottles of Tusker Export beer.

By the time we finally tracked down Sabina, I boasted an entourage of twelve Kenyans, or the 'Dirty Dozen' as I dubbed them. With the exception of Brush, they were all curious to meet the women. However, there was not enough room for all of them in Sabina's hut; I asked them to return to Odinga's in Isibania where I promised to meet them later.

Sabina and the young women – her wives, Coleta, Elizabeth and Grace – lived in a stockade made up of four huts fortified by a high wall of thick, dead branches which stuck eight feet up in the air like clumps of tentacles.

In the days leading up to the meeting, I had begun to imagine that they could indeed be witches dressed in tall black hats, and that their homes might be filled with cauldrons, broomsticks and strange recipes for spells. At first glance, however, there seemed nothing untoward.

Elizabeth poured Fred and me some hot milky tea and gave us both a bowl full of *ugali*, a thick porridge made from ground maize flour. I presented Sabina with the radio cassette. As she turned the tuning knob, the voice of a newsreader came on, followed by static. Finally, she found a local station and the familiar sound of Swahili kettle drums. Grace, Elizabeth and Coleta peered over her shoulder watching the multi-coloured bulbs flashing in sequence around the speaker.

Sabina placed the cassette recorder on the ground, instructing her wives not to touch it. She leaned forward in her chair and the seat creaked under her weight.

'Now what do you want with me?' she asked Fred, who translated her words into English.

'We would like to know whether it is true that you marry other women,' he said.

'Very well,' she replied.

Massaging her throat gently with one hand, the old woman started to tell us about her extraordinary life. 'We are not lesbians,' began Sabina in a croaky voice, 'but we do marry each other. It is an old custom of our tribe which allows us to raise families without having to live with men. It is very ancient.'

Sabina spoke slowly and carefully, as if she were divulging a great secret. 'It can happen for many reasons. It is usually old women like me who marry women. I cannot have children and so these young ones have them for me. They sleep with men, but I am the father of their children. I look after them all. It is a good arrangement.

'Sometimes, rich women choose to take a wife,

227

whether or not they can or cannot have children, instead of marrying a man. They marry young women who have lost their virginity before marriage or those who are unable to find husbands. Some even refuse to marry men.'

Sabina asked one of the young women to pour us some more tea. 'There is no limit to the number of wives a woman like me can have,' she continued, 'although the more wives there are, the more money we have to have.'

Sabina, her three wives, and the household's twelve children resembled the conventional three-generation family: grandmother Sabina, and daughters, Coleta, Grace and Elizabeth, together with their children.

'I was once married to a man,' said Sabina, scratching the tip of her wrinkled nose. 'He died fighting with the white men.'

This, I thought, might have been in World War Two or during the Kenyan struggle for independence in the 1950s, but as with her birthday, she had forgotten the date – if indeed, she ever knew it.

'I had two sons who died in a car crash. All my family were gone and I became very sad. I inherited all my husband's land and possessions. Then my dead husband's brothers and father came to see me. They became my "watchmen", my guardians. Although they had wives and families of their own, they suggested that I sleep with one of them in order to have more children who would take my dead husband's name and inherit the land.'

Sabina chose one as her lover; sadly, she was too old to conceive. 'I did not know what to do. It was very worrying because it was horrible not to have any friends or children with me,' she said. 'My home was empty, and I wanted to give my land and cattle to my children. I went to my husband's family and asked them what I should do. The family suggested that I "marry" another woman so that she could have children for me.'

In Kurialand, as in most of African society, producing

children, especially boys, is considered mandatory. Not only are they deemed to be a great blessing, they also secure ownership of land and the male family name. Given this rigid prerequisite, there is nothing embarrassing or strange about using a surrogate mother: Kuria tradition allows it. As I discovered, families made up entirely of women and children can be found in villages throughout Kurialand. Some homes also exist in which an elderly husband and wife live with a surrogate mother and 'her' young children.

'There is nothing wrong with it. No one in the village thinks anything bad about us,' said Sabina.

As I was writing down what the old woman had been telling us, the door to the hut suddenly flew open. Bright sunlight poured in, half blinding me; it was impossible to make out the face of the figure standing in the doorway. The women hid their eyes from the glare.

'Tarquin, are you fine?' asked a voice.

It was Brush. He was carrying a stick. 'Brush. What are you doing here?' I asked.

'I have to make sure you are fine. Are you fine?'

'Yes, I'm OK. What are you doing with that stick?'

'Are these women trying to possess you?' he asked.

I looked around the mud hut. Fortunately, none of the women spoke English. 'No. Not that I know of. We're just having some tea.'

'Why are they hiding their eyes? Do they fear light?' he asked, still clutching his stick.

'No, Brush, it's just that the sun is very bright. Why don't you come in?'

'I will wait outside. Call if you need me.' With that, he pulled the door shut.

It had been brave of Brush to come to the hut, considering how frightened he had been of Sabina and her kind. I was sure, though, that I was not in any danger. The women had been welcoming and didn't seem to mind talking about their lives. In fact Coleta was enjoying it, especially when asked about her marriage.

'I was dressed by my mother in tanned goat skins, beads and small painted bells,' said the twenty-six-year-old who was breastfeeding her baby. 'The watchmen came to my home with twenty-seven cattle which Sabina gave to my father. In the old days, one of them would also have carried a spear and the other a shield, but they brought a stick and a cassette player instead.'

Fred told me later that while the stick has replaced the spear and shield in these more peaceful times, very few households own tape recorders. They are still seen as a novelty, and the party centres around them.

'In the evening, many men came to my house,' she continued, 'and I invited a lot of my girlfriends. We danced and danced. Lines of men and women faced one another, bouncing and jumping up and down and moving their arms. The men wore skins, many beads, masks, ostrich feathers ...'

'... and thick-heeled, wooden shoes,' added Sabina.

When Sabina wanted Coleta to have a child, she called the family's watchmen. 'I asked them to come separately,' said Sabina. 'They would talk with Coleta for a long time. Then we talked about which one it would be. I wanted one that had many sons already. The watchmen can be of any age.'

The lovers' identities are generally kept a secret from the community. Coleta refused to reveal her partner's name. She did tell me, however, that the same man was responsible for each of her three conceptions. This does not necessarily have to be the case; sometimes wives grow tired of their chosen watchmen or the man may prove impotent. Another is then selected. This is a convenient and comfortable arrangement for the men. Yet, they do not pay to sleep with the wives; instead, they are fed for their 'services'.

'It is their duty to see that the land is properly inherited by men who will carry the family name,' said Sabina.

Naturally, this 'noble' sense of duty is not always shared by the men's wives. Although it is accepted that men are unfaithful even within a polygamous marriage, it does not mean their wives are always prepared to turn a blind eye. Watchmen who spend too much time indulging in their 'duty' sometimes find jealous and angry wives when they return home.

'If the men are not good in bed, I give the girls some *irihabia*, a herbal aphrodisiac, which I can buy from the *abaganga*, or medicine man,' Sabina told me later. 'It gives the men a lot of energy when they are in bed.

'Coleta has had two boys and a girl,' Sabina said. 'She can never leave with them. They are really mine and they have my dead husband's name. They will inherit his land.'

We had been sitting in the hut for more than two hours and Sabina now wanted to go outside and stretch her legs. She raised herself slowly from her chair. Grace helped her up, leading the old woman, her 'husband', to the door. Fred and I followed them into the compound. Outside, the air was filled with the strong scent of a flowering vine growing on the roof of Sabina's hut. A group of long-horned cows stood in a group near the entrance. Thick roots were being boiled in a blackened pot hanging over a nearby fire. Brush was sitting on a granite bolder, entertaining some of the family's children.

I walked over to Brush who had put down his stick and was looking more relaxed.

'These children say that old woman is their father – isn't it?' said Brush.

'I know. She told me. They don't know who their real fathers are,' I replied. 'She says the biological fathers play no part in their everyday lives except when she needs advice on unusual matters such as disputes between the family and the community over land and water rights, and rights of passage through other people's property.'

'Don't the younger women mind not owning their children?' asked Brush.

'It doesn't seem so,' I told him, 'they just accept it.'

The young wives left the compound and headed off into the fields to tend to their crops. As Fred introduced Brush to Sabina, the old woman pointed out a grave next to her hut. It belonged to one of Grace's young boys who had died. She was not sure what killed him. In that part of Africa, it could have been anything.

'When a person dies, they enter another place,' she told me. 'They also remain spirits in our world. Sometimes, we can see them when they want us to. Otherwise, they act as our hidden guides. They are buried inside the compound because they still live here. We cannot bury our dead outside the compound, otherwise they would be lost. Soon I will join them ...'

Watching Sabina in the sunlight, it was impossible to tell how old she was. She looked one hundred and ten. Perhaps she was. Perhaps she possessed supernatural powers after all. It was easy to see how the terrible stories had grown up about the women, and even after returning to Nairobi, Brush was not completely convinced they were untrue.

Before we left Sabina and returned to Odinga's hotel where the others were eagerly awaiting us, I asked her how long she thought this remarkable system would continue, given that the modern world was beginning to encroach upon Kurialand.

'It cannot stop,' she said. 'It must go on because this is a very hard place to live in and people are always dying. Without our tradition, many women would not have children or families ... and those are the most important things of all.'

SIXTEEN

Confessions of a Mau Mau

...the great thing about journalism is that you get
to meet and talk to people from such a variety of
backgrounds: from ministers to road sweepers,
from priests to prostitutes. I can't think of another
profession that gives you such access. Sometimes,
it's amazing who you come across. Last week, on
a plane to Zimbabwe, I recognised the Sudanese
rebel leader John Garang, and sat down next to
him for a chat. Today, I was on a bus sitting next
to a woman who sells vegetables for a living ...

Diary, 1 May 1992

Threatening black clouds loomed over the Mau Massif
east of Lake Victoria. Above the hills, forks of lightning
flashed downwards from the heavens. In the distance,
thunder rumbled, grumbled and clapped like balls career-
ing down a bowling alley. The waters in the lake grew dark
and choppy and waves crashed against the shoreline.

As the thunderstorm approached, the air became thin
and cold and the first drops of rain skimmed across the
windows of our *matatu*. We were destined for Kakamega,
Brush's home. Women gutting a catch of Tilapia covered
their heads with brightly coloured cotton scarves and
headed indoors. Muscular fishermen pulled in their nets
and paddled their canoes towards land. A cyclist leant
over his handlebars and pedalled for all he was worth.

With another burst of thunder and lightning, the rain
came tumbling down. The passengers wiped the steamy
windows and glared out onto the sodden landscape, as

water poured over the side of the *matatu* and muddy torrents coursed down the pot-holed tarmac. With the Japanese engine straining, we climbed the steep hill north of Kisumu. Looking back, I could see Lake Victoria meeting the horizon like a sea at the end of the world.

It was on this general route, I recalled, that Speke had trekked while searching for the source of the Nile. Since then, western Kenya has changed immeasurably, only its unique climate remaining constant. The population inhabiting this area are fortunate in the fact that clouds forming off the lake meet cold air from the hills, which provides plentiful rainfall. The western part of Kenya is by far the most fertile part of the country with lush hills and farmland planted with coffee, tea and sugar cane.

It is also the most densely populated district with the highest birthrate in the world. Throughout western Kenya, whether on streets and roads, or in the bush and villages, women are rarely seen without babies hanging in bundles from their backs. Ask a Kenyan in Nairobi where he or she is from and, if they are not Kikuyus, chances are they will say either 'Kisumu' or 'Kakamega'.

It took us two hours to reach Kakamega where Brush was eager for me to spend a few days with his father and watch an African bullfight, a 'sport' unique to the area. As we arrived, the population was busy preparing for a visit from the Kenyan president, Daniel Arap Moi. National flags, still drenched by the earlier downpour, drooped from the fronts of shops, and a gang of workers arranged seats on a platform where he was due to address a crowd the next day.

Brush's father, Sunday, the former decorator, lived in a row of concrete homes built for factory workers during the 1970s by a local brewery. His wife, who had worked on a nearby farm some years before, was tragically struck by lightning and died as a result. Brush's father had neither the resources nor the inclination to find a new wife, so he remained alone. As we entered his home,

Sunday, who spoke a colourful form of English often confusing his adjectives, adverbs, nouns and tenses, greeted us.

'Welcome, please,' he said, offering me a seat on the knitwear-covered sofa, 'it is essential to greet you. I hope you is feeling in the mood.'

Sunday, who was retired, offered us a drink, disappearing into his kitchen for a moment before returning with some glasses, three bottles of Tusker beer and a bottle opener. 'Nearly most of these bottles is good, some though is unsatisfactory, so drink them guarded.'

Brush asked after his health. His father, who sported a wide-brimmed baseball cap like those worn by American truckers, poured his beer. 'Things is OK,' he said, 'though I feel drowsy all the times, when it's not necessary.'

As Brush explained, in all his fifty-two years, Sunday had never travelled beyond the confines of Luyia land in western Kenya; nor, for that matter, had he ever met an Englishman. He had only seen a few at a distance, mainly during his childhood, when there had been white settlers farming nearby. Brush's father, by his own admission, had always been somewhat prejudiced against the British and until he learnt that his son was working for me, he had no enthusiasm for meeting one. He had, after all, grown up through a time when Kenya was struggling for its independence.

'Wazungu people alighted on our land and pushed us people out,' he said.

Sunday remembered vividly one evening in the 1950s when a trio of Mau Mau fighters, who were on the run from British soldiers, had come to his family's home seeking food and refuge. During that period, the Kenyan countryside was swarming with guerillas who were fighting a terrorist war against the colonials.

I had read that the Mau Mau uprising started in 1948, principally amongst the Kikuyu tribe who lived between the Kiambu district and Nyeri on the foothills of

Mount Kenya. Their movement was called Mau Mau, a corruption made up from '*Uma! Uma!*' which means 'Out! Out!'. Their aim was to drive the British from Kenya, or at least from their own tribal land, which they had temporarily abandoned during a smallpox epidemic at the turn of the century and had been seized by the British. Somewhat conveniently the British believed that the Bantu African tribes, like the Kikuyu, do not hold land as property.

'My father contributed them Mau Mau things for eating and sleeping in the dwelling and they were dreaming heavy. If we had declined, they can come and automatically make a finish to our lives,' said Sunday.

Brush's father and grandfather objected to the way in which much of their land had been taken away by the British and were consequently anti-colonial – or rather pro-independence. However, at the time, they believed that there should have been a political settlement, and to their family, and many more like them, the Mau Mau were anything but heroes. They had committed untold atrocities, often against their own people, and were feared and dreaded for their use of black magic.

The Mau Mau, a secret society, carried out ritual murders under the terms of an oath. Kenyan villagers who opposed the terrorists' strategy, even fellow Kikuyu, were eliminated. A favourite Mau Mau technique was to trap people in their huts and burn them alive. Anyone trying to escape was cut to pieces with *pangas*, or machetes.

One such attack, which was well documented by the British authorities, was carried out at Lari, near Lake Naivasha in 1953, when over a thousand men attacked a powerful chief who opposed the Mau Mau movement and hacked him to death. Seven of his eight wives were also killed; the surviving woman saw her husband split in two halves in front of her. Another woman, who had lost an arm, watched as the attackers decapitated her baby.

'Them Mau Mau was very so strong, strong enough,' continued Sunday. 'I am in the opinion that they was fighting because they felt like essentially being in control of Kenya, but they did not feel like coming to the assistance of Kenya.'

'Yes,' added Brush, 'they just wanted power for themselves – isn't it?'

Noting my interest in the Mau Mau, Sunday told me that he knew an ex-Mau Mau fighter who lived on a small farm on the very edge of the Kakamega rainforest only half a day's walk away. 'If you are feeling in the mood, would you be willing to greet him?'

Of course, I said I would, but Sunday said that he would be unable to take me for two days.

* * *

In the meantime, Brush, who had taken me into Kakamega town where we met up with his friend, the local surveyor, found out the date and time of a bullfight. It was staged the next morning at six o'clock in a field still covered in a thick mist. As we arrived at the scene, hundreds of barefoot locals crowded around a mammoth bull called Abraham, jumping up and down on their toes, waving sticks and small branches in the air, blowing horns and whistles, cheering and hollering.

'*Simba ilarira, yaya ilarira*,' they chanted in unison, '*mama ing'ombe yaya, Ing'ombe ing'ombe* (the lion is bellowing, yes, he is bellowing, mother of the bull, the bull, the bull).'

The giant black bull paid only coincidental attention to the hollering crowd; a more formidable adversary awaited and it sensed that a fight was in the offing. A fight, perhaps, to the death. Abraham's owner, Ewosi, who worked for a local dairy and was wearing his blue uniform, had brought his six-year-old brute to this neutral spot after having received a written challenge from another bullfighter in a rival village. Ewosi patted his 'pet' on the head and stroked his blunted horns while talking into his ear like a coach encouraging a boxer before a fight.

'When I tell Abraham the day before that he is going to fight,' said Ewosi, who also grunted and made bull-like noises when informing the animal of an impending contest, 'he understands and then he rests so that he is strong. He knows my language.'

Owners have an intimate relationship with their bulls. Abraham even responded when Ewosi called his name. 'If I was not here, Abraham would chase you and tear you apart,' he chuckled.

Ewosi also gave his bull a 'special medicine', a herbal concoction, made from the bark of the *munyama* tree mixed with hippopotamus excrement. This, he claimed, understandably made his bull acutely hostile – I hoped only towards other animals.

In a far corner of the field, another bull and a cow, together with an equally enthusiastic crowd, took up their positions, bellowing a challenge. Brush explained that the cow was on heat and, as an outsider, I began to wonder whether this might result in a different form of 'match', but as my friend explained, the cow was there to inspire and rouse the other bull, a notorious brown champion called Blaze.

Seconds later, the spectators were diving in all directions as Abraham stampeded towards the cow, who was happily munching on a clump of luscious grass. Noticing Abraham's oncoming charge, the cow made good her escape by jumping over a fence and disappearing down the lane. A frustrated Abraham attacked the fence, uprooting shrubs and small trees and baying at the sky. Then he turned.

The other bull, Blaze, was now out in the open. Abraham saw him and lowered his head. The crowd shouted, '*Ushwa* (charge)!' The referee, dressed in a white butcher's coat, had arrived during the commotion and blown his whistle. As the Kenyans screamed encouragement, the Herculean beasts bolted towards each other, meeting head on with a thud. The two bulls locked in frenzied combat, violently digging their hooves into the turf as they shoved and thrust against each other, occasionally withdrawing their heads and then smashing and hammering them together again like battering rams.

After nearly one hour of intense conflict – fights can last from between a few seconds to six hours – with neither bull breaking the deadlock or taking the advantage, Blaze slipped in the mud and Abraham triumphantly seized his opportunity, propelling himself at his opponent's haunches and stomach.

The brown bull was butted backwards, unable to find his grip on the sodden pitch and, reeling from calculated, strong blows, he managed to turn and tore away towards the nearest gate. Abraham followed in hot pursuit, dispersing the crowd who fled for their lives.

Ewosi's villagers shrieked, hollering their heroes' names. The losers were gloomy, but they were fortunate that Blaze was still alive. The referee declared it a fair fight. The loser paid Ewosi two hundred shillings, the pre-arranged amount, and Ewosi and his friends headed victorious towards their village where the celebrations lasted all day and well into the night. The others moved away in a slow, melancholy procession with Blaze the bull looking somewhat depressed and perturbed. His fans tried to comfort him.

'Don't worry,' they told him, 'you will win next time, Great Bull. We still love you.'

I asked Ewosi what would happen to Blaze.

'He will fight again, probably several times. But if he does not win soon, he will be eaten,' he said.

Was there no alternative?

'The people might object and trade Blaze for two cows,' he answered, 'otherwise the owner can sell him. If he does, he must buy another bull, so they have a fighter.'

I discovered later that if Blaze were to be served up on a platter, the owner would be prohibited from eating him. He would, however, retain his horns; if he were ever to lose them or if they were stolen, superstition has it that the village would never again possess a winner.

By the time we reached the village, news of the win had already spread and the women were there to congratulate Ewosi and Abraham. The prize fighter was rewarded with his favourite culinary delight: maize leaves. Glasses of *changa'a*, an illegal, highly alcoholic drink brewed from rotten maize and molasses, were purchased with the winnings. Soon the crowd was drunk and singing songs about their bovine heroes.

* * *

It was two days before Sunday and Brush were able to set out to see the Mau Mau warrior. To reach his home, we had to walk through a section of the Kakamega tropical forest, one of the few remaining in East Africa. Set at an altitude of five thousand feet, with the tops of the trees shrouded in mist, the terrain is hilly and scattered with swamps and the occasional grassy glade. The forest is home to the deadly Gabon viper and for this reason, Brush, who hated snakes, walked between Sunday and myself. Fortunately, as we made our way through the thick woods, we avoided any encounters with these slithery residents, although the odd brightly coloured parrot fluttered up into the branches and a bush-tailed porcupine scampered across our path.

Even though Sunday had not been in the forest for some years, he knew it well, having played there during his childhood. Along the way, I asked him about the Kikuyu, the largest of Kenya's forty-eight tribes and the one that had spawned the Mau Mau. This time, he spoke to his son in Swahili and Brush translated.

'The first Kikuyu was a woman called Muumbi and her husband Gikuyu who lived in Kenya's Fort Hall district seven or eight hundred years ago,' he said. 'Ngai, the Kikuyu's god, who they believe inhabits Mount Kenya, gave Muumbi nine children; each of these lent their names to one of the nine clans.

'They were mainly agriculturists and goatherders. They believe that their ancestors and the spirits of the Earth are ever present, loitering in their land and intervening in the affairs of the tribe. Religion plays a big part in Kikuyu life as does ceremony and ritual.'

However, Western methods of exploiting nature have, in the past, undermined the Kikuyu's traditional reverence for forests, rivers, waterfalls and mountains – once the haven of spirits and now the source of new wealth.

We walked for a number of hours and just after noon we reached the Mau Mau's home. He lived in a hut made entirely from natural materials, positioned on the edge of the forest and surrounded by a thicket of twisted bushes.

Sunday, who was nervous about the reception we might receive, suggested that Brush and I waited in a field while he went to see if the Mau Mau was at home. We watched from a distance as he disappeared inside. A few minutes passed before Sunday emerged. 'Let us alight inside,' he said, although Sunday explained that I would not be able to take photographs.

Walking into the Mau Mau's hut, we had to bend down to avoid knocking our heads on a mirror hanging over the door along with several strings of cowrie shells which, we were told later, had been placed there on the advice of a local medicine man to ward off evil spirits. The inside was barely large enough to hold four people. The walls were plastered with torn pages from a Bible and a home-made cross hung from the back of the door. In one corner, a portrait of Jomo Kenyatta, who was imprisoned by the British for allegedly organising the Mau Mau movement, was propped up against a shield, together with a few unwashed pots and pans and a pair of ram's horns.

On a log in one corner sat a melancholy looking African albino who was squinting in the sunshine. He had skin as pasty as an Irishman's, with white, curly African hair and clear eyes. His hands were chalky, the dirt showing clearly under his fingernails. Not stirring from his log or saying anything, he gestured for us to close the door.

The Mau Mau lay on the other side of the room on a piece of foam on the floor covered by a grey, stained blanket. Now an old man in his late sixties, he was ill and frail; his hair stood up in clumps above his head as if he had been given an electric shock, and his lips were thick and cracked. He sat up on one elbow when I entered and stared at me with an expression which was not one of joy nor of anger, but of relief. Indeed, if anything, the former Mau Mau, whose name was Waruhiu, seemed glad to see me.

Sunday suggested we sit down on the floor. Speaking in Kikuyu, which Brush had picked up during his childhood, Waruhiu spoke quietly about a recent dream in which he had met a *mzungu*, a white man. Now regretting much of what had happened during the 1950s, he propped himself against the wall, fingering a copy of the Bible, and he asked me to stay and listen to the story of his life. Getting out my pen and note pad, I readied myself.

'I grew up in Kiambu in the old Kikuyu heartland,' said the Mau Mau slowly. 'That was the place where all the trouble began with the British so many years ago ...'

He stopped talking, no longer looking at me or Brush or Sunday or even the albino. His cheeks quivered, his eyes were fixed on the ceiling.

'It was a time when our traditions were under threat from you. Many young men were wild, like lions. They had strong views, views which made them angry.'

Waruhiu was a peace-loving young man and, although he had friends who he knew were involved with the Mau Mau movement, he refused to join.

'Darkness fell over our land,' he said. 'The British came and they took it. When we tried to live there, we were told to leave ... Why did you come?' he asked.

'It was a long time ago,' I said. 'I cannot answer for those people.'

'But you put many people in camps in the middle of the desert. Many of my people died. Why did you do it?'

I found myself apologising for the actions of my forefathers. 'I'm sorry it happened. I wasn't alive,' I said.

Brush translated my words and there was an ominous silence. The Mau Mau continued: 'One night, it was in 1953, I was asked by some friends to go for a walk. We went into a field. My friends took me to an arch, an arch made from two banana trees. It was surrounded by a group of men with half their faces painted white.

'I was scared, scared to death,' croaked the old Mau Mau. 'There was nothing I could do but agree. Otherwise they might have killed me and my family.

'I and three other men were told to remove our shoes and our shirts. Then we had to pass through the banana tree arch seven times while another Kikuyu held up the lungs of a goat over our heads.'

While being anointed with blood, each one was instructed to repeat a series of oaths. After much persuasion, the Mau Mau told it to us:

'I speak the truth and vow before God
And before the Mau Mau,
That I shall go forward to fight for the land,
The lands of Kiringaya that we cultivated,
The lands which were taken by the *mzungu*,
And if I fail to do this
May this oath kill me.'

Afterwards, Waruhiu was made to mix some of his own blood with the goat's blood and was then required to eat a piece of the goat's lungs. The climax came when each newly initiated member called upon an oath-stone to bring about the death of all his clan if he should be guilty of perjury or false evidence.

'Even though I didn't agree with the Mau Mau,' said Waruhiu, who, like most Kikuyus, feared and believed in the power of black magic, 'I was now a member of the Mau Mau. What could I do?'

As the guerilla war with the British escalated, Waruhiu became more deeply involved with the Mau Mau, who now had a psychological hold over him. Eventually, he served under Dedan Kimathi, a man labelled by the British as a psychopath who believed that he was destined to be the leader of all the Kikuyu.

Born illegitimate in 1920, Kimathi had been brought up by an old man whom he later murdered before joining the Mau Mau. After escaping from prison, he hid in the forest around Mount Kenya, taking with him a copy of the Bible written in Kikuyu. Reading this, he came to the startling conclusion that he was Abraham, Moses and Jesus all rolled into one and that he had a divine mission.

Impressed by this conviction, numbers of men thronged to his ranks and he organised them into an effective guerilla force, the Land Freedom Army, quickly becoming one of the most powerful commanders in the Mau Mau movement. Ruling by fear and killing off any opposition, his power increased until he had himself proclaimed 'Prime Minister Sir Dedan Kimathi KCAE, by God Knight Commander of the African Empire'.

'He was mad,' continued Waruhiu. 'At the time I began to admire him. Now I know he was mad. He murdered people all the time, even those who were his friends.'

Waruhiu had, by this time, become a conscript in Kimathi's forces after being displaced from his home village during the fighting. He and the other Mau Mau lived in the forest and, as Kikuyu, they enjoyed being close to the spirits of the mountains and trees. Gradually, though, as they became completely self-sufficient, they degenerated, like the children in *Lord of the Flies* and were eventually cut off from the main Mau Mau movement.

'For a long time we did not come out of the forest except to attack *mzungu* farms. I forgot much of the Kikuyu language as we did not use it very much. I did not care how I looked or how I felt and often went for many days without food.

'We did terrible things – things I can remember too well even now – but I could not stop myself even though I wanted to.'

For several years, Kimathi's forces managed to evade the British bombings and the raiding parties which were sent into the area to root them out. Eventually, in 1956, a posse of former Mau Mau captured Kimathi and brought him to justice.

It was a further four years before the State of Emergency in Kenya was officially lifted. In all, over ten thousand Mau Mau fighters were killed. Waruhiu remained with some of his comrades in the forests, but for them the fighting was over. When Kenya finally gained its independence in 1963, the remaining guerillas were granted pardons by the new president, Jomo Kenyatta.

'I came down from the mountain,' said Waruhiu. 'Life seemed very strange on the farms so I went back to the forest.'

Eventually, as the forests around Mount Kenya receded and tourism encroached on the area, Waruhiu moved to the Kakamega hills. Since the end of the war, the Mau Mau warrior had never married or stayed in contact with his family or clan. In over thirty-five years, he had experienced barely any human contact and lived a life of solitude and regret; the albino his only friend in the world. They shared the hut together, growing their own food and, when Waruhiu had the strength, they hunted in the forest.

'I was touched by evil,' said the Mau Mau. 'It got hold over me and it has never let go ...'

* * *

We left the former guerilla and the albino in their hut on the edge of the Kakamega forest, walking in silence. It was difficult to imagine such a man terrorising the countryside, murdering both white and black, as he and his fellow fighters had done.

Brush and his father told me that there remained a number of former Mau Mau members at the forefront of Kenyan society, although their involvement with the group had never been officially proved. As we walked back towards the town, I wondered if the movement would ever rear its ugly head again, perhaps even in another form. After all, groups like the Ku Klux Klan in the United States have often disappeared and re-emerged years later. All it would take, I reflected, would be for some fanatic to stir up the Kikuyus' tribal instinct, and the Kenyan countryside might once again tremble at the very thought of the ruthless Mau Mau.

SEVENTEEN

The White Woman
of Southern Sudan

... once in a while, I'll get paid a big cheque. Other times, smaller amounts. The problem is cash flow. Accountants are so damned slow at paying. It's unfair. The more you work, the more you spend out in expenses, the slower the cash flow, the harder it is to keep working. Can't win ... Went to Naivasha for the day and the car got stuck in volcanic ash. Quite a job getting it out ...

Diary, 7 June, 1992

A towering Sudanese man stood in front of the customs counter at Nairobi's Wilson airport. He was at least seven feet tall, his legs were as long and thin as stilts, and his jeans had been tailored to his extraordinary proportions.

'How's it hangin'?' he asked in a voice that boomed down as if from the heavens. My neck strained back as I tried to gaze up at his face lost amongst the glare of the ceiling's strip lights.

'Good, thanks!' I called up to him.

He introduced himself as Peter. Originally from the Sudan, he was a basketball 'pro' for a Philadelphia team.

'I'm heddin' for the South myself,' he said. By the 'South' he meant southern Sudan. His family had emigrated when he was fourteen to escape persecution from the northern Sudanese government.

'I want 'a see what I can do for my people. They're in some bad shit, man. Real bad. Where you heddin'?'

As I explained to Peter, it was somewhere in the vast-

247

ness of his country that I hoped to locate an extraordinary twenty-six-year-old English woman called Emma McCune. She had 'gone native', abandoned her comfortable middle class life and married a guerilla commander. The only hope of reaching Emma was to fly to a dot on the map of sub-Saharan Africa called Nasir, on the east bank of the Nile, west of the Ethiopian border.

The trip was something of a gamble as Emma had a reputation for exhibiting an intense dislike of journalists. I risked travelling over fifteen hundred miles for nothing. Still, it was an intriguing story and had aroused the interest of a number of Fleet Street editors who promised a fat fee if I could land a full-blown photo-feature.

Peter and I were both waiting to board the same plane which had been charted by Salvation Medicine, a German non-government organisation assisting displaced Sudanese. Gunter, the agency's director, was from Hanover. He had bloodshot eyes, bristly sideburns, and spoke English with a strong Teutonic accent:

'Did you hear ze vun about ze two Sviss UN assessment officers who came to Keenyar for ze looking of ze projects?' asked Gunter, who had a sadistic sense of humour.

'Zey vere crossing ze river over a bridge, ven zey looked down into ze vater. Zere zey saw an African being eaten by a crocodile vith its mouth all ze vay up to his vaist.

'Vun of ze Sviss turned to ze other and said: "Vat a vaist of a gud Lacoste sleeping bag."'

The basketball player looked at me and shook his head as if to say 'what manner of being is this?' But as we walked across the tarmac to the plane, Gunter laughed his sadistic laugh; it wasn't our appreciation of his joke that caused us to smile.

The pilot, who was dressed in shorts, a white shirt with breast pockets and striped shoulder straps, was a British colonial woman called Cynthia Watkins.

'Won't be a minute, chaps,' she said as we got ready to board her plane, 'just got to run a few checks and that sort of thing. Then we'll be on our way. Fine day for a trip.'

Although I didn't realise it at the time, Cynthia was something of a legend throughout East Africa; one of the only women pilots to fly mercy missions into war zones. For twenty-five years she had been going in and out of some of the most inhospitable regions on the African continent. In any one week, her adventures were enough to last most people a lifetime; contending with the threat of northern Sudanese anti-aircraft fire, hostile Somalia warlords, navigational logistics of nightmare proportions ...

Recently, she had been shot at during a take-off at Mogadishu airport. A gang of thugs had somehow got the idea that she was leaving without permission and opened fire.

'I could hear bullets hitting the ground underneath the plane and the propellers,' she told me. 'One penetrated the windscreen and shot through the roof of the cockpit, missing my head by millimetres.' Somehow, though, Cynthia nursed her aeroplane back to Nairobi – a two and a half hour flight. She parked in the hangar and asked the mechanics and engineers 'to fill in the holes'.

Even during this age of 'equality', I was surprised to find a mother of five flying in such circumstances. The pilots who usually venture into these parts tend to be single, swashbuckling males, complete with Indiana Jones-style stubble and steel-rimmed Ray Bans. Cynthia was far more original, however. She had travelled the world, left one man at the altar, been married more times than she cared to remember, brought up a family, and mixed with the richest and the poorest, the famous and the unknown. Like Emma McCune, she was the sort of idealistic, romantic woman you occasionally come across in Africa.

Cynthia invited us to board her twin-prop. 'Mind your head, ducky,' she warned Peter, who had to climb in on all fours and took a seat towards the back, his legs and feet protruding well into the aisle. Cynthia, earphones on and navigational maps at the ready, invited me to take the co-pilot's seat. The engines putt-putted into action as she pulled out four or five stops and pressed a number of buttons. The plane jolted onto the runway. She handed me a pair of earplugs: 'Better put these in during take-off. It can get pretty loud up here.'

The wheels left the tarmac and, with a roar of propellers, the plane entered a steep climb. To the left, Nairobi's skyscrapers stretched up into the stratosphere. Below, lay plains criss-crossed with tracks like the lines on the palm of a hand. These had been made by buffalo and wildebeest migrating to the Serengeti in northern Tanzania.

The propellers cut through the thick cloud belt above the city and the cockpit was splashed with sunlight. Cynthia adjusted her instruments. She flew without radar or guidance of any kind, relying almost completely on her familiarity with the landscape. From a basket, she produced two mugs, a flask, a bowl of sugar and a silver spoon and, as we sipped steaming Earl Grey, she pointed out the dramatic landmarks.

'We're just over the Nairobi race track, chaps,' she shouted back to her eight passengers while pointing out the window. Looking down, I spotted the perfect green course and the lawns and gardens of 'Karen', where Karen Blixen, author of *Out of Africa*, spent much of her adult life.

A few miles on, the land suddenly dropped away below us and the needle in Cynthia's altitude meter flicked violently upwards. We were over the edge of the Great Rift Valley. One of the most dramatic features on Earth, it looks like a gigantic toboggan run with steep, curved walls and a flat floor patched with fields. Below us, amongst the red and brown lunar landscape, I could make out Kenya's white satellite ground station; next to it stood the dormant Longonot volcano with its round, lop-sided crater and sides scoured with thousands of ruts made millions of years ago by flowing lava.

As we flew up the rift, our plane lost in the landscape, we passed over the shimmering waters of Lakes Naivasha, Bogoria and Baringo before reaching Lodwar and the western shores of Lake Turkana.

I had driven along this same route a year before, and now, seeing it from the air, I was once again struck by its vastness. There can be hardly anywhere else in the world where you can see so much land that has been barely touched by mankind. Moving across never-ending plains and huge valleys, you feel as if you have gone back in time to the very birth of the planet. In places, it is so flat and the sky seems so close, the horizon is swallowed up and the land stretches out forever.

* * *

It was almost dark by the time we reached the Sudan border. Contrary to United Nations policy, Salvation Medicine had not informed the Sudanese Government in Khartoum of our proposed flight plan. From the Kenyan border to Nasir, Cynthia would have to fly under the radar at ground level. If detected, we risked being shot out of the sky by northern Sudanese MiG fighter-jets based at the city of Juba.

Pushing hard on the joystick, Cynthia, her tongue curled up over her lip, flew the plane down to tree-top level. It was now pitch dark and we had no lights, only the faint glow of the Moon through the cloud line to guide us.

'What do we do if we're attacked?' I asked Cynthia.

'I don't know, ducky – pray I suppose.'

'What about parachutes?'

'Oh dear. I forgot to bring them,' she said, smiling at me. 'If we have to jump out, we'll just have to hope we land on the soft belly of a hippo.'

251

Like a group around a camp fire listening for the rumbling of a distant thunderstorm, Gunter and the others terminated their conversation. The propellers hummed, the wind whipped over the wings, and the ground slipped away below us. We skimmed over the occasional collection of straw huts set in round compounds, and wide rivers that flowed dark brown, as if filled with chocolate sauce. Four tense hours later, we flew over another, wider river which Cynthia recognised as the Sobat. On its banks stood a group of concrete buildings with gaping holes in their roofs, which the British had built during the days of Empire.

'Toodle pips. It's Nasir,' said Cynthia.

The plane made a pass just twenty feet over the runway. A lone long-horned cow stood in the middle; startled by the screeching propellers, the animal charged off in a cloud of dust.

'The strip looks OK, chaps!' shouted Cynthia over the roar of the engines. The plane veered sharply to the right.

We landed and she opened the cockpit door and Gunter got out to check in with the airstrip official who lived in a nearby tent. No sooner had we stepped outside, than we were set upon by thousands of insects attracted by the lights of the plane. Grasshoppers smacked into my face; bloated mosquitoes that seemed to relish the taste of insect repellent bit through my shirt sleeves; bugs crawled in my hair, down my back and up my legs; it was every child's nightmare. Peter, Cynthia, the aid workers and I scratched ourselves as if we had rolled in a bed of nettles.

There was no sign of life near the dirt airstrip except the forlorn cow who had been unable to contain her curiosity and stood somewhere in the darkness 'mooing' incessantly. Gunter and the aid workers unloaded their materials and, after having refuelled the plane, Cynthia was ready for take-off and her return trip to Kenya. Not wanting to overrun the airstrip in the darkness, she asked

Peter, by far the tallest amongst us, to stand at the end holding up a kerosene lantern, and with a wave and a 'cheerio', she lined up the plane and took off again into the darkness.

* * *

Exactly a year had passed since my first visit to southern Sudan where the guerilla group, the Sudan People's Liberation Army (SPLA), were locked in a seemingly never-ending battle against the mechanised army of the Islamic north. The southerners were fighting for the right to live as free Christians while the Islamic Khartoum Government sought to control their land. Much of it was rich with oil and, if properly irrigated, had the potential to be the bread basket of Africa.

After thirty years of conflict, southern Sudan had degenerated into one of the most backward parts of the world, with no infrastructure, little health care and few educational facilities. Most of the population were displaced and many women and children had taken refuge in Ethiopia under the patronage and protection of Mengistu Haile Mariam, the Marxist despot of Addis Ababa.

In 1991, however, Mengistu was overthrown and the Sudanese refugees were forced out of Ethiopia at gunpoint. For over a week, three hundred thousand people – mainly women and children of the Nuer tribe – walked in the extreme heat towards Nasir. Harassed by militia and bandits, they followed the sluggish, winding course of the Sobat, a tributary of the Bahr, itself a tributary of the Nile. Thousands survived by eating grasses and roots which constituted part of their normal diet, yet without meat, fish and other sources of protein, many fell by the wayside. To make matters worse, this mass exodus occurred during the rainy season and the route of the fleeing refugees became a sea of mud and marsh.

To reach relatively dry land, the returnees needed to cross the Sobat river which, fuelled by the rains falling in the Ethiopian highlands, was running in a torrent. Most were too weak to swim. They tied bunches of giant water hyacinths together and paddled across, but in the confusion, dozens were swept away.

The refugees who made it to Nasir arrived with virtually nothing. They had no food, no cooking implements, no livestock – just the bare hope of survival. The United Nations were making the best of a disastrous situation, prescribing what medicine was available and handing out high-energy biscuits. However, fresh water was in short supply and people were drinking from the river, which was contaminated with rotting bodies and human excrement. As one aid worker put it: 'The river's so full of cultures, it's thick enough to eat.'

On the south bank of the Sobat, as far as the eye could see, huddles of scrawny, dying people lay about on the cracked, sunbaked earth; skeleton-like figures crawled across the landscape on all fours, too weak to stand. In order to protect themselves from the sun, the returnees covered their bodies from head to toe in a mixture of ash and mud. The substance turned their skin a deathly grey which made them look like corpses awaiting burial in a mass grave.

I walked amongst them, thinking back to a recent conversation with a white Kenyan who had been complaining about being overweight. Before me were children who had never once had their bellies filled with a solid meal. I had never seen such human suffering, not even in the Afghan refugee camps.

The sun was so bright that you could hardly raise your eyes above ground level. It was a crushing equatorial heat that whipped across the plain and could dehydrate a person within a matter of minutes.

Near the river bank, I stooped down to photograph a child whose starving mother slowly raised her head to look at me like one of the living dead. Her teeth jutted out of her mouth and her eyes bulged out of their sockets, the pupils tiny and black, surrounded by dozens of little red veins like the trunk roads on a map. As if it had been glued on, the skin on her face clung to her skull and cheek bones; her breasts hung bare, like two flat balloons the morning after a party; tropical ulcers festered on her thin legs and arms, pus-ridden and septic. Dried up and brittle, it was a wonder her fragile frame had not been blown away by the light wind.

Her child was roughly four years old but had never developed into anything more than a large baby. His head needed support, two trickles of the greenest bile ran from his nose, and his limbs resembled thin twigs. I was afraid to pick him up; afraid that he might snap in two.

As the mother continued looking at me, never blinking or looking down even for a moment, I realised that her child was dead. Surely she must have noticed. Or perhaps she was just spending a few last moments with him, despite the lack of privacy.

All I could do was to offer her some water. Slowly and precisely, she took my bottle between two long, ghostly fingers, her expression never changing. I left her cradling her dead child, knowing that she would soon join him.

A French politician, who had arrived a few hours earlier in a plane loaded with coconut milk, which UN nutritionists later informed me was unsuitable for the Sudanese, stopped to talk to a group of children. The Parisian was dressed immaculately for the TV cameras, his comb never far from his already blow-dried hair. He stopped to pick up a child and held it, tears coursing down his face.

'I will take zhis girl back with me to France!' he announced. 'Zere she will be cared for. Even if I can only save one girl, zat is something – *n'est-ce pas?*'

The infant's mother looked on in dismay. A UN representative discreetly drew the minister aside and delicately explained that it would be wrong to take the child from its mother without her consent; besides, there were thousands of others in the same condition and preferential treatment was frowned upon.

Towards evening, I felt a cool breeze rush against my face. It felt like someone had opened a fridge door in a hot kitchen. Seconds later, torrential rain pelted down, washing away the mud and ash mixture on the Sudaneses' skin. Most had no shelter as the UN had only been able to provide a small number of plastic sheets and there were no trees under which to take cover, no shop awnings.

One man who had a cooking pot put it over his head and in a fast rhythm, the drops pinged off it; others sat still, with opened mouths, swallowing the rain, waiting.

'This is a blessing!' called out one old man crouching under a piece of plastic, lifting his hands to the heavens. 'The first we have had for a long time.'

In the midst of this human disaster, Emma McCune had married the chief eastern military commander of the SPLA. It was a story right out of the pages of a Mills and Boon romance novel.

Emma was from Richmond in Yorkshire, the daughter of an heir to a fortune who lost his money and later died. She was brought up by her mother who had to sell their large home to raise some cash. They moved into a two-up-two-down. The children were put through private schools and Emma was sent to a convent where she developed an interest in art, later gaining a degree at Oxford Polytechnic.

By the age of twenty-three, she remained uncertain about her future career. Through several twists and turns of fate, however, she found herself working in southern Sudan on educational projects for Street Kids International.

Young and impressionable, and coming from a sheltered English background, Emma, like so many before her, fell in love with Africa. In southern Sudan she found a cause, a cause with which she identified and one which gave her a sense of purpose.

Weeks before the Sudanese exodus from Ethiopia, Riek Machar, her future husband, whom she had already met once before in Nairobi, invited her to visit him in Nasir. Emma, who had developed a taste for adventure, drove up from Kenya, the first person to make the journey by land in over eight years. It was an epic fifteen hundred mile trip. Emma moved through territory controlled by the hostile Toposa tribe, along heavily mined routes, across the front line and through thick bush and swamp.

Amidst the horror of the flight from Ethiopia, a courtship began between the English aid worker and the guerilla commander. It is often under the most extreme conditions that the strongest human bonds are formed. Even in war zones, people fall in love. At first, however, the likelihood of the relationship lasting for any length of time seemed remote. The SPLA are generally distrustful of foreigners and Riek was already married to a woman living in Bradford. The reversed geographical position of the two women was ironic: the Sudanese who grew up in the bush living in England, and the woman who grew up in Yorkshire living in a mud hut. When Riek proposed to Emma, she accepted without hesitation.

Their wedding ceremony was held at dusk as the locals were herding their long-horned cows into cattle camps and burning dried dung, sending thick, sweet-smelling smoke drifting across the landscape. On the way to the straw hut which served as a church, their Land Rover was stranded in the mud. Abandoning their shoes, they struggled barefoot for nearly an hour through the quagmire to the church, where they were joined by a choir. Emma was married in a wash of mud.

The groom wore his military uniform: purple beret and fatigues. The bride had no 'nice clothes'; only a white piece of Ethiopian cloth which she wrapped around her shoulders. Two UN aid workers, whom Emma had invited earlier that morning to act as witnesses, picked wild grasses along the way and made her a bouquet. The short service was conducted in the Nuer language by a priest wearing a pink dressing gown, and outside a new Moon lit their path to the river where a motor boat had been sent to collect them. There was no celebration, no killing of a cow as Nuer tradition demands – given the poverty of Riek's people, it would have been insensitive. There was no honeymoon either. Emma settled down to a polygamous marriage in one of the most isolated parts of the world, where she faced the threat of bombings, where an offensive from the north was expected any day, and where only the bug-eating lizards could be assured of a regular meal ...

* * *

All this had taken place one year earlier. So what had become of Emma now? Had the fairy-tale marriage survived the rigours of a civil war? Or had the inevitable realities and problems of such an unconventional relationship forged in such precarious circumstances brought disillusionment or even tragedy?

I had discovered that the couple were still very much together despite the fact that their roles and status had changed beyond recognition. Shortly after their marriage, Riek accused the SPLA leader, John Garang, of human rights abuses and of forcing children to become soldiers. In an unsuccessful bid for the leadership of the SPLA, he formed a breakaway group, splitting the movement in two. Fighting soon broke out and Riek's Nuer forces attacked the town of Bor, massacring five thousand of Garang's tribe. He was perceived by many observers as a traitor to the cause; some said he had made a deal with the north to preserve his position.

Emma was in England during the split and swore that she was unaware of her husband's plans beforehand. Many aid workers and observers found her protests difficult to swallow; however, none was more vocal in their condemnation of Emma than the Garang faction who accused her of master-minding Riek's coup attempt. Emma now found herself embroiled in the middle of a propaganda battle. Garang accused her of being a British spy and the in-fighting was dubbed by journalists as 'Emma's war'.

She was considered a clever, scheming foreign woman and the influential wife of a commander with many ene- mies – enemies who would be only too happy to see her dead. Left with little choice, her employers fired her as they felt she was jeopardising the success of their projects.

No longer an aid worker, Emma was forbidden from flying in the UN planes and her only chance of getting out of the Sudan was if a pilot agreed to carry her secretly on board.

* * *

It took me four days of travelling to track down Emma. She was in a village in a forest on the Ethiopian border monitoring the distribution of UN food and discreetly involving herself in local politics.

When I first spotted her in the distance, I saw a tall, thin, dark-haired woman feeding an ostrich. She was dressed like an actress in what looked like an absurdly incongruous Victorian period costume, consisting of a floppy felt hat, blue Hush Puppies with pink socks, a flower-print skirt, sleeveless black felt blouse and a neck- lace made from sunflower seeds. She carried a parasol and around her waist she had fastened a *tic*, a string of colourful Sudanese beads.

Despite the fact that I had been searching for Emma, there was something startling about coming across this English woman, who looked as if she was about to set off for a garden party, in the depths of Stanley's darkest Africa.

I introduced myself as a journalist and she was welcoming, although she didn't seem the least bit amazed that I had travelled all the way from Nairobi to meet her.

'Do you like ostriches?' she asked. 'I call this one Burty because he reminds me of one of my old teachers. Burty used to have a mate, but she was killed in a cross-border raid not long ago. Oromo raiders ate her.'

A number of journalists had flown up to Nasir to interview Emma; she had turned them all away. Now, however, the Garang propaganda battle was intensifying and she wanted to tell her side of the story. She found me sympathetic and, I suppose, trustworthy; also I was young and, no doubt, she imagined that she would be able to persuade me to write her version of events.

We walked back to where she was staying in an SPLA compound. Locals waved and called out greetings to her. '*Maley* (hello),' she called back. Everywhere I went, the Sudanese seemed happy to see Emma even though she had learnt little of their language. She enjoyed the sort of star attention usually afforded only to royalty and celebrities. In villages, people would run up to her car as she drove past, bring her presents and ask her for advice. When she went to meet her husband's family, the local women were so delighted that she was carried on their shoulders for several miles to Riek's home.

'I feel like a bit of a celebrity, although it hasn't gone to my head,' she told me as we tucked into some roasted goat which had been slaughtered and prepared for us by the SPLA soldiers guarding her. 'The people here are so much friendlier than they are at home.'

* * *

I spent nearly two weeks with Emma and found that beneath her smiles, there was a tough, driven woman who had survived malaria, typhoid, hepatitis and bombing and the ridicule of many of her former friends and colleagues.

We travelled back to Nasir together in her Land Rover, which was packed with health experts. It took a further two days to reach her husband's military headquarters, a sprawling compound of mud huts surrounded by a high straw wall. Soldiers lazed in the shadow cast by a Soviet-made juggernaut upon which was mounted an imposing four-barrel anti-aircraft gun. Artillery pieces were positioned nearby, half hidden by camouflaged tarpaulins. As we approached, the soldiers sprang to attention.

With the exception of Emma, there were no women allowed inside the compound, only men, or rather giants, many well over six and a half feet tall, machine guns at the ready. They looked menacing, but called out 'Hello Emma!' grinning like friendly neighbours over the garden wall. Out of a *tukel*, or hut, sauntered 'Come On', Emma's brown and white one-year-old dog, tail wagging. She was so named by the soldiers who heard Emma continually calling 'come on, come on', so the name stuck. The dog was very pregnant and so was the eldest of Emma's two cats. 'I'm going to start a zoo,' she joked, but the soldiers, who were tired of looking after her animals, did not find this amusing.

'We got the cats so they would kill all the rats,' said Emma, who had woken one night to find a rat gnawing at her forehead, 'but now they eat all the chickens. The soldiers keep threatening to kill them because they say they are too expensive. But Riek has forbidden it.'

Apart from the cat question, Emma had formed a rapport with the soldiers. 'When I first came, they thought it was all a bit odd, but after we married and they realised I was here to stay, they were very welcoming. They gossip like crazy about us and they say the commander has gone a bit soft. I think he is liberated; if he wasn't, I would be cooking every night and out the back washing up.'

We had to bend down to get through the door and into the *tukel*. The furniture was simple: a long table top balanced on bricks, chairs made from old ammunition boxes, a bookcase, and a bed surrounded by a mosquito net. Much of it had been made by local women who also decorated the walls with paintings and cartoons. Life was basic: no running water, no bathroom and everything cooked over wood fires.

As we sipped sesame-flavoured Kenyan tea, Riek joined us. His full name was Riek Machar Teny Dhurgon; his grandfather's surname was Pot but, for some unknown reason, it was changed. Emma was grateful for this: 'I don't think I would like being called Emma Pot.'

Riek took off his beret. They said a fond hello. He was welcoming, his handshake firm. He looked me straight in the eye; then he slouched back into his armchair, placing his ivory cane on the table. A young soldier entered, stood rigid to attention and saluted enthusiastically. He then bent down on the floor at Riek's feet and removed the commander's combat boots, changed his socks and laced on a pair of trainers. Meanwhile, Riek was asking Emma about her trip, smiling occasionally around the gap in his front teeth. The soldier withdrew.

Riek was very composed. Compared to other SPLA commanders, who were austere and forbidding, he appeared open and congenial. He had taken his MSc at Glasgow, his PhD at Bradford and gone on to lecture in mechanical engineering. In a country with less than two per cent literacy, this inspired respect. His English was good, although more importantly, he was practised at dealing with Westerners, especially journalists.

A jug of water was brought and we washed our hands. Then a tray of food was placed on the small table in front of us, one bowl containing grilled Nile perch, their staple diet, another fresh tomatoes which Emma had grown in her garden, and the third a brown paste which they ate with their hands with sour, flat bread made from sorghum.

Watching the couple together, I wondered why Riek had married Emma. Was he as smitten with her as she was with him? Or had it just been a public relations stunt? Certainly, the fact that he was married to a white woman earned him respect in the community.

Finishing the meal, Riek sat down to write messages to his command on a computer powered by a car battery and I began to take some pictures of him.

'I can see the caption now,' he said, as I adjusted my flash, 'High-Tech Warrior'.

* * *

Emma and I left him and walked towards Nasir. The town had changed a great deal in the year since I had last been there and the conditions were generally better. One thing was familiar: the hundreds of children who loitered by the airstrip, waiting for the UN food to be off-loaded so they could scoop up loose grain that had spilled onto the ground.

A market had sprung up. Metal workers, tailors and carpenters were doing a roaring trade and there were even ten small 'restaurants' all offering the same menu. Emma took me to the 'office' of the Women's Association of Southern Sudan where dozens of women were repairing the building which had suffered from extensive aerial bombardment. Emma had earned their trust and become the leading force behind the organisation, having travelled in the bush, encouraging women throughout Riek's territories to elect local representatives.

'It has been important for me to help these people,' she said. 'I feel like I'm in a very unique position now because I share their lives every day and I'm not just another aid worker pretending to understand their position and telling them how to live.'

The longer I stayed in Nasir, the more I found myself becoming fascinated by Emma. She was one of the few people I had ever met who was prepared to take the most extraordinary risks for what she believed in. She was planning on spending the rest of her life in southern

Sudan and no matter what else I really thought of her, this alone seemed a tremendous sacrifice. I wondered, though, what she found so attractive about the place.

'I like the simplicity here, although it is dangerous at times and the life is basic,' she said. 'You realise how the life you leave behind in the West is so geared to materialism. The southern Sudanese are very romantic in a way and people live here like they always have. Not much has changed. They're survivors and I respect that.

'I'm not going to pick up a gun myself to fight,' she said, 'but I married someone who is committed to a cause, so I have a certain amount of commitment to it myself.'

She found many of the tribal customs refreshing, like the fact that women who bear three children cannot be divorced. How did she cope with being a second wife?

'Polygamy is legal here and most men have more than one wife. There's nothing wrong with it. Look how much divorce there is in the UK and how many people commit adultery. Nearly everyone. You don't get that here because of the system.'

Most aid workers, no matter how involved they become in the affairs of any country, rarely stay for more than a few years. By marrying Riek, Emma achieved something that few other ex-patriates had ever managed. She had put herself on the inside. She got under the skin of the place: the ultimate cultural experience.

* * *

A week passed and liberation celebrations began in Nasir town. Thousands crowded into the main square and a line of chairs and tables was put at one end. These were the first festivities since the liberation of Nasir by the SPLA three years earlier.

At mid-day, Riek's white Land Rover, surrounded by an armed cavalcade, drove into the main square. One hundred and fifty or so heavily armed soldiers jumped down from the trucks and marched in formation around us. A sergeant shouted out commands and the men dispersed to their posts. Ammunition and a rocket launcher were positioned nearby.

Like royalty at Ascot, Emma and Riek and their entourage took their seats to preside over the games of tug-of-war, soccer and bag racing. It was like a school sports day. Other officials made speeches and then it was Riek's turn. He took the hand-held loud-hailer and, shouting at the top of his lungs, launched into an hour's tirade about his glorious troops and their operations. Ten soldiers faced outwards in a circle around him, their Kalashnikovs held firmly across their chests.

At the end of the day, Emma and I had a drink in her hut and I asked her how she felt about Riek's role as a man who made military decisions and inevitably had people killed.

'War is ugly,' she said. 'I don't think Riek is in the war because he loves it and because he loves fighting. He hasn't joined the army like a British officer who wants it to be his career ... Riek has chosen it because of a principle, as a means to an end. Once they have achieved their liberation, then I think he will stop being a soldier. Of course, that doesn't detract from the fact that lots of people I know will be killed. And that's obviously not very nice.'

It was difficult to ascertain what Emma knew about her husband's involvement in the Bor massacre; clearly he was not the saint she had made him out to be. But however much she seemed to blot out sides of his character, she was adamant about remaining by his side whatever happened.

Emma took me to the airstrip the next day to see me off. She asked to be sent seeds for her garden, cigarettes, glossy magazines, a few good novels, sugar and soap.

'People are always asking me what it's like being married to a guerilla leader,' she said, just as I boarded the plane. 'But I don't know what it's like being married to a stockbroker, so I've nothing to compare it with.

'I am so happy here. Whatever happens, I'm glad that I followed my instinct, married Riek and came to live in Nasir. I have no regrets.'

At those words, I boarded the UN Twin Otter plane and we took off over the Sobat. Looking down on the dry river bank, I could see Emma's Land Rover returning towards Riek's compound. I wondered what would become of her.

* * *

Many months after my photo-feature about Emma appeared in *YOU Magazine* in *The Mail on Sunday*, I opened a copy of *The Times* and, casually turning the pages, an obituary caught my eye.

Emma McCune was dead.

I was deeply saddened by the news, although I was hardly surprised, for Emma had chosen to remain in a part of the world where lives are often cut short. The tragic ending to Emma's story was that she did not lose her life for the cause, as she would have wished and many others expected; instead, she died in a mundane car accident on a Nairobi road.

Emma's coffin was flown to southern Sudan where she was buried in a ceremony attended by hundreds of villagers. The Sudanese came from far and wide, many walking for days, to pay their last respects. Sitting in the relentless sun for hours on end, they sang songs about Emma, a white woman who, for a variety of reasons, had chosen to make her life with these people and would live on in their songs for generations to come.

EIGHTEEN

A Few Lines from the *Qat* War

Mogadishu is the scariest place I've been. It's the unpredictability that worries me. At least if you're caught in the middle of a fire fight in Afghanistan, you can take cover. Here, chances are some crazy Somali will walk straight up to you and blow your head off .... We went to the beach this afternoon. You would never have known we were in the middle of a civil war, except that some lunatic was fishing with plastic explosives near the swimmers ...

Diary, 17 July 1992

When I arrived in Mogadishu, I went immediately to see Stephen, an experienced aid worker whose name I had been given as someone who could fill me in on recent events in Somalia. Unfortunately, however, he had little time for me as he was desperately searching to find a suitable vehicle for use as an ambulance, a task that was proving particularly trying.

Earlier, he had been visited by a merchant and a gang of unruly teenagers with a Land Cruiser for sale. The vehicle was just what Stephen required so he looked over the engine and took it for a test drive. Satisfied that it was in good working order, the aid worker, who had been living in Somalia for a decade, asked the salesman how much he was asking.

'The man quoted me a figure that seemed quite reasonable,' said Stephen, who spoke fluent Somali, 'and I was about to start bargaining when one of the teenagers interrupted, saying, "Oh brother! That is far too little. I want what is rightly my share, for it was I who stole the car ..."

'The salesman attempted to silence his associate, promising to give him his cut. But then another of the gang jumped in: "What about me, oh brother? For was it not my Kalashnikov which was used to hold up the people to whom the car belongs?"

'Then another interrupted: "But was I not the one who provided the bullets with which the Kalashnikov was loaded?"

' "But it was I," interrupted yet another, "who provided the car you used to reach the house ..." '

Soon they were all clamouring to be heard, one above the other. Not wanting to purchase stolen property, and concerned that the gang would soon start fighting amongst themselves, Stephen left them as they threatened each other's lives.

'Now, they say I've insulted them by not buying the thing and the whole lot of them are baying for my blood,' said the incredulous aid worker. 'Have they all gone mad?'

While I was in Mogadishu, I continually asked myself the same question: are the Somalis mad? I had just finished reading *The Africans*, by David Lamb, the *Los Angeles Times* correspondent who was in Somalia during a period when Mogadishu was the only city in sub-Saharan Africa where you could walk safely at night. Since then, the once beautiful capital on the Indian Ocean, with its golden beaches, whitewashed Italian villas and sandy streets, had been destroyed.

There was barely a square foot of wall in all the city that had not been riddled with bullets or punctured by shrapnel. Even the lampposts were full of holes, as if they had been gnawed at by metal-eating termites; at dawn the sun shone through them forming laser-like beams of light.

Trees had been strafed by machine-gun fire, homes

levelled by anti-aircraft guns and bazookas, tanks and artillery. It would be easy to believe that a demolition team had systematically set out to level each neighbourhood. No wonder Mogadishu was now known as the 'Beirut of Africa'.

The city had been thoroughly and professionally looted, picked clean like the bones on the plate of a starving man. There was little left of the foreign embassies except the flag poles where colonial powers, which had once flown their proud standards, had vied for control of Somalia during the scramble for Africa and, later, the Cold War. The presidential villa, where the former dictator, Siad Barre, made his last stand before sneaking away in the belly of a tank, had been blown to pieces, its entire contents carted off and sold, right down to the light fittings and tiles in the bathrooms. Anything that remained was not worth taking, like the hundreds of letters which lay strewn across the floors, written by parents pleading for their sons to be released from prison.

The telephones no longer worked as the entire network of copper lines had been torn down and rolled up into bails and flogged for a goodly sum to a certain Gulf state. The city stadium stood roofless and open to the sky, and the manhole covers from the streets had been melted down and made into ingots. The fridges, which once housed the hospitals' blood banks were, no doubt, for sale in some Mombasa bazaar.

The old port looked like pictures I had seen of Dresden in 1945. Rubble was strewn across roads, severed cables and wires hung from crooked telephone posts, gutters were filled with shattered glass. The gaping five-foot holes in the side of the old cathedral gave it the look of a ruined medieval church.

Throughout the city, whether in the hospitals or on the beach, outside the hotels or in the markets, there was a stench of death. It stuck in my nostrils as if someone had rubbed a piece of rotting dog in my face. There were corpses and bodies everywhere. People ignored them as if they were no more than discarded rubbish. Along the side of every main street, you could see hundreds of little mounds in the sand where men and women, children and babies had been buried where they dropped, in graves only a few inches deep.

The city had been without electricity for months. Medical personnel in the hospitals did their best to patch up the wounded. Less could be done for the tens of thousands of people who had flooded in from the countryside in search of food. There was hardly a single person in the city who was not suffering from malnutrition. Starvation was widespread and many feared that if they closed their eyes at night, they might never wake again.

The city's fairground had become a camp for thousands of displaced mothers and their children whose only water supply was one dripping tap. Amongst the ruins of stalls where men had once sold sweets and stuffed toys, they lived in makeshift shelters made out of twigs and plastic. In their midst was a Ferris wheel, a squeaking hulk of metal that had been stripped of its chairs and looked rather undignified, but it provided more enjoyment than any Ferris wheel in the whole wide world. Clinging to the steel girders, skinny children, barely covered in rags, smiled and laughed for possibly the last few hours of their wretched lives.

How many of them would survive was impossible to predict. Aid workers were hopeful, as they must be. But there was little food getting through to the city from Kenya and most of what was sent by the UN and the International Committee of the Red Cross was looted between the airport gates and the distribution centres.

Meanwhile, warlords bringing in food from the Gulf and making hefty profits by preventing free, internationally donated food from reaching the markets, paid anyone wanting to earn an easy five dollars to fire rocket-propelled grenades at the planes. There was nothing easier in Mogadishu than finding someone else to do your dirty work. This forced humanitarian aid organisations to cancel or delay their flights while they negotiated with the politicians.

Everyone in Mogadishu was armed. I saw old women carrying Kalashnikovs – they looked prepared to use them. Six-year-old children were being taught how to protect themselves. Anyone with the money could buy an assault rifle for a mere hundred dollars and any cigarette vendor, on any street corner, would happily sell you enough ammunition to wipe out a whole neighbourhood; the country was awash with Cold War bullets, the cheapest commodity. An egg, on the other hand, cost you nearly two pounds and you needed a whole suitcase full of notes to pay for one night in a hotel. The same was true all over Somalia.

The death and destruction had been caused by a few greedy men and gangs of teenagers who grew up with nothing, but had made money looting and were now armed to the teeth. Known as Technicals, they roamed the streets in jeeps and open cars with sawn-off roofs mounted with anti-aircraft guns. They wore cheap sunglasses and loose, Hawaiian-style shirts; the Technicals had no qualms about killing, much like the young Khmer Rouge in Cambodia.

'Don't mess with these guys,' an American cautioned me, 'they're like New York crack addicts. You can't reason with them.'

One morning, as I was taking a picture of some Technicals in their jeep, a teenager not a day over thirteen, pointed his rifle at me. Through my lens, I could see him aiming at my head, so I slowly lowered my Nikon and waited, frozen to the spot.

He squeezed the trigger.

'Click!'

I will never know whether he knew if his rifle was loaded or not.

He looked at me and laughed, a terrible, crude laugh. Then everyone around me started guffawing like a flock of crows. The jeep sped away, the driver firing his gun into the air.

Later, as I drove in a Save the Children Land Cruiser surrounded by five armed guards, I spotted some children playing on the burnt-out carcass of a tank, so I stopped and started taking pictures. A teenager wielding a seven-inch machete came running out of a building and shouted that this was 'his' tank and I was forbidden to photograph it. If I continued my blood would 'mingle with the sand'.

Many of the Technicals were vicious renegades who owed little allegiance to anyone but themselves, and others were 'controlled' or used by the principal Mogadishu godfathers, Ali Mahdi Mohamed and General Muhammad Farrah Aidid. Months earlier, Mahdi and Aidid, in a united front, had ousted Siad Barre. Since then, they had fallen out and split their party, the United Somali Congress, or USC, and were now fighting each other for control of the city and ultimately the country.

Mahdi, a former hotelier who had styled himself president, enjoyed a marginally cleaner image than his opponent and, recognising the power of public relations, had invested in a satellite phone which he used regularly to call the BBC. In countless interviews, he had claimed to have brought peace to Mogadishu. However, he was forced to drop that line after one of his long-winded radio interviews was interrupted by the sound of a fierce and noisy gun battle.

I went to see Mahdi in his grandiose villa built during Mussolini's occupation of the city.

The 'president' was struggling to piece together a new government and his reception was filled with Somali elders and politicians, some in suits, others swathed in flowing cloth, all sitting on imitation Louis XIV furniture and resting their glasses of cardamon-flavoured tea on beautifully polished mahogany tables.

I waited in the air-conditioned reception and was handed a list of the ministers in Mahdi's new cabinet. Amidst all the chaos, it had been prepared using desktop publishing and a laser printer. There were some sixty ministers, representing every clan and sub-clan in Somalia. There was even a minister for fruit and another for tourism. It was a ridiculous effort to appease his enemies and potential trouble makers.

I sat there for over three hours, exasperated, listening to the humming of petrol generators and, finally, was asked by an apologetic, glib-tongued secretary, who spoke faultless English, to be kind enough to return the following day as 'Mr Mahdi has a headache'. Under the circumstances, it hardly seemed surprising.

I drove to the other side of town to Aidid's armed house and asked to see the general. His cardamon-flavoured tea was bitter-tasting compared to Mr Mahdi's; he didn't make me wait so long, however. We sat alone on two cushions at the far end of a long, otherwise empty room.

Aidid was a short man, in his sixties, balding, with shifty, slightly sunken eyes, who carried a cane. He spoke shaky English, but we managed. I asked him what action he was taking to bring peace to the streets of Mogadishu. He claimed to be trying to disarm the population – especially the teenagers – but as I pointed to the court-yard behind his house where a dozen vehicles, manned by Technicals who appeared to be working for him, were stationed, he grew agitated.

'No, no, no. You must understand,' he said, his head bent down, his eyes staring at me from the top of their sockets, 'that they are part of my army. They are not involved with looting.'

As I left, I inspected these same vehicles which looked no different to the hundreds of others cruising the streets filled with boys who would kill for a Seiko watch.

* * *

Before leaving Mogadishu for Kismayo, a city to the south, I met a Somali doctor called Abdirazak who had trained and worked in the United States and England. A seemingly open-minded man, I felt that if I asked him whether the Somalis had an overriding crazy streak, he would give me an objective response. By way of an answer, he told me the following story:

'I'm setting up a health care centre in Baidoa, a town to the south-east,' he said. 'I've worked there before and went down there last week for the first time in six years.

'I met with the local leaders and had a constructive meeting. But as I was heading back towards the airstrip where a plane was waiting for me, a gunman ran in front of the car and told me to get out, calling me by name.'

The doctor was forced onto his knees and told to make his 'peace with Allah'. Abdirazak was about to be executed, for no apparent reason, when someone rushed up behind the gunman and wrestled him to the ground.

'It turned out that this lunatic held a grudge against me because I didn't give him a job he had applied for six years ago. Just for that he was prepared to kill!'

The gunman's family now dragged Abdirazak's attempted murderer off into some side street where they meant to put an end to him. 'They said he had disgraced their family,' continued the doctor, 'and I now found myself pleading for his life. They only agreed to spare him if I accepted their invitation to dinner and agreed to let the gunman serve me personally.

'In this situation both our lives were saved because people intervened who stood by our customs and traditions. Elsewhere they are disregarded. The whole culture has broken down. It is like the end of the world ...'

What I found puzzling about Somalia was that it is the only country in Africa, a continent often ruptured by tribal divisions, that can truly claim to be a real nation.

The Somalis are one tribe, they speak the same language, and belong to the same religion, Islam, believing that their Muslim clerics are descended from Aquil Abu Talib, cousin of the Prophet Mohammed.

Yet the Somalis are predominantly nomadic pastoralists who live their lives on the edge of starvation, often having to fight one another. They are defiant, tough and fiercely nationalistic and they have been invaded continually throughout their history – by the Ethiopians, the Egyptians, French, English, Italians and Portuguese – and therefore perceive life as a battle for existence.

Somalis are more concerned with their genealogy rather than where they live or have lived. As children, they are taught the names of their ancestors going back twenty generations and when they meet a stranger, they recite the names of their forebears until they reach a mutual ancestor and therefore common ground.

Although usually extremely hospitable, the Somalis will unite to beat off any outsider when the need arises and the rest of the time, fight amongst themselves. They have a saying: 'My cousin and I against the outsider; my brother and I against my cousin; me against my brother'.

The adventurer Sir Richard Burton, during his search for the source of the Nile, travelled across Somalia. He called the people he found a 'fierce and turbulent race' and was scarred for life by a member of a raiding party who stuck a spear through his cheek. Later, the British tried to bring the Somalis to heel, but they rebelled for twenty years under Mohammed Abdille Hasan, 'the Mad Mullah'. At that time, a Ugandan soldier warned his commanding officer not to antagonise the Somalis. 'Bwana, they no good,' he said. 'Each man his own sultan.'

Traditionally, if internal fighting breaks out, the elders settle arguments using a system of compensation.

'Nowadays,' said Dr Abdirazak, 'with all these modern weapons, the killing is so great that no one can keep track of the body count. Our whole system of chivalry, which we inherited from the Arabs and was designed to stop this kind of bloodshed, has totally broken down. If we are not careful we will completely wipe each other out.'

Somalia was caught up in a vicious circle of politics, war and a breakdown in tribal traditions, much like the situation in Afghanistan. But these were not the only elements fuelling the civil war. The Technicals chewed *qat* – pronounced in the Arabic 'kut' and often incorrectly spelt by journalists as 'khat' – which is grown in parts of Ethiopia and Kenya. Chewed throughout East Africa and parts of the Middle East, the leaves are a mild amphetamine. Although not officially classified as a drug, they seem to have a strange effect on the Somalis, acting like caffeine, suppressing hunger and increasing alertness while at the same time dyeing the mouth green.

Before the civil war, only affluent Somalis could afford to chew *qat*. But during the unrest in Mogadishu, it had become available to teenagers earning cash from looting. Each morning, fresh supplies were flown in from Nairobi's Wilson airport and were quickly on the streets. A couple of bunches of *qat* was enough to raise the adrenalin levels of a Technical, and they had grown addicted, requiring more and more money to fuel their dependency.

As I sat on the roof of the Save the Children office, writing my notes, I could see young Somalis buying *qat* from the street vendor down below. From time to time, I could hear the thud of artillery and gunfire, and I wondered if there was a solution to this terrible mess. This was my first and, I hoped, last experience of watching an entire culture spiralling out of control. Sitting there, I realised how lucky I have been to have grown up in the relative safety of England.

Below, a policeman stood in the middle of the street trying to direct traffic. He could do nothing to discipline the green-mouthed Technicals who jeered at him as they zoomed past. Nearby, a nomad was leading his camel to water, and a group of women in black were burying a child.

NINETEEN

Pilgrimage to Maralal

... it seems like a long, long time ago that I sat with Frank in Marty's in New York. A lifetime ago, in fact. For a while there, I thought things wouldn't work out. Publishing in the British press seemed like such a distant possibility ... I can see certain disadvantages. Not having a degree in the UK will, no doubt, prove difficult, even with the experience I now have ... but I wouldn't have missed the past four years for anything.

Diary, 2 August 1992

As my plane pulled up over Lake Victoria from Entebbe airport in Uganda, and veered away toward Kenya and Nairobi, it struck me that exactly four years had passed since I had arrived in New York. During that time, I had seen little of my family and friends in England and I was eager to pay them a visit.

Before returning to London, however, I wanted to meet a boyhood hero, the man who had been described by St John Philby, the Arabist and traveller, as 'probably the greatest of all the explorers': Wilfred Thesiger.

Thesiger was the only great wanderer left alive who could testify to the amazing age of African discovery, as Burton, Livingstone and Stanley had known it. He was the first European to journey into the lands of the deadly Danakil in Abyssinia; one of the first Arabists to wander with the Bedu through Arabia's hostile Empty Quarter, and one of the few Westerners to have ever lived for extended periods amongst indigenous peoples such as the Marsh Arabs of southern Iraq.

I knew that Thesiger still lived in a hut made from cow dung and mud in central Kenya. I knew, also, that he was elderly and that the opportunity to meet him might never present itself again. Discovering the name of the town in which he lived, I wrote to the old explorer, mentioning my adventures in Afghanistan, a country through which he had also travelled. Who could forget the description of Thesiger at the end of Eric Newby's classic, *A Short Walk in the Hindu Kush*. Would he be interested in hearing about the current situation in that war-torn country? I addressed the letter: 'Wilfred Thesiger, Maralal'.

A month passed with no answer and, as the days went by, I began to wonder whether my letter had ever arrived. In the event, however, I needn't have worried as I later learned that correspondence with less detailed addresses had reached Maralal many times. One, sent from France some years ago, was simply marked 'Wilfred Thesiger, Africa' and that found its way to the Englishman's door, in spite of the fact that it took many months.

At length, Thesiger's eagerly awaited reply arrived in the form of a blue air mail envelope with a picture of a rhino printed on the front. 'Do come to Maralal and I will be happy to put you up,' he wrote in a barely legible hand. 'I feel sure you will enjoy seeing this part of Kenya, which still has a character of its own ... Come as soon as you can.'

A day's drive in a *matatu* along a gravel road that crossed the equator took me to Maralal, a dusty two-street town which serves as a capital for the Samburu tribe. I was grateful that the uncomfortable journey had ended, yet apart from my fellow passengers, who seemed to disappear in all directions, the town was deserted.

The *matatu* pulled away and I was left standing alone, clutching Thesiger's letter which lacked any further directions. Lugging my backpack and cameras, I knocked on the doors of a few of the closed shop fronts. Then, at the end of one of the two tree-lined streets, I saw a gaunt Samburu striding towards me, a small dust cloud forming at his heels. Putting one hand over my eyes to cut out the dazzle of the sun, I glared in his direction. The man seemed to be waving an object over his head and calling to me.

'Are – you – here – to – see – Kissinger?' he shouted.

'Kissinger?' I asked, as he grew closer.

'My little joke,' he said, now just a few feet from where I stood. 'You're here to see Wil-fraid.'

'Yes. But how did you know?' As far as I was aware, no one, with the exception of Brush and a few friends in Nairobi, knew of my trip. Even Thesiger had no idea when I would be arriving.

'You're a *mzungu*. You must be here to see Wil-fraid. Wil-fraid is my pal. He's giving me this coat.'

The Samburu, whose cheeks seemed to be partially covered in orange make-up, modelled the Savile Row tweed jacket like a drunken mannequin on a cat walk, twisting proudly in his rubber sandals, showing me the back. Although the jacket was of superior quality, its fine tailoring hadn't stood up to the rigours of bush life, and it hung in shreds from Thesiger's lanky lackey, barely held together by patches upon patches, like a dervish cloak.

Holding up his pet locust, which he carried about in a transparent plastic bag, the Samburu led me to the local garage owned by an Asian whose grandparents had been amongst the first Indians brought to Kenya to work on the construction of the Mombasa to Uganda railway line. A humble man, he had a collection of vintage cars. I wondered how, in the middle of Kenya, he had managed to get his hands on them.

'It's amazing what you come across,' the Asian told me over a glass of cool water while we awaited the return of his son who had gone off with the family's Land Rover, 'sometimes you come across some real treasures.'

Only recently, a friend of his had been driving through Uganda in a vintage Rolls-Royce when the axle broke. 'He went along to the local garage and asked if they had one that would fit,' continued the Asian. 'The old man seemed to think he could help and rummaged around in a shed full of old rubbish. Lo and behold, he found a gold-plated axle for a Rolls still in its original wooden box. It must have been left there by some colonial, donkeys years ago ...'

The Asian was showing me some of his cars when his son returned. He drove me to Thesiger's house, up a river bed two miles out of town. Built into the side of a lush hill, it was guarded by a tribesman who carried a six foot long spear and wore a red blanket and rings of plastic multi-coloured beads around his neck.

As we approached, I saw the Englishman pruning some flowers in the garden. Despite the blazing heat, he was dressed like a man expecting the imminent arrival of a heavy winter blizzard, wearing sturdy brown walking shoes – which he later claimed to have owned for some twenty-five years – faded tan trousers, a tweed jacket with a blue spotted handkerchief protruding from the breast pocket, and a distinguished trilby.

'Who the devil may you be?' he barked, giving me a frosty, unwelcoming stare as I got out of the Land Rover. I gave my name, swallowing back the lump in my throat. 'Tarquin Hall, sir,' I said, feeling very much as if I was on school report.

'Who?' he bellowed. I repeated my name, gently reminding him that I had written to him and that he had replied.

'Oh, yes, yes, yes, the Afghan man.' His face relaxed. 'Do come in. Do come in. I'm afraid it's not the Ritz, but quite interesting nonetheless ...'

Thesiger's face showed strength, but at times he looked menacing. His dignified demeanour conveyed an air of nobility. His crooked nose, which made several sharp turns down his protracted and sagging face, seemed almost to reach his chin. His ears were like an elephant's, enormous and floppy, and when the Sun was behind him, they appeared to blush red.

With great pride, he showed me around his house, a shack with a green corrugated-iron roof whose walls were made of baked mud and cow dung; it had been built by Thesiger and a group of locals. There was no electricity and no kitchen as such, only a brazier and a few pots and pans on the floor in one of the rooms. There was no running water, either, just rain water which ran off the roof and collected in a metal barrel. A few yards from the house, a hole in the ground and a small, rickety cabin with a threadbare curtain made out of potato sacking served as a toilet. To take a shower you had to walk three miles to the nearest house owned by a friendly neighbour on the next hill; and in the winter, if it grew cold, the only comfort was a blanket and, perhaps, a hot mug of coffee.

Now officially retired, Thesiger might well have chosen to live out his last years in the comfort of his Chelsea flat, which had been left to him by his mother. However, he was indifferent to comfort and these were the perfect surroundings for a man who still cherished the exotic.

'We can walk up into the forest beyond that far hill,' said Thesiger, pointing in the distance, 'and see elephants. Many Samburu still live a traditional way of life and this house is always full of young people. The secret to longevity is to surround yourself with young people. Don't you think?'

Thesiger, who never married, shared the house with his adopted Kenyan family, a group of mainly unrelated, formerly homeless or parentless Samburu locals whom the Englishman had chanced upon over the years and taken under his wing. They lived together day in day out, cooking, cleaning, sharing each others' problems and lives while Thesiger provided the money to keep the household going.

Thesiger invited me to sit down in the basket chair in the sitting room. The walls were plastered with photographs taken with two Leica cameras, the only ones he ever owned; the shelves were packed with some of his favourite books, including Conrad's *Lord Jim* and Kipling's *Kim*, copies of which he had carried with him all over the world.

As the great traveller told me proudly about his family, one of the youngsters, a mischievous three-year-old, ran into the room, pulling books off tables and using Thesiger as a human climbing frame. 'Get out of here, Little Horror,' he shouted.

The child's real name was affectionately ignored; Thesiger had given nicknames to all the members of the family. One was known as 'Nandi Bear' after a mysterious animal fabled to live in the Nandi Hills; another 'Bush Baby' after a furry rodent; and the 'Little Horror's' father was called 'Prester John', after the legendary priest-king thought by Europeans during the Crusades to rule Abyssinia. Another child was dubbed 'the Mini Moran', a *moran* being a young Masai warrior.

Thesiger turned on a radio which he had borrowed from a friend. 'Do excuse me,' he said, 'I usually hate these blasted things, but my eyes are going and, unfortunately, I can no longer read the newspapers.'

Thesiger tuned in to the BBC World Service. The announcer spoke of fighting in the former Yugoslavia. 'The world is in an incredibly disturbed state, isn't it?' he frowned, making gruffing noises under his breath, like a growling dog does when it first senses the presence of an intruder on its territory. 'I was hostile to the Gulf War and I can't see that it has achieved anything. I think there is no means on Earth of stopping the proliferation of weapons ...'

Thesiger was not a man to qualify his opinions. He spoke abruptly and enjoyed shocking people. Indeed, I have never met anyone with quite so many enemies as

Thesiger claimed to have. But like many of his generation, he was a man of his word. Although unfashionable these days, he believed strongly in the concepts of service and duty.

Slouching back in his favourite armchair, a tatty object with springs hanging out of the bottom, he toyed with the top of his cane, and began to relate adventures which have spanned his long lifetime. He was still able to recall in great detail exciting and dangerous episodes.

Born in Abyssinia, now Ethiopia, in 1910, Thesiger was witness at an early age to the exploits of the army of Ras Tafari – later to become the Emperor Haile Selassie – going forth to war and returning in triumph. Thesiger made his first expedition when he was just twenty-three into the country of the Danakil, a murderous race whose men measured their stature by the number of enemies whom they had killed and castrated. In 1935, Thesiger joined the Sudan Political Service. The war took him to Abyssinia where he fought in the Gojjam Campaign with Colonel Wingate, the maverick officer, and later Thesiger joined the SAS, operating in the Western Desert.

'I came to Keenyar in 1961 when this was still known as the Northern Frontier District,' he said. 'I came here by camel. No Samburu had ever seen a camel before and they thought they were very strange creatures indeed. Now they have lots of them.'

In his later years, Maralal became a base and home from where he journeyed to Afghanistan, Pakistan, India, Indonesia, Malaysia, as well as much of East Africa.

But Thesiger was best known for his journeys in the Middle East where he had spent years with the Arabs. Fascinated by these people and possessing tremendous strength of mind, he had learnt to fit in to their hard way of life, learning Arabic, their traditions and customs, at the same time remaining incredibly British and refraining from 'going native'.

Thesiger might have settled with his Arabs had it not

been for various wars and the march of modernisation. 'I went to Iraq to shoot some duck and ended up staying for eight years,' he reflected. 'When I left, I said I would be back in three months. I was in Ireland having tea with some cousins and someone came in and said, "There's a revolution in Iraq, they've killed the Royal Family and they've burnt the British Embassy." So I realised that my travels in Iraq had come to an end.'

Thesiger got up to go to bed. 'I hope you get up early. We wake very early here,' he said. 'And I hope you like porridge, we'll be having porridge for breakfast.'

* * *

Sure enough, the following day, I woke to a bowl of hot porridge. Thesiger loved porridge; had loved it ever since his Eton days, a time he spoke of with much affection. He drank his tea out of a tin mug, horrified to learn that I didn't like coffee. 'You young people are very odd,' he said disapprovingly. 'We had one old Etonian here recently who didn't drink coffee, didn't drink tea and didn't like porridge, so he went very hungry, I'm afraid. He hadn't read the *Jungle Book* either. Very strange.'

We walked to Maralal, a fair distance for any eighty-two-year-old. We passed a herd of cattle. Bells hung from their necks, making a soft clanging sound. Herds of frisky zebra romped through the valley. We passed some trees with branches which had been broken off during the night by a herd of elephants.

A camel derby was being held in the town and we were just in time to see the start. Along the dark brown, dirt road enthusiastic Japanese tourists, cheerful British ex-patriots, determined Americans, as well as a handful of native Kenyans, sat atop an agitated collection of white, black and brown camels. Among the four-legged contestants, there was much snorting and grinding of teeth.

Thesiger and I stood by the starting line as a pistol

sounded. Several camels promptly relieved themselves of their riders, some made a bolt for the bush, while others decided that the race had already gone on long enough and planted their hooves in the dust, refusing to shift.

Thesiger was much amused by the scene. He was a great camel expert, having travelled on them for many years. 'There are two kinds of camels: one-humped Arabian or Dromedary and the two-humped Bactrians,' he told me. 'The Arabian is native to India, the Middle East and Africa and is longer-legged. The Bactrian is indigenous to the highlands of Central Asia.

'If you don't treat camels well,' continued the Englishman, 'they will either just crouch down and do nothing or are liable to fits of rage. They spit when annoyed and can bite and kick quite dangerously. But well treated, they are the finest mounts on Earth.'

Leaving the derby behind, we walked into the centre of Maralal where a group of Samburu, all wearing colourful beads, were waiting for Thesiger because they wanted to borrow some money from him. One of them, whom the Englishman called 'the Missing Link', called him *mzee juu*, chief elder, a term of tremendous respect.

Thesiger was the local attraction for the Samburu and the occasional tourist alike, and from time to time foreigners would arrive in the town, much the way I had, in search of the legendary traveller.

My host once recalled having been sent an urgent message to meet an American couple at the Maralal airstrip. He had no idea who they were, but decided to meet the plane. When they landed they invited him to join them for lunch.

'I had just finished eating when the husband asked me whether I was wondering why they had flown up here. I admitted that I was curious. He said: "Every year I ask my wife what she would like for her birthday, and this year she asked to have lunch with you. So here we are – all the way from New York".'

* * *

At home that evening, Thesiger supervised the prepara-
tion of thick goat stew, chapatis and soup prepared over
glowing braziers which sent flickers of light darting across
the floor. The Little Horror played on a mattress and the
Mini Moran studied an English text book while his surrogate father explained the meaning of the words to him.

In many respects, Thesiger's family recognised that
they were living with an extraordinary if not eccentric
man. They considered him to be just another one of the
family, however, and treated him like any grandfather. 'He
is the only *mzungu* who really treats us as equals,' said
one of them when we were alone. 'He looks after us and
we look after him just as much. He very much lives the
life of his choice.'

Thesiger was only too happy to tell his captivating
stories and this evening was no exception. No doubt his
talent for spinning a yarn had flourished and developed
due to Irish ancestry and the privilege of having generations of eager listeners. Like a magician, he conjured up
memories and images from countries long since modernised or destroyed. He described the pageantry of Haile
Selassie's victory parade in 1916 with minstrels singing
war songs, slaves on mules beating battle drums, thousands of followers cheering, and defeated chiefs led in
chains. He regaled us with tales of death-defying episodes
with the SAS during the war; being lost in the desert with
no water and shooting man-killing lions in Kenya and
Sudan; reminiscences of treks through the mighty Hindu
Kush; and descriptions of the Karakorams and Tibet.

One of his less cherished memories was of sailing
through the South China Sea on a yacht with an American
companion called Mac whom he detested. Thesiger woke
one morning to the sounds of screaming on deck.

'I asked Mac what the hell was going on. He shouted
that the only thing he could be certain of was death. Well,

to be told that the only thing certain is death just after you have woken up is not very comforting. Great waves were sweeping over us, the engine was out, the dinghies were useless and we were heading for a coral reef upon which the boat would last no more than two minutes ...'

I asked Thesiger whether he missed travelling.

'No, not now,' he sighed, 'because travelling as I knew it is gone. Travel and exploration as they were are extinct.

'A lot of people would do anything to have made the sort of journeys that I did ... A few years ago, you could go into a remote village and you would find the natives there as yet untouched by our so-called civilisation. Now you would find a tour operator and thirty tourists with him.'

During his travels, Thesiger learned to value one thing more than any other, more even than the wildness or beauty of the lands he had visited: the simple companionship of the few who chose to accompany him. He found in them qualities he most admired: endurance, courage and loyalty, qualities that in his own life he desired to emulate.

In that respect, for people such as myself who have grown up in this increasingly modernised, industrialised, overpopulated world, travel is very far from dead. As Thesiger himself put it: 'It has always been, in fact, the people and not the places.'

Towards midnight, he checked that the hurricane lights had sufficient paraffin and wished everyone a good night.

'Please do remind me to buy some more sugar tomorrow,' he said to me over his shoulder, as he disappeared into his room.

In the darkness, the Little Horror was screaming.

'Oh, will you give that damn child a good spanking!' roared Thesiger. And then, in the silence, all that could be heard was the distant barking of dogs.

* * *

After a week with Thesiger and his adopted family, I returned to Nairobi. There, I wrote a feature about the last great explorer and got down to the tedious and laborious process of selling my work, which is ninety-nine per cent of a freelance journalist's lot.

My four years were up. I was now a practised photographer, interviewer and burgeoning journalist, having achieved nearly everything I had set out to do. Some of my articles from East Africa had appeared as major spreads in British newspapers and magazines and a few had even been syndicated worldwide.

The question was what to do next. Could I really see myself back in London on a newsdesk eight or more hours a day? Or should I stay on in Africa?

While I was mulling it all over, the telephone rang. It was an old friend who had just moved to Istanbul. Would I be interested in spending some time in Turkey?

I told him that I would have to think it over but, as I hung up the phone, I had already made up my mind. I called my parents to tell them that I would be returning home – for a break.

The world map on the wall stared down at me, beckoning. There was still so much to see and I was only just twenty-three. The city of Constantine and Sinan awaited, and beyond it, Turkey and the Middle East ...